Praise for *Cultivating Co...* *in the Classroom* by Lisa Johnson

These days, young people seamlessly shift between modes of communication and sharing with emerging technologies, applying a deftness that those who remember a time before ubiquitous computing and networking will never fully comprehend. However, this does not necessarily mean that these students natively know how to apply their embedded habits in meaningful, context-drive, and generative ways. In this book, Lisa Johnson provides memorable anecdotes mixed with actionable steps. It is full of engaging imagery, clever templates, and thoughtful quotations, which are sure to leave a lasting impression on today's teachers who are meeting students where they are and leading them where they want to be.

—**Reshan Richards,** Adjunct Assistant Professor
Teachers College, Columbia University
New York, NY

In my opinion, Lisa Johnson's book is a must-have publication for both learning about the skills needed by students, as well as utilizing all the great examples and ideas in each chapter in the classroom. A combination of a practical guide and a research review, I can see the content and activities in Johnson's book being used with students as early as middle school, as the basis for a study group or PLC by educators at all levels, and as a grad school textbook at the university level. The set-up of each chapter—including research and resources, planning and preparation, challenges for educators, and a student self-assessment checklist—makes it easy to digest all the new skills both our students and we need to acquire. I learned so many new things while reading this book that will make my practice of training teachers better!

—**Kathy Shrock,** Educational Technologist, Adjunct Instructor
Wilkes University, PA

We communicate 24/7 these days. But do we really use the right tools for communicating our message? Clear communication is a key skill. This book asks the right questions and helps students to really use technology to enhance their learning. Teachers from all over the world get practical examples on how to work on core skills. After reading this you will be able to give your students a voice to clearly communicate their stories.

—**Kurt Klynen,** Content Coach
ICT Atelier
Belgium

This book has an unbelievable amount of tips, ideas, and great advice for communicating in the 21st century. It's not only helpful for teaching students to be better communicators, but adults as well! Some of these tips are so exciting and thoughtful, I want a tip-a-day calendar version of this book!

—**Jennie Magiera,** Chief Technology Officer
Des Plaines School District 62
Des Plaines, IL

All teachers will find insight, ideas, and inspiration in this book. Lisa Johnson provides an enthusiastic, thoughtful approach to needed skills in the digital age. She highlights the value of different approaches and tools and shows us how to best use them. The provided Communication Catchers are a real bonus!

—**Julie Willcott,** Educator
Kennebec Valley Community College
Fairfield, ME

This is my new favorite professional read! The TechChef has cooked up a delicious meal I will want to enjoy again and again. There are so many great ideas for supporting digital communication, digital citizenship, and digital footprint in the classroom. The ready-to-go activities and templates make it easy for teachers to start implementing tomorrow! I want this book for all of the teachers I support!

—**Terra Graves,** Program Specialist, 21st Century Learning
Washoe County School District
Reno, NV

As someone who grew up in the 1980s, this is the resource I need to help me prepare my students to be "future ready." Great information and practical, use-immediately ideas for the classroom!

—**Jerri Michaelsen,** Teacher
Briscoe Middle School
San Antonio, Texas

The world would be a better place if everyone who sends and receives email reads Lisa Johnson's email etiquette in Chapter 1. Furthermore, Lisa follows her own advice in Cultivating Communication—much of the information in this book is presented in bulleted lists and visuals!

—**Tony Vincent,** Teaching and Technology Specialist
learninginhand.com
Council Bluffs, IA

This book is the most practical guide I have seen to truly help secondary students be "future ready." The advice and tips that Lisa Johnson shares should become a standard digital literacy read for all middle school and high school students.

—**Kyle Pace,** Instructional Technology Coach
Grain Valley School District
Kansas City, MO

Full of convincing rationales, practical tips, and classroom solutions, this book will leave your head spinning with easily implemented ideas that will energize and enrich your instruction. Johnson has compiled and created a vast array of resources that will improve both the teacher and student experience in lasting and meaningful ways.

—**Melissa Dupre,** Teacher
Westlake High School
Austin, TX

My career has taken me from ESOL to tech specialist. My colleagues used to question why certain students were in the ESOL program because they spoke so well. They talked conversationally, not academically. It was my job to move them into academic language. Now as a tech integration specialist, the same type of conundrum is occurring. Students use technology but do not incorporate it. Many tech curriculums include how to type, how to insert a picture, spacing but not when, why, nor discussions. Lisa Johnson's book effortlessly builds the bridge between the basic knowledge or "how-to" of technology into synthesizing technology applications. Seventeen years into the 21st century, technology is exponentially assimilating in our careers, lives, even our refrigerators. Lisa's book makes the skills needed to navigate the vastness and sometimes caverness pool of technology tangible. Technology is simply a tool, but a tool that makes education, jobs, and lives more efficient and engaging. This book would give knowledge to the educators in order to empower their students to garnish the power of these "gadgets."

—**Tana Ruder,** Instructional Technology Specialist
Wichita Public Schools: Cohort II and VI
Wichita, KS

Stop talking about technology, and focus on communication! Loaded with practical tools and useful pedagogical approaches honed through experiences in the classroom, Lisa Johnson's book seeks to define and support the literacies our students need now, and for a lifetime of learning.

—**Cathy Hunt,** Visual Art Educator
iPad Art Room and St Hilda's School
Gold Coast, Australia

Lisa Johnson truly recognizes the need for teaching communication and bringing authentic learning to education. Through reading this book, I discovered practical lesson ideas, my interest was piqued, and a call to action ignited by Lisa's articulate observations and insightful suggestions. I highly recommend this book for any educator.

—**Don Goble,** Multimedia Instructor
Ladue School District
St. Louis, MO

Lisa Johnson has written a book that finally puts into words what our students *and* teachers need to know to incorporate and mirror true, 21st century teaching and learning! This book needs to not only be in the hands of our current educators, but our future educators studying to teach our future leaders!

—**Anne Beck,** Instructional Technology Specialist
University of Oklahoma, Jeannine Rainbolt College of Education
Norman, OK

With her book, Lisa Johnson has her fingers on the "pulse" of educators when it comes to cultivating communication with today's students. Her diverse experiences, and expertise as an Educational Technologist gives her insight into the fears that educators and administrators face, and her experiences can equip those same educators with the tools to overcome then.

—**Lucas Loughmiller,** Director of Library and Instructional Media Services
Manhattan-Ogden USD 383
Manhattan, KS

Lisa Johnson is a longtime leader of technology integration, and this book distills the complicated mess of technology use in secondary schools down to a clean, lean, and easy-to-follow book. While all the concepts are based on sound pedagogy and the "why" is certainly addressed, Lisa doesn't waste any time getting down to the classroom level to make it clear to all of us how best to support our students. As danah boyd points out in her book *It's Complicated,* "most teens aren't addicted to social media; if anything, they're addicted to each other," and Lisa's book is here to help encourage the communication through the use of technology. Lisa puts the needs of students first, pedagogy second, and places the technology in its proper place as a tool and not an obsession. This is the book we've been waiting for that rises above button pushing and gets to the heart of what we need and want for our students.

—**Michelle Cordy,** Third-Grade Teacher
Thames Valley District School Board
London, Ontario, Canada

Cultivating Communication in the Classroom

To my boys Hayden and Gavin. . . . My hope for you is that you can share your innate gifts and passions with the world to cultivate your own success in, outside of, and beyond the classroom and communicate effectively with whatever tools you have in your hands.

Cultivating Communication in the Classroom

Future-Ready Skills for Secondary Students

Lisa Johnson

Foreword by Guy Kawasaki

CORWIN
A SAGE Publishing Company

A SAGE Publishing Company

FOR INFORMATION:

Corwin

A SAGE Company

2455 Teller Road

Thousand Oaks, California 91320

(800) 233-9936

www.corwin.com

SAGE Publications Ltd.

1 Oliver's Yard

55 City Road

London EC1Y 1SP

United Kingdom

SAGE Publications India Pvt. Ltd.

B 1/I 1 Mohan Cooperative Industrial Area

Mathura Road, New Delhi 110 044

India

SAGE Publications Asia-Pacific Pte. Ltd.

3 Church Street

#10-04 Samsung Hub

Singapore 049483

Acquisitions Editor: Ariel Bartlett

Editorial Assistant: Kaitlyn Irwin

Production Editor: Melanie Birdsall

Copy Editor: Lana Arndt

Typesetter: Hurix Systems Pvt. Ltd.

Proofreader: Alison Syring

Indexer: Marilyn Augst

Cover Designer: Anupama Krishnan

Marketing Manager: Anna Mesick

CONTENTS

FOREWORD   xiii

Guy Kawasaki

PREFACE   xv

ACKNOWLEDGMENTS   xxvii

ABOUT THE AUTHOR   xxix

CHAPTER 1: EMAIL ETIQUETTE   1

Why Are We Talking About Email for Students?   1

How Do We Ensure Best Practices for Using Email?   2

How Do We Support Clear Communication Through Email?   5

How Can I Troubleshoot Email With My Students?   10

How Can I Provide Authentic Curricular Opportunities
    for Email Communication?   11

Chapter Resources   15

    Email Etiquette Preparation Inventory Assessment   15

    My Students' Self-Assessment Checklist   15

    Additional Resources and Reading   16

    References   16

**CHAPTER 2: COLLABORATION AND
POSITIVE INTERDEPENDENCE**   19

Why Is Collaboration a Necessary Skill for
    College and Career Readiness?   20

What Is Collaborative Learning?   21

How Can I Set the Stage for Positive Collaboration
    and Interdependence?   22

How Do We Build a Community?   27

How Do We Support Students With Determining Their
    Signature Strengths and Core Competencies?   30

How Can I Ensure and Measure Ongoing Collaboration?   34

What Curricular Collaborative Tasks and Activities Can Groups Do? 35

Chapter Resources   38

    Collaboration and Positive Interdependence Preparation
       Inventory Assessment   38

    My Students' Self-Assessment Checklist   39

    Additional Resources and Reading   39

    References   39

CHAPTER 3: VISUAL LITERACY AND PRESENTATION SKILLS   **43**

Why Is Visual Literacy So Integral for My Students?   44

Why Are Presentation Skills Important for My Students?   46

What Are the Three Elements of Presentation Skills?   47

What Are Some Best Practices for Drafting a Presentation?   49

    Content: How Can My Students Effectively Organize
       Content and Information Throughout Each Stage
       of the Presentation?   50

    Visuals: How Can My Students Effectively Communicate
       With Visuals (e.g., Images and Icons) and Color?   56

    Delivery: How Can My Students Effectively Deliver Content?   61

What Tools and Applications Can Be Used in Conjunction
    With Student Presentations?   65

Beyond Sharing These Resources, How Can I Model
    Best Practices in My Instruction?   65

Help! I Have a Few More Questions About
    Presentation Skills and Visual Literacy!   65

Chapter Resources   69

    Presentation Skills Preparation Inventory Assessment   69

    My Students' Self-Assessment Checklist   69

    Additional Resources and Reading   70

    References   70

CHAPTER 4: STUDENT PUBLISHING AND PROJECTS   **72**

How Can I Provide Autonomy and Choice Within a Project?   74

How Can I Provide an Authentic Audience for Students' Projects
    and Publishing?   84

How Can I Ensure Appropriate Use (of Incorporated Elements
    and Original Ones)?   86

How Do I Revise an Existing Project?   92

Chapter Resources   94

    Projects and Publishing Preparation Inventory Assessment   94

    My Students' Self-Assessment Checklist   95

Additional Resources and Reading   95

References   95

CHAPTER 5: PORTFOLIOS AND RESUMES   **97**

What Is a Digital Portfolio?   98

What Challenges Can Digital Portfolios Solve for Me
    and My Students?   101

How Can Digital Portfolios Directly Benefit My Students?   102

What Is the Main Goal of a Digital Portfolio?   102

What Will Be Included in a Digital Portfolio?   103

What Is an Easy Entry Point Into Portfolios?   104

How Can Students Reflect on Their Learning Journey?   106

How Can I Involve Peers in the Iterative Process of Learning?   110

How Can a Portfolio Impact Future Career and
    College Readiness?   113

Chapter Resources   119

    Digital Portfolio Preparation Inventory Assessment   119

    My Students' Self-Assessment Checklist   120

    Additional Resources and Reading   120

    References   121

CHAPTER 6: SOCIAL MEDIA   **123**

How Do We Teach Students to Practice Emotional
    Hygiene When Consuming Content?   126

How Do We Teach Students to Be Critical Consumers
    of Social Media Content?   128

How Do We Teach Students to Carefully Craft Their
    Digital Doppelgänger?   131

How Can I Support Students With Positively Integrating
    Social Media?   132

Chapter Resources   137

    Social Media Preparation Inventory Assessment   137

    My Students' Self-Assessment Checklist   137

    Additional Resources and Reading   137

    References   138

CHAPTER 7: CURATION   **141**

What Is the Value of Curating for My Students?   142

How Can I Design Lessons to Explore Curation in the Classroom?   145

What Is the Value of Critically Evaluating Curation
  for My Students?   152
What Are the Risks Associated With Curation?   154
Chapter Resources   156
    Curation Preparation Inventory Assessment   156
    My Students' Self-Assessment Checklist   156
    Additional Resources and Reading   156
    References   157

APPENDICES

    Appendix A: Book Study and Communication Cohort Challenges   158
    Appendix B: Communication Catchers   162
    Appendix C: SEL Index   179
    Appendix D: Industry Insights   182

INDEX   184

Visit the companion website at

https://resources.corwin.com/cultivatingcomm

for downloadable resources.

FOREWORD

My mantra is to empower people. I try to help others use the skills and knowledge that I have acquired through experimentation, diligence, and good (and bad) luck. If I could impart one skill to students before they graduate, it would be the ability to communicate effectively. Factual knowledge is easy to obtain in a post-Google and post-Wikipedia era, but the ability to communicate this knowledge is still a challenge.

Fortunately, Lisa has crafted a resource for educators to empower students to become better communicators. This book seamlessly and cleverly delivers the why, how, and what educators need to deliver college and career-ready communication skills to students. Working with Apple, Motorola, Canva, Wikipedia, and Mercedes-Benz, I know that Lisa's methods are valuable and effective.

You will be able to garner her knowledge and do amazing work with your students by reading this book.

—**Guy Kawasaki**

Guy Kawasaki is the chief evangelist of Canva, trustee of the Wikimedia Foundation, and brand ambassador for Mercedes-Benz and an executive fellow of the Haas School of Business (UC Berkeley). He is also the author of The Art of the Start 2.0, The Art of Social Media, Enchantment, *and nine other books. Kawasaki has a BA from Stanford University and an MBA from UCLA, as well as an honorary doctorate from Babson College.*

"The world economy no longer pays for what people know, but for what they can do with what they know."

—Andreas Schleicher, OECD Deputy Director for Education

Is There a Communication and Content Divide?

As a child of the 1980s, I remember researching using the public library and our home collection of Funk and Wagnall's encyclopedias. I remember corresponding by actually writing letters using Lisa Frank stationery and mailing them with stamps, typing research papers and printing them on a dot matrix printer, and getting our first cordless phone so I could be free to roam beyond a 20-foot tethered radius. I remember waiting for dial-up to check my AOL Mail, waiting for film to be developed before I could see and display my vacation photos, and waiting for my parents to drive me to the local Blockbuster so I could rent a movie for the weekend. Many educators remember this reality in some form. Conversely, most of our current students have no understanding of an era or a life without immediacy of digital content and accelerated communication.

Our students' current reality is an era where information is simply a click or a search away. Our students grow up with a digital doppelgänger (that is, a version of themselves that lives online), can binge-watch entire seasons of shows with a click of a button, and are instantly able to communicate with friends and family in a variety of ways. Our students' new normal is Google for research, making instantaneous edits to a collaborative document, and downloading books on a whim to a mobile device for immediate consumption. Our students have moved beyond digital natives to become mobile natives. While students may feed their digital doppelgänger with tweets, posts, and videos, they may not realize that immediacy of online communication and access to content can be permanent. Neither does their familiarity with mobile devices and technology preclude their knowledge of appropriate and purposeful use of these tools.

Many times they also don't realize that the tools they use to communicate informally might be the very same tools that they will also use to communicate formally . . . beyond our four walls. As educators, we have to prepare our students

> *"The illiterate of the 21st century will not be those who cannot read and write, but those who cannot LEARN, UNLEARN, and RELEARN."*
>
> **—Alvin Toffler** *(Author and Futurist)*

for a successful future in beta. While we won't know what types of college and career paths students will seek and obtain, we do know that effective communication and the ability to learn will be tools that will last a lifetime.

Author's Note: I'll be honest. I am not a huge fan of buzzwords and labels. I realize they are used in research and publications to achieve a shared vocabulary and understanding, but I also find they tend to be overused and sometimes confuse common understanding rather than make it more transparent. So for the purpose of this book, consider 21st Century Skills and the 4 C's (that is, Communication, Collaboration, Critical Thinking, and Creativity) as ultimately future-readiness skills for students. Perhaps one day we can just refer to them as "readiness" skills.

What Is the Future of Learning?

Three recent experiences of my own drove me to write this book and advocate for the need for such a resource.

> *"We cannot build the future for our youth— but we can build our youth for the future."*
>
> **—Franklin D. Roosevelt**
> *(32nd President of the United States of America)*

First, I had the opportunity to sit in on several student mentorship presentations. Students had spent a semester of high school observing and working with a professional in a career field that interested them. The most fascinating and impactful insight came when the teacher asked each student: "What characteristics should you possess to be successful in this field?" As you can imagine, no one said expertly completing a worksheet, acing a test, or the ability to write in cursive, type 60 wpm, or memorize the quadratic formula . . . the responses ranged from being empathetic and a good communicator to being able to work in groups and manage time. One student even mentioned the ability to be an effective communicator through email.

Second, I observed a MAPS (Methodologies for Academic and Personal Success) course—essentially a study hall with benefits that is provided to support students with determining their individual learning styles and abilities and acquiring successful time management, organization, note-taking, and study skills. Interestingly enough, this course is typically only offered as an elective to ninth and tenth graders. One would think that all secondary students could benefit from these strategies.

Third, I have witnessed the shift of content expectations gradually trickle down grade level to grade level. As a mom of two elementary-age boys, I have first-hand experience with *Why Kindergarten Is the New First Grade* (Nadworny & Kamenetz, 2016). Though this book is tailored to an audience of secondary educators, I think we would be foolish to ignore the trickle down of academic expectations. Soon our college and career readiness skills will be simply good teaching. Being proactive in teaching these skills ensures that we won't be blindsided in the next decade when we encounter an article that reads "Why Seventh Grade Is the New Freshman Year."

If we are truly teaching learners and preparing them for a future not yet written, then we need to consider the critical need for all students to receive a viable education that not only includes core content but also purposeful integration of the 4 C's. It is not enough to retain knowledge and information. Our students are now expected to effectively analyze, critique, and communicate content and information in a variety of ways to very diverse audiences. Interestingly enough, these verbs are also used in every set of standards to describe the actions that students should be comfortable taking as they interact with content.

Having personally and professionally witnessed the shift from Student A to Student B (Figure P.1), I have to thoughtfully ponder, are we teaching content or are we teaching learners? Yes, students still need to know content, but all of this content is now accessible to them with a quick search . . . it doesn't have to be solely committed to memory. The past two decades of rapid technological innovations have also caused what we knew to change as information and studies challenge our

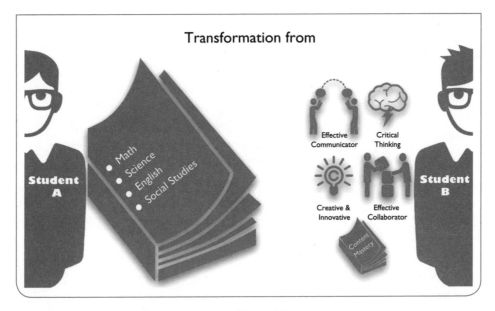

Figure P.1 Transformation From Student A to Student B

Source: Adapted from Ken Kay's ASCD 2013 Session "4 Keys for Becoming a 21st Century School or District"

current beliefs on brain research, planets that exist (sorry Pluto), and even beloved dinosaurs (is the *Brontosaurus* real or not). The most astounding discovery is that of IBM, which found that 90% of the data in the world has been created in the last two years ("IBM—What Is Big Data?," n.d.). We have to thoughtfully consider that the content we currently teach may not be relevant or even accurate in the next 10 years, so equipping students with a firm foundation to positively and professionally access and interact with whatever content and communities they may engage with is a necessary and noble pursuit.

> *"Our largely singular focus on academic achievement has resulted in a lack of attention to other components of a successful life. . . . These traits frequently described as 21st century skills, have and will continue to serve students well into the next century."*
>
> **—Denise Pope, Maureen Brown, and Sarah Miles,** *Overloaded and Underprepared: Strategies for Stronger Schools and Healthy, Successful Kids*

Students are now expected to know much more than the narrowly defined core content areas; they are expected to be prepared for a future that is unknown and yet imminent. Both the Office of Educational Technology (2016) and the Learning Curve Report (2014) touted 21st Century Skills as integral to student success. Interestingly enough, these same skills are not only important within our classrooms but beyond them. In a recent study of 768 managers and other executives in regard to the importance of the 4 C's in their organization (Figure P.2), these competencies were not only agreed to be relevant, but would become more important in the next 3–5 years (American Management Association [AMA], 2012).

Although the idea of 21st Century Skills is more than a decade old, educators are still searching for ways to support this movement and the workforce still reports

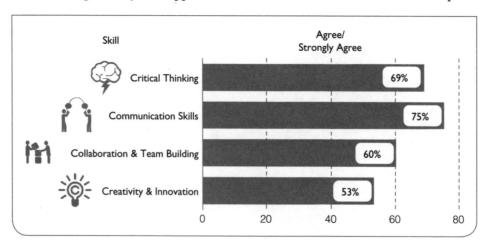

Figure P.2 Results of a Study of 768 Managers and Other Executives in Regard to How Important the 4 C's Are in Their Organization

Source: Graph adapted from the American Management Association (AMA) 2012 "Critical Skills Survey" conducted December 2012

that high school students are deficient in many of the skills needed to be success-ful in the 21st century global economy. In fact, the study *Are They Really Ready to Work?* (2006) found that writing in English and written communications were not only deficits in high school graduates, but in 2-year and 4-year college graduates as well.

If we are truly cultivating future-ready learners, then we have to carefully craft our lessons to support them beyond our classrooms. Rather than looking out the win-dow to the university or the trade school or lamenting that the computer lab at the elementary didn't sufficiently prepare students, we have to consider looking in the mirror to see how we can leverage our content-specific curriculum to support crit-ical skills like Critical Thinking, Communication, Creativity, and Collaboration.

A pillar of the ISTE Nets ("Standards for Students," 2015) and International Baccalaureate program, threaded through education standards and expectations as early as first grade, and a component of both the National Education Association's guide to "Preparing 21st Century Students for a Global Society" and "The Global Digital Citizen Foundation," communication skills are integral in the classroom, digital environments, and a global economy. Communication skills aren't just a critical component of standards, but they also rank higher than critical soft skills like adaptability and teamwork ("Millennial Branding Student Employment Gap Study," 2012).

Before the technology that teams use to communicate globally and even asynchro-nously was developed, communication was more seen in a collegiate framework. Even the Partnership for 21st Century Skills acknowledges it as somewhat neglected in the framework of the 4 C's. (National Education Association, n.d.). While there are multiple books available to support creativity, critical thinking, and collaboration, very little content is available to support students with communication—the highest rated of the critical 4 C's among employers. There are tools to think critically, collab-orate, and create content online, but the fundamental foundation for all of these skills is . . . communication. Consider the innovative idea that couldn't be communicated effectively or two students trying to collaborate without an effective framework for establishing social contracts and positive interdependence. Communications can also be misconstrued without attention to tone when using social media.

Furthermore, curricular content can be easily threaded through the art of commu-nication, which will inevitably incorporate the 3 other C's. Consider presentations. I haven't met a teacher yet who didn't require some type of presentation during the year. Presentations require students to communicate their knowledge of the con-tent effectively, *but* they typically also foster collaboration through group projects, critical thinking during the research and planning phases, and creativity in the formats and choices they make to display the content. While students may not collaborate or engage in creative tasks each and every day, they do communicate in a variety of modes and formats with multiple audiences daily.

How Will This Book Support Communication Skills Within and Beyond the Classroom?

As more and more secondary students are taking advantage of CTE courses, in-school incubators, semesters of mentorship, and even Capstone AP courses that mimic and provide real-world authentic learning experiences, the need for technology and communication skills to be threaded and intertwined through these experiences increases. As access to mobile devices and technology steadily skyrockets, more and more schools are opting to remove or revamp computer labs and the traditional methods of teaching with technology.

> *"The conversation has shifted from whether technology should be used in learning to how it can improve learning to ensure that all students have access to high-quality educational experiences."*
>
> **—The Office of Educational Technology,** *Future Ready Learning: Reimagining the Role of Technology in Education*

The intent of this book is to serve as a springboard—a springboard for students to navigate from middle school to high school and from high school to college or a potential career. The intent of the book is *not* to teach isolated communication skills, but to select types of communications that are necessary to be successful beyond the educational institution and that can be cultivated and nurtured within the classroom.

For the purpose of this book, we will focus on types of communications that

- directly correlate with classroom content and process standards,
- can be influenced by positive classroom interactions,
- are supported with mobile technologies and a variety of tools, and
- are skills that students ultimately need to be successful beyond our institution.

To support educators with navigating this resource, I have focused on one of seven communication skills in each chapter. While one could digest them one communication skill at a time, this book is more intended to be a well-crafted stew. Each one of these topics could stand alone but they are far more powerful when brought together. To honor your time and expertise, each chapter section begins with a question. This helps you easily navigate the chapter and possibly skim over sections that you feel you know the answer to or have more experience with. Whether you digest this resource like a meal served

> *"Students must be able to communicate not just with text or speech, but in multiple multimedia formats. They must be able to communicate visually through video and imagery as effectively as they do with text and speech."*
>
> **—Global Digital Citizen Foundation**

on a sectioned plate or a flight of cheese and wine, my wish for you is to cultivate an appreciation for the critical role communication does and will play in the future and discover the motivation and tools to support your students with this integral and attainable skill.

Each of the seven chapters (e.g., email ettiqutte, collaboration, visual literacy and presentation skills, projects and publishing, digital portfolios and resumes, social media, and curating) are skills that the majority of adults use in their jobs and careers (and even personal lives) in some form or fashion. Additionally, these are types of communications that have either been directly impacted by technology (e.g., visual literacy and presentations, collaboration, portfolios) or have origins in recent technologies (e.g., social media, email etiquette, curation, student publishing). To narrow in on the goal of college and career readiness (rather than classroom readiness), industry examples have been thoughtfully selected over student examples in some activities.

The ultimate goal of this book is to provide a success-ready resource that will support educators with designing learning experiences that allow students to flex these communication competencies, while providing students with tools and authentic opportunities to foster the continued growth of these skills throughout and beyond their secondary education.

To support instructional design of lessons to integrate these communication competencies, each chapter includes:

- Practical hands-on resources, research, and examples
- A Communication Catcher (like a fortune teller—not the cookie, but that little origami children's game that folds paper to provide eight questions or activities for the player) that can be easily implemented in the classroom with students
- Chapter Planning Preparation Inventory: A summary of the chapter in question/checklist form to help with planning
- My Students' Self-Assessment Checklist: A quick resource that can be used as a pre- and post-class assessment
- Additional Resources and Reading (found on the companion site as these will be updated and adapted over the years)
- Communication Cohort Challenges: A collection of challenges to support teachers with being intentionally introspective and flexing and exploring these skills individually or with fellow colleagues correspond to each chapter's focus. These are included in the Appendix A rather than at the end of the chapter as they are designed for teachers as optional professional development. These could be completed individually, but I tend to think completing them alongside fellow professionals whether in your building or online provides far more insight.

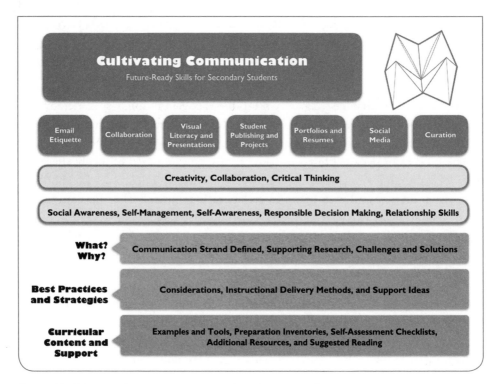

Cultivating Communication
Future-Ready Skills for Secondary Students

| Email Etiquette | Collaboration | Visual Literacy and Presentations | Student Publishing and Projects | Portfolios and Resumes | Social Media | Curation |

Creativity, Collaboration, Critical Thinking

Social Awareness, Self-Management, Self-Awareness, Responsible Decision Making, Relationship Skills

What? Why? Communication Strand Defined, Supporting Research, Challenges and Solutions

Best Practices and Strategies Considerations, Instructional Delivery Methods, and Support Ideas

Curricular Content and Support Examples and Tools, Preparation Inventories, Self-Assessment Checklists, Additional Resources, and Suggested Reading

Figure P.3 *Cultivating Communication* **Book Map Weaves in 4 C's, SEL, Research, and Actionable Resources**

A visual book map has been provided (Figure P.3) as an overview of all seven chapters and how each one will contain a rich pedagogy and resource sandwich of the other 3 C's, social-emotional skills, defined rationale and purpose for each chapter's topic deeply rooted in research and flavored with industry experts, a wealth of best practices and strategies, and finally garnished with a heavy helping (hopefully not-heavy-handed) curricular content and support.

I am of the mindset that more is more when it comes to resources, research, and relevant information, so I sought to support you and your students with a variety of additional accoutrements:

- **Supporting All Learners:** To cultivate communication for all learners, this book embeds some of the best practices for ELLs and students with learning disabilities such as visual cues, multimodal directions, mentor models, rubrics, and multiple ways to communicate understanding. After all, supporting these students effectively is not done through watering down content and standards, but by providing authentic learning experiences to communicate in a variety of fashions (e.g., oral, written, visual, nonverbal, multimedia) and with a variety of audiences.

- **Supporting Social-Emotional Skills:** In addition to baking in communication best practices for all students, I felt very emphatically about including social-emotional learning skills (sometimes referred to as emotional intelligence) within every chapter. In a round of industry interviews I conducted, I found SEL skills to be important. In particular, self-management, responsible decision making, and relationship skills led the pack. I think Justin Hammond, Clouds Networks Engineer, said it best: "No matter the industry you work in, your position in it, or the remoteness of your workplace, everything eventually ends on people. Masterful use of people-skills can create success from nothing." How we communicate with people oftentimes is directly related to our own self-awareness and management. In fact, one study determined that 90% of top performers were also high in emotional intelligence as compared to 20% of bottom performers. The same study also found that people that possessed higher levels of emotional intelligence also garnered higher incomes ("About Emotional Intelligence," 2016). The good news is that these skills can be taught. Threading these social-emotional learning competencies throughout the book is also clearly vital to students building the foundation for effective communication skills in college, careers, and beyond. A quick reference for these skills has been included in Appendix C. Interestingly enough, both Harvard through "Making Caring Common" and Stanford through "Challenge Success" have recognized a need for these social-emotional skills and created organizations to cultivate and grow them in students, staff, parents, and the community.

> *"Unfortunately, we've moved away from teaching the emotional forms of communication. But if you want to get along in this world, you need to have a heightened sense of emotional intelligence, which is the equal of your intellectual intelligence."*
>
> **—George Lucas**
> *(Filmmaker and Entrepreneur)*

- **Supporting College and Career Readiness Skills:** Full vignettes from the interviews I conducted are in the Industry Insights spotlights woven throughout this book (and explained in Appendix D) to offer a clear perspective as to how valuable these skills are now and even some tips on how to polish them.

- **Supporting Teachers and Their Own Professional Learning:** While this book is designed to guide teachers' practices, these very same best practices can be reimagined within our own communications as well. Multiple additional readings and resources as well as a book study template and communication cohort challenges (Appendix A) are provided to support your journey cultivating 21st century communicators.

I am a firm believer that the vast majority of teachers know what works, but find taking those big ideas and translating them to day-to-day instructional practices can be difficult without proper support or real-life examples. Sometimes there can be a disconnect between knowing what works and making what works actually happen. Hopefully, that's where this book fills a need. Sometimes we look at other teachers and think they got a little extra magical dust or found some hidden fountain of awesome. When in reality, there is no great and powerful Oz—truly just great teachers in need of inspiration and guidance to redefine their classroom and support their learners to be successful communicators and lifelong learners.

Beyond reading this book and utilizing its best practices, ideas, and resources with your own students, consider sharing what works, what you have learned, and questions and insights you have using some of the suggested teacher challenges found in Appendix A. I know what it feels like to teach on an island with no mentor, no curriculum, no scope and sequence, and no clue. While I learned a lot from that experience, I wouldn't wish that struggle upon anyone.

> *"The smartest person in the room is the room itself."*
>
> —**David Weinberger**
> *(Technologist and Author)*

Using social media to ban together and support each other allows everyone to have access to a collective Oz, a connected group of educators that is far more powerful and transformative together than individually. While I realize that not all of you are online or use social media as a means of professional development, my hope is that through this book, you are moved and inspired to get connected and redefine what communication looks like for you and your class. After all, our future is not powered by *my* students, but *our* students.

References

About Emotional Intelligence. (2016). *TalentSmart*. Retrieved October 20, 2016, from http://www.talentsmart.com/about/emotional-intelligence.php

Are They Really Ready to Work? (2006). Retrieved from http://www.p21.org/storage/documents/FINAL_REPORT_PDF09-29-06.pdf

IBM—What Is Big Data? (n.d.). Retrieved from https://www-01.ibm.com/software/data/bigdata/what-is-big-data.html

Kay, K. ASCD 2013 Session "4 Keys for Becoming a 21st Century School or District." Retrieved from http://mollybestge.com/tag/edleader21/

The Learning Curve: 2014 Report Summary (2015). Retrieved December 28, 2015, from http://thelearningcurve.pearson.com/2014-report-summary/

Millennial Branding Student Employment Gap Study. (2012). *Millennialbranding.com*. Retrieved July 7, 2016, from http://millennialbranding.com/2012/millennial-branding-student-employment-gap-study/

Nadworny, E., & Kamenetz, A. (2016). Why kindergarten is the new first grade. *NPR.org*. Retrieved January 24, 2016, from http://www.npr.org/sections/ed/2016/01/08/462279629/why-kindergarten-is-the-new-first-grade?utm_campaign=storyshare&utm_source=facebook.com&utm_medium=social

National Education Association. (n.d.). *Preparing 21st century students for a global society: An educator's guide to the 4 C's.* Retrieved January 24, 2016, from http://www.nea.org/assets/docs/A-Guide-to-Four-Cs.pdf

The Office of Educational Technology. (2016). *Future ready learning: Reimagining the role of technology in education.* Retrieved January 24, 2016, from http://tech.ed.gov/files/2015/12/NETP16.pdf

Pope, D., Brown, M., & Miles, S. (2015). *Overloaded and underprepared: Strategies for stronger schools and healthy, successful kids.* San Francisco, CA: Jossey-Bass.

Standards for Students. (2016). *Iste.org.* Retrieved January 24, 2016, from http://www.iste.org/standards/ISTE-standards/standards-for-students

ACKNOWLEDGMENTS

All my love and gratitude to my "boys" (Scott, Hayden, and Gavin), my family, friends, colleagues, and PLN. A special thanks to Carl, Rafranz, and Ariel for all of your clarity and insight. And I can't forget . . . my Starbucks on the hill, Blue October, Macklemore, and Twenty One Pilots that kept me moving and motivated through this journey.

Publisher Acknowledgments

Corwin gratefully acknowledges the contributions of the following reviewers:

Natalie Cannon
Latin, Mythology, and
    Credit Recovery Teacher
Westlake High School
Austin, TX

Jennifer Casa-Todd
Literacy Consultant
York Catholic District School Board
Aurora, ON

Mandy Frantti
Physics, Astronomy, and Math Teacher
Munising Middle/High School
Munising, MI

Lauren Gehman
Twelfth-Grade AP Environmental
    Science Teacher
Westlake High School
Austin, TX

Brianna Henneke Hodges
Instructional Technology
    Integration Educator
Stephenville High School
Stephenville, TX

Kacy Mitchell
Educational Technologist
Eanes ISD
Austin, TX

Sara Stewart-Lediard
21st Century Learning
    Instructional Coach
Washoe County School District
Washoe, NV

Mandy White
Eighth-Grade Science Teacher
Fort Riley Middle School
Fort Riley, KS

ABOUT THE AUTHOR

Just Google "iPad Lessons," and **Lisa Johnson's** creations and curations can be readily found across a variety of social networks. Recognized as an Apple Distinguished Educator in 2013 and Lead PBS Digital Innovator for Texas in 2016, featured in both editions of *iPad in Education for Dummies* and Corwin's Connected Educators Series *The Missing Voices in EdTech*, Lisa thoughtfully and diligently models and shares the transformational power of mobile devices and professional learning networks within the global edusphere.

Creator of the TechChef4u blog, co-host of "Appy Hours 4 U," and coauthor of the professional development hit "Hot Apps 4 HOTS" with close to 20,000 international downloads, Lisa offers a unique perspective as she is embedded at the intersection of where all stakeholders in technology integration meet.

Mother of two mobile natives, Educational Technologist supporting a K–12 1:1 iPad school district, nationally recognized speaker, international curriculum writer, Book Creator Ambassador, Tackk Advocate, and Thinglink Expert Educator, Lisa has the ability to see and share how technology can impact and redefine pedagogy, assessment, instruction, and the four walls of the classroom.

Blending purposeful technology integration with wit and a dollop of app-thusiasm, Lisa addresses hot topics ranging from SAMR and 21st century learning to formative assessment, fostering students as authors, differentiated instruction, digital portfolios, workflow, curation, collaborative cultures, device neutral classrooms, college and career readiness, and the ever-evolving classroom dynamic. Bringing her own unique home-roasted blend of pedagogy and perspective, Lisa empowers educators with the critical ingredients to cook up a new recipe for learning.

Connect with Lisa via these channels:

- Website: www.techchef4u.com
- Twitter: @TechChef4u, #cultivatecomm
- Facebook: www.facebook.com/techchef4u
- Pinterest: www.pinterest.com/techchef4u

Lisa is also available for keynotes, conferences, and professional development.

Industry Insights

How important is email in your business? What are some best practices you use for email with customers, clients, colleagues, etc.? Explain.

Email is essential to ...

Pass on information that is hard to retain in a conversation: "It is a way to communicate with clients and pass information that is hard to retain from a conversation. I try to keep emailing concise."

—Brandon Mitchell (Veterinarian)

Serve as an official conduit for multiple audiences: "Emails can have legal and business repercussions, and therefore every employee must carefully consider everything that is stated or conveyed in emails. Oftentimes emails may be filtered through a few representatives such as project engineers or project managers to be the official conduit for communication."

—Matthew Guerrieri (Electrical Engineer)

Make decisions: "Email is extremely important. All communication with clients is done through email. All call sheets, mood boards, inspirations for advertising and marketing is done through email sent by the clients directly to us. It is crucial for our job."

—Judy Jacomino (Makeup and Hair Artist)

Document timelines and processes: "It's one of the primary ways that we communicate with other members of our team outside of our company (e.g., title companies, realtors). We are also communicating via email with our customers. Being able to quickly know where we are in a transaction is very important to running our business efficiently."

—Melissa Johnson (VP/CFO in Real Estate)

Email must ...

Be accurate and impartial: "Particularly in health care, written communication with patients and fellow practitioners must be 100% accurate. The information conveyed should be factual and impartial, not based on personal emotions or opinions. Also, patient confidentiality and legal concerns such as maintaining HIPPA compliance have to be at the forefront of every electronic communication."

—Kati Ohlmeyer (MS, RDN, LD)

Strike the right tone: "In law and related fields strong written communication skills are imperative. So much of business is conducted via email that consistently striking the right tone and conveying the right (and right amount of) information determines whether your message is really 'received.'"

—Kristy Peters (Principal at Litigation Finance Company)

Value the recipient: "The tone of electronic communications can easily be misinterpreted. We begin every communication with a thank you—the recipient needs to know we appreciate the value of their time. Second, we utilize 'I' as few times as possible. In order to avoid or prevent miscommunication from escalating, if something emotional is being discussed, the conversation is moved to a phone or video call."

—Jacob Hanson (Managing Partner With PR with Panache)

Be courteous: "Email is our primary tool for external communication. We always hedge on the side of courtesy and clarity, never assuming that tone can be interpreted. We are respectful of the reader, and keep messages succinct, with a call to action to read further (or click a link) below the sign off."

—Reshan Richards (Chief Learning Officer at Explain Everything)

Prioritize clarity over brevity: "Email is often used to communicate with people who lack the technical depth to understand the content of the message. Even if the message is targeted to a technical audience, it may still be distributed to those who are not. It is important to prioritize clarity over being concise in almost all situations because of this."

—Justin Hammond (Cloud Networks Engineer)

Email Etiquette

Communicating with peers and professionals to elicit an action or response through clear communication, self-advocacy, and due diligence

"What really leads to miscommunications is a lack of empathy."

—**Sasha VanHoven (Social Media Producer at the Wirecutter)**

Y ou might find it odd to devote the first chapter of this book to email. However, if you view email as the on ramp to other forms of digital communication, you will quickly see that it impacts every other chapter, whether it be with email correspondences or having an email account to create another account (e.g., Evernote, LinkedIn, Twitter). Furthermore, for better or worse, the brevity and accelerated nature of text messages and a variety of social networks has naturally bled into the way we communicate through other channels. Additionally, based on the findings from *Are They Really Ready to Work?* that discovered deficits by both high school graduates and 2- and 4-year graduates in the areas of English and Written Communications, it seemed as best a place as any to journey into communication innovations (*Are They Really Ready to Work?*, 2006).

Why Are We Talking About Email for Students?

When I first started with iPads in 2011, my campuses had several carts and were using iPad 1's as shared devices. As students created something or needed to email off a product, they had to use a class email account or a class Dropbox account, as our district did not provide email addresses to the students at that time. The workflow process from the device was cumbersome to say the least. Now with the growing prevalence of mobile devices in schools, the idea of email for students is less of a nice to have and more of a must have. Students now require email accounts for access to GAFE (Google Apps for Education) tools like Google Docs, Sheets, Slides, and Calendar, as well as other apps and tools like Canva, Tackk, and Thinglink that are used in the classroom.

While many of us can remember a day without emails . . . a day that might have included handwritten or typed communications and addressing envelopes, this reality is a science fiction flashback at best for your students. I imagine most of you are like me and find email to be a necessary evil. Most adults have been marinating an email account for 15–20 years or more in some form or format and have sent countless electronic correspondences. Some of you may have even experienced email overload and sought out creative life hacks to remove the electronic clutter. But the majority of our secondary students are just emerging into this reality. Some of the best practices of this communication tool may seem obvious to us, but not to the novice.

Interestingly enough, the majority of our secondary students have a school email account (and many times a personal one) and rarely check either one, only to find out that this seems to be the main mode of communication in college and most careers. There is little question that it is an integral part of the adult world and most likely will continue to be for the foreseeable future. College and career readiness doesn't mean replicating college and career settings in high school. This means providing opportunities to not only stress the importance of this type of communication, but also leverage our curriculum to support clear messaging with this form of writing and literacy.

How Do We Ensure Best Practices for Using Email?

If you have ever read the circular tale *If You Give a Mouse a Cookie,* where the mouse asks for something, which then leads to asking for something else, then you might feel that way about emails. If I give a student an email, they might send out something inappropriate. If they send out something inappropriate, we might have a parent complain to the district. If a parent complains to the district, then we might have to shut down emails for all of the students. In fact, I actually worked with a district that had restricted the camera on all of their mobile devices for this very reason. Teachers had to submit a work ticket request to allow use of the camera for a 24-hour period on their classroom devices. I know this may seem extreme, but it may also resonate with some of you. Sometimes we have to take the parenting view though. If we give students email accounts, then they will be able to make mistakes and also learn with our support. If they make mistakes in a walled garden and learn appropriate use, they will be less likely to inappropriately use this technology when they leave our institution. Let's face it. An inappropriate email in school may cause them a suspension and some embarrassment, but an inappropriate email in their career could cost them their job.

Understanding the nature of when and why email should be used in the first place is essential to beginning this journey. For example, if I am sending an attachment or longer communication, an email might be preferable. But if I just need a quick answer to a question, need to address a concern, or have an ongoing discussion, then I might text someone or send a direct message on Twitter, Facebook, or Slack. We do have to remember that recipients aren't always on or available and having the "text a peer or professional" option doesn't necessarily support personal problem-solving either. That being said, I was recently sitting in a classroom when a student (not in the classroom) texted another student (in the classroom) to ask the teacher if she could make up the test fifth period. Like you I was first shocked and appalled at the casual nature of this communication. But then I flipped the perspective a bit. If I know my co-worker is with another co-worker and I need a quick answer to a question, I might text that co-worker to ask the other one the question. Too often we prepare curriculum for the world we live in and don't consider that the format of existing communications will naturally evolve as our students become that future. We can't future proof them, but we can provide them with the ability to problem-solve and think critically about how they communicate now and in the future. Posing the question to your students, "In what situations would email be the best tool and in what situations would it not be?" not only honors their current communication practices, but opens the door for discussing best practices (with whatever tools they use).

Students do in fact communicate using a variety of tools, but these tools do not necessarily support them with college and career communications. Texting is typically used to inform someone or give him or her a heads up (e.g., "hey I will be staying late for tutoring today") or to gain a response (e.g., "hey can you bring my lunch . . . I forgot it at home"), but texts are typically brief and informal. Emails tend to be more formal, longer, and they are on the record as they are through a school-issued service. Additionally, we typically only get a few texts at a time because only friends and family text us (or a few co-workers), but everyone in your place of work has your email, so this adds an extra layer of importance as you then have to prioritize your responses. If you are supporting a profession with a customer service or client component, then email becomes a vital way to provide support in a clear, timely, positive, and efficient manner.

Part of this future proofing is providing frameworks for students to problem-solve and make educated decisions before they enter college and the workforce. Rather than dictating rules in a campus or district email contract, having discussions that lead students to the answers through thoughtful discourse with peers and professionals (e.g., teachers, counselors) can be far more powerful. This idea of "Conversations Before Contracts" was the impetus for me to create an Email Etiquette Communication Catcher (Figure 1.1) to facilitate these types of conversations. It is intended to be used with students to spark thoughtful discussion and dialog around these topics. The resource is included in Appendix B and can be downloaded at https://resources .corwin.com/cultivatingcomm.

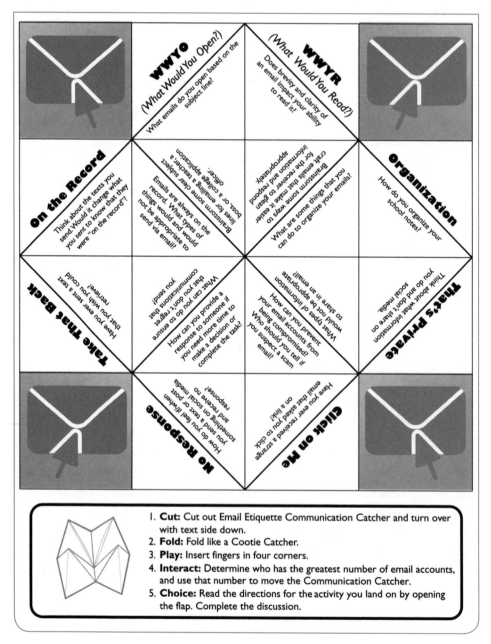

1. **Cut:** Cut out Email Etiquette Communication Catcher and turn over with text side down.
2. **Fold:** Fold like a Cootie Catcher.
3. **Play:** Insert fingers in four corners.
4. **Interact:** Determine who has the greatest number of email accounts, and use that number to move the Communication Catcher.
5. **Choice:** Read the directions for the activity you land on by opening the flap. Complete the discussion.

Figure 1.1 Email Etiquette Communication Catcher

Available for download at **https://resources.corwin.com/cultivatingcomm**

While conversations are integral, our current reality does have to ensure legal responsibility for inappropriate use, so having a district email contract or an acceptable use policy is necessary in addition to these conversations. Just remember that students have a lot more buy-in when they are front-loaded with conversations before contracts.

How Do We Support Clear Communication Through Email?

While the Communication Catcher in Figure 1.1 dives into acceptable use and briefly delves into clear communication (e.g., "What would you open?"; "What would you read?," No Response), additional conversations and support will most likely be needed to scaffold this skill. Email is ultimately an invitation for communication. The very nature of invitations is asking for some sort of response, whether it be an acknowledgment or a specific action. If the email or message is cluttered or unclear, the response may be less than what was requested. We can't predict how long we will have email and if this generation of texters and tweeters will slowly impact this form of communication as they enter the workforce. What we can do is provide them with guides and opportunities to craft communications that invite the desired response. In my experience, the desired response ultimately hinges on two things: audience and action.

- **Audience:** If the audience is a professor, then they will most likely want to have a more formal approach. If the audience is a co-worker or a friend, then a less formal, more casual approach that includes emoticons might be applicable. Audience can get even more granular if you look at it in the context of differentiated instruction. People use different strategies to communicate with different types of people. When it is appropriate to use Reply versus Reply All or CC and BCC is also a useful skill to teach as choosing the wrong one can be a social faux pas.

- **Action:** Because I have received so many bad emails and have to sift through paragraphs of wonkily formatted vague text to figure out what information is important and what I am supposed to do with said information, I have been hypersensitive to designing my emails to juxtapose this condition. Students write in some form or format K–12. Reminding them that emails are just another form of writing and that this type has a delineated set of rules and best practices, much like a persuasive essay, tends to make this acclimation easier.

Here are some guidelines you can pass along to your students:

- **Actionable Descriptive Subject Line:** Subject lines are key. Make them descriptive and give the recipient a heads up on the action requested (e.g., "Please Review My Assignment" or "Discussing Extension on Project").

- **Questions/Action Items:** I don't ever want someone to read my email and have no idea what I was asking them to do. I try to make my requests and notices easy to digest by including questions that are then answered within the email (see Figures 1.3 and 1.4 later in this chapter).

- **Clear Formatting (e.g., bullets, bold, spacing):** While grammar and spelling is important, most email services will scan for these. Much like a textbook uses formatting to draw attention to questions, important words, and ideas, I use bullets, bold, and spacing to organize the message (see Figures 1.3 and 1.4).

- **Clear Self-Advocacy and Due Diligence:** Sometimes emails can feel just like a laundry list of to-do's, each one with a specific task. Students should be reminded that email is an important way to advocate for themselves by communicating issues with completing deadlines or quandaries with a project. Many teachers' biggest pet peeves are not student or staff emails, but people not doing due diligence. If you send me an email about something discussed in class, consider approaching the email with the "Ask 3" model (e.g., "Dear Mr. Bronsan, I will be out next week for ACL surgery. I looked at the online class calendar, reviewed the course website, and asked one of my third-period classmates about assignments for that week, but couldn't find any. Please let me know what work I will be missing, so I can begin collecting those assignments prior to my absence.") This type of communication honors the recipient's time and allows our students to be proactive self-advocates.

I know it may seem silly or redundant, but if your email address is only on your teacher website or some handout you had at the front of the room

Figure 1.2 "We Are Away But Not Absent" Email Tear Sheet

on parent night, odds are that students won't remember what it is. As I am in a support position and not assigned to a classroom, I have students drop by my office each and every day. When the light is on, but I am not there, they may complain and lament I am "never there" rather than being proactive and finding alternate means to communicate with me, especially if their needs or inquiries are time sensitive. To facilitate their self-advocacy, I have a flier that has my picture, a communication that makes it clear that just because I am not in my office does not mean that I am not on campus, and tear sheets that provide students with quick access to email, shown in Figure 1.2.

While this may look slightly different for a classroom teacher and might include class periods present and the teacher's website, the idea is one that ultimately takes away excuses and puts the ownership of communication and problem-solving back in the student's hands.

Audience and action are important, but ferreting out specific guidelines utilizing actual examples is vital to supporting clear communication and to even trouble-shooting revising emails. Take the example given in Figure 1.3. Both essentially say the same thing, but the one on the bottom uses bullets and bolded text to make it easier for the recipient to decipher the information.

When asking for a favor rather than just alerting someone of a change or an event, you want to be very specific with your communication as well as respectful and

---

Before

Subject: Future Student Devices: Final 4

The final 4 devices are set up and ready for review in the library. The contenders are a MacBook Air 11", iPad Air 2 with Keyboard Case, Dell Latitude 3350, and Dell ChromeBook. Each device is charged, ready for you to explore, and has a placard with detailed specs. We are also providing a spreadsheet with additional specs of all 4 devices side by side. Mandy and/or I will be available during 4th and 5th to answer questions and provide additional clarification as needed.

After

Subject: *** Future Student Devices: Final Four ***

The Final Four devices are set up and ready for review in the library.

- **Contenders:** MacBook Air 11", iPad Air 2 with Keyboard Case, Dell Latitude 3350, and Dell ChromeBook.
- **Explore:** Each device is charged, ready for you to explore, and has a placard with detailed specs.
- **Deeper Details:** We are also providing a spreadsheet with additional specs of all 4 devices side by side.
- **On Site Ed Tech:** Mandy and/or I will be available during 4th and 5th to answer questions and provide additional clarification as needed.

Come and kick the tires. ;)
M&L

Figure 1.3 Revised Email Example 1

grateful of their time. The email in Figure 1.4 is what I used to send out to fellow colleagues when I was gathering contextual feedback for the book. The one on the top has a subject line that sounds pushy, whereas the one on the bottom acknowledges the value that the recipient will add to the intended response. The email on the bottom uses bullets, bold formatting, and questions to make it very clear what is needed from the recipient and when it is needed. Finally, the email on the bottom also clearly states how long the intended action will take (e.g., "It should take no more than 5–10 minutes to complete.") and expresses gratitude for this time and effort (e.g., "Thanks in advance.").

Before

Subject: Hey, Hey Fill Out My Survey

I am finally getting to the final stages of the book. I would love for you to complete the survey based on the work you do with Explain Everything (especially with global collaboration and teams) . . . The book is titled "Cultivating Communication in the Classroom" and will be published by Corwin. It is designed to support secondary teachers with best practices, research, and practical ways to support college and career readiness skills within their core curriculum. The book focuses on Communication skills (e.g., email, collaboration and teams, presentation skills, social media, curation, resumes, online portfolios . . .). I am looking to gather information from a variety of careers and industry leaders to support the book with real-world contextual examples and anecdotes. I have crafted the survey below. It should take no more than 5–10 minutes to complete. I would greatly appreciate your support with sharing your insight and expertise from your career and industry lens. The book is nearing the final stages so I would greatly appreciate your kind but expedient attention to providing feedback.;)

Communication Skills Survey Google Form

After

Subject: *** Your Input Matters: Communication Skills Survey ***

So . . . finally getting to the final stages of the book. I would love for you to complete the survey based on the work you do with Explain Everything (especially with global collaboration and teams) . . .

- **What is the book about?** The book is titled "Cultivating Communication in the Classroom" and will be published by Corwin. It is designed to support secondary teachers with best practices, research, and practical ways to support college and career readiness skills within their core curriculum. The book focuses on Communication skills (e.g., email, collaboration and teams, presentation skills, social media, curation, resumes, online portfolios . . .).
- **What do I need?** I am looking to gather information from a variety of careers and industry leaders to support the book with real-world contextual examples and anecdotes. I have crafted the survey below. It should take no more than 5–10 minutes to complete. I would greatly appreciate your support with sharing your insight and expertise from your career and industry lens.
- **When do I need it?** The book is nearing the final stages so I would greatly appreciate your kind but expedient attention to providing feedback. ;)

Thanks in advance!

Communication Skills Survey Google Form

Figure 1.4 Revised Email Example 2

Sometimes we miss an email or need more time to complete the action or make a decision. Teaching students that a response is better than no response at all is vital to clear communication and setting clear expectations. The following examples highlight simple ways to supply an interim response in lieu of no response at all. Elizabeth Grace Saunders has fantastic quick default response emails (Figure 1.5)

When you need more time to write a thorough response:	When you need additional time or want to request a deadline extension:
Thank you for your message. I'll get back to you shortly with a more thorough response.	I want to keep you updated on the current status of the project. We've made some great progress but in the process discovered that [fill in the issue] takes longer than we had initially anticipated. Would it be reasonable to have an additional week to account for the unexpected delay?
When you need additional time to make a decision:	**When someone has requested your support or help with a project but you feel like you can't take on any additional projects:**
Thank you for your email. I'll take some time to consider the alternatives and get back to you with my decision.	I really appreciate your coming to me. I would love to help, but unfortunately I'm at capacity right now and can't give this project the time and attention it requires.
To apologize for a delayed response:	**When someone asks you to complete an additional project but does not provide any clarification as to the resources needed, the process utilized, or the timeline:**
Thank you for your understanding about my delayed response. [XYZ] has been happening.	Thanks for sending on this project. I would be happy to move forward on it but need more clarity on the scope of the work. Can we set up a time to discuss this more?
When you would like to provide project updates but are not finished with the project:	**When you don't feel comfortable responding via email:**
I've completed [bullet point, bullet point, bullet point]. On Friday, I'll send a status update on my additional progress.	[Pick up the phone or schedule an in-person meeting.]
When you need additional support or materials to complete a project:	**When people ask you about everything instead of directly contacting the appropriate person:**
I'm excited to start on this project, and I'll need this additional support and materials to move forward [list out specifics].	Just wanted to let you know that I received your email, and [fill in the person] is the best person to help you with that request.

Figure 1.5 "Email Is for Setting Expectations" by Elizabeth Grace Saunders

Source: Elizabeth Grace Saunders, time management coach and author of *How to Invest Your Time Like Money*

that provide helpful wording to acknowledge an email and ask for more time to provide a solution or informed response.

Try pairing some of the strategies for clear communication and setting expectations with the authentic curricular opportunities detailed later in the chapter.

How Can I Troubleshoot Email With My Students?

While the bulk of this chapter has focused more on global questions, which are great fodder for conversations, and granular practices for clear communication within the body of an email, there is always a need for practical troubleshooting strategies. As more and more student creations are generated digitally, students will inevitably encounter technical issues that will need to be resolved. As file storage increases (a decade ago a 128 MB flash drive would suffice for a whole year's worth of documents, and now a 4 GB flash drive will barely hold a few videos and a slide deck), students will have to utilize file management and storage to their advantage. While this may not be an issue for schools and districts that utilize GAFE (Google Apps for Education) or a LMS (Learning Management System) like Canvas or eBackpack, it is a reality for those that don't have access to these tools.

- **What types of formats are acceptable to send in an email?** Many times students send emails with an attachment to an assignment. Due to the variety of devices and software applications, mismatches occur. For example, a student sends a Pages document, and the teacher only has Word to open it. A good rule of thumb for students is to always send a .pdf version of the document to be reviewed. While .pdf requires an extra add-on or tool like Adobe to annotate or comment, it is an universal format that all devices can easily access.

- **What will you do when a file is too large for email?** This is by far one of the most prevalent issues I have seen. Many times it involves students trying to share videos. The easiest fix is to upload the video to a site like YouTube, Vimeo, or Google Drive and then share the link.

- **What protocols need to be set up for file sharing?** If a student is working on Google Doc and wants to allow the teacher or fellow student viewing or editing access, they have to set that up within the document. Oftentimes mismatches occur when students try to share a document from a school account to someone's personal account that is not within the school domain. While it is a pretty easy issue to resolve, file sharing will continue to be on our radar as more and more content becomes digital in nature and stored in the cloud.

- **Will you use your personal or school email to create accounts?** I always encourage students to use their school email to create additional accounts. However, as students get to be juniors and seniors, they tend to want to transition their accounts for life beyond our 12-year academia. This is especially important for the portfolios and blogs that students would like to continue to groom. It is also essential for students to have an email that they have access to year round if they are applying for college or jobs.

Each one of these questions directly relates to an encounter I have had with students, whether it be scenarios students have shared or overarching issues I have observed or had to troubleshoot.

How Can I Provide Authentic Curricular Opportunities for Email Communication?

Teaching email can be a pretty bland topic, unless it is used in context. Below are a few options for teachers to weave this type of communication into the classroom:

- **Emails From the Past:** Have students compose an email from someone in the past (e.g., Lincoln, Napoleon, Marie Curie, Shakespeare) to address an issue or a concern. What would F. Scott Fitzgerald email his editor? What would Andy Warhol email his mother? What would Muhammad Ali's coach email him? What would emails between Richard Nixon and his secretary look like? For more information, ideas, or research on this topic, check out *The Who, the What, and the When: 65 Artists Illustrate the Secret Sidekicks of History*.

- **Future Me:** Have students write an email to their future self to be delivered at a future date. The website futureme.org allows them to achieve this. This is also a fantastic goal-setting exercise to explore at the beginning of the year.

- **Ask Me:** While most students aren't familiar with the Dear Abby letters, the idea is a good one to reboot. Consider having students practice handling concerns via email. This is less about email and more about problem-solving and persuasive language through the vehicle of email. Many careers handle customer emails or employee concerns. Using a framework like CARP (e.g., Control, Acknowledge, Refocus, Problem-Solve) is useful. Carl Hooker, Director of Innovations for Eanes ISD, uses three email challenges to screen candidates for educational technologist positions. Responding to student, parent, teacher, and administrator communications is an integral part of the job.

- **Persuade Me:** Many emails embody strategies similar to that of a persuasive paper. Rather than having students write a persuasive letter, consider using a RAFTS (e.g., Role, Audience, Format, Topic, Strong Verb). The format is an email, so we have that part covered. One example from the WritingFix.com generator was: "You will write as though you are . . . *a history textbook writer* . . . writing something to be read or heard by . . . *the local school board*. The writing will take the format of . . . *an email* . . . and will be about '*The Bill of Rights.*' Your piece of writing's purpose will be to . . . *INSPIRE* your audience to act now" ("HistoryFix," 1999).

- **Miss Me:** One way to foster relationship skills and social awareness is to have students send an email to a classmate who was absent. The email both acknowledges that the missing student is a valuable asset to the class but also provides them with notes from the day or maybe a link to resources so they can easily catch up. This could be applied to students who are homebound as well.

- **Anticipate Needs With an Autoresponder:** It was bound to happen. As email is one of the predominant forms of communication, not providing a response within a 24–48-hour period can appear like a form of negligence. Figure 1.5 does provide some simple standard responses to navigate these delays. Others have adopted a more creative approach and crafted custom autoresponders that not only inform recipients that a response might be delayed, but also anticipate their recipient's needs, and even provide tips for getting a quick response. The beginning of the year is a hectic time and I receive heaps of emails that I can't answer in a timely fashion and that tend to be similar requests. To expedite support and clear messaging, my colleague and I created an autoresponder (Figure 1.6) while we were on campus so teachers were aware of what we were doing, but also might be able to come to a resolution with the information we provided.

Subject: We Are on Campus and Will Be With You Soon…

Thanks for the email! We want you to know that we will get back with you, but it's taking a little longer than usual due to the rush at the beginning of the school year. We thought it might be helpful to add this autoresponder with a few frequently asked questions and our answers to them so you might be able to find answers sooner:

- **Students Having Issues Logging in to Turnitin:** Check out this video tutorial to support you.
- **Students Not Able to See Folders in Google Classroom:** Check out this video tutorial:
    - Sharing files and folders in Google Drive and Classroom (computer version)
    - Sharing files and folders (computer version with closed captioning)
    - Sharing files and folders in Google Drive and Classroom (iPad version)
- **Students Who Did Not Pick Up iPads:** Have them Email Phillip Gallagher (pgallgaher@anyschool.net) or visit his office.
- **Students Without Google Login or With Faulty Google Login:** Email the Tech Services Help Desk (TSHelpDesk@anyschool.net).
- **Self Service:**
    - **Students Without Access to Self-Service:** Make sure students are on ESCHOOL network and that their date and time in settings is set to automatic. Self-Service should appear in a few hours. If it does not, please send students to the new Juice Bar (in the old attendance office next to the Commons.)
    - **Students and Teachers With Inoperable Self-Service:** If a student or teacher's Self-Service app is not working, delete it and it should reappear in a few hours and be operable. If it does not, please send students to the Juice Bar in the library during 4th and 5th period.
- **Suggest Apps for School App Store:** Here is a direct link to the Google Form.
- **Prompt Replies and Technological Emergencies:** Technology Services is working diligently to complete existing work orders. Please continue to submit work orders in this manner. If you are experiencing a technological emergency, please call the help desk directly at #021891 or email the Tech Services Help Desk directly (TSHelpDesk@anyschool.net).
-  Click here for Hold Music (if you like). ;)

We look forward to talking with you. Have a great year!

Figure 1.6 On-Campus Autoresponder

CULTIVATING COMMUNICATION IN THE CLASSROOM

While I don't imagine most students will create these for themselves, I do think drafting samples for their own teachers or for a historical or political figure gives them some experience with anticipating needs and discovering the best formats of communication. I have included a professional example (Figure 1.7) to highlight the variety of content that can be included in one. This activity could also be easily paired with generating emails from the past.

Subject: TechChef App-solutely Awesome Autoresponder

I realize that autoresponders may seem impersonal and obnoxious, but I also realize that we have limited hours in our day to complete personal and professional tasks and respond accordingly. I am currently in the final stages of editing my first book, *Cultivating Communication in the Classroom*, and want to ensure the quality of this resource for educators before it goes off to typesetting shortly.

I sincerely apologize for my delayed response. In an effort to connect you with the answers and resources you may be seeking, I thought it might be helpful to provide a few frequently asked questions and my answers:

- **I am looking for a slide deck you shared at our event:** All of my slide decks, infographics, and handouts are posted on my portfolio linked here: https://techchef4u.com/portfolio
- **I want to book Lisa Johnson to speak:** Please complete the Google Form.
- **I want Lisa Johnson to write a guest blog post:** Please email me the specifics of the request (e.g., website, topic, timeline, length of post).
- **I am looking for your bio and head shots for our program:** Visit my site for multiple versions of my bio and some options: https://techchef4u.com/speaking
- **I would love to meet up at an event:** I love to connect with educators in person. I have all of my upcoming events posted on my site. Let's chat on Twitter (@TechChef4u) and set up a time to meet.

If you are still reading . . . I would love to share a few more alliterative inspirations with you:

- **Passions on Pinterest:** I love adult coloring books, slide design, graphic novels and much more. Follow my boards on Pinterest.
- **Curated Conferences:** One of my favorite pastimes is sketch note summaries. I have Thinglinked many of my notes with additional resources.
- **Helpful Hacking:** I am all about life and productivity hacks. Check out my posts on email bankruptcy, custom desktop wallpaper organization, and handy ways to reboot your handouts.
- **Step-by-Step Student iPad Base Camps:** Students need professional development too, so I have posted a guide to how to create iPad Base Camps for secondary students that will totally knock your socks off!

I sincerely app-reciate your time and patience and will craft an original response shortly. ☺

Figure 1.7 Personal or Professional Autoresponder

- **Embrace Emoticons and Abbreviations:** Let's face it. Emoticons are here—for a while at least. As an educator, I see this less of a perversion of the serious literary form and more of a way that visual literacy has seeped in to written communications. I will be the first to admit that I have embraced this art form as a vehicle for context clues and tone and even use it to soften or clear messages that could be misinterpreted otherwise. A simple activity for this would be to have students write the same phrase with three different emoticons and then discuss how the recipient might react or respond to each phrase and emoticon (e.g, "you got a letter today" ⊙, "you got a letter today," ⊗

and "you got a letter today" ☺ [emoticon images courtesy of Creative Commons, https://creativecommons.org/licenses/by/3.0/us]). While these statements in textual form are all clearly the same, they convey a very different thought and feeling from the sender. A few books to get you started considering this format in a curricular mindset are *Yolo Juliet*, *srsly Hamlet*, and *Macbeth #killingit*.

- **Class Newsletter:** Have students create and maintain an email newsletter of classroom learning and activities, then track and discuss the analytics. Or have students generate a newsletter for the student body to address communication best practices or digital health and wellness for teens. Beyond providing an authentic experience for students and beefing up parent communications, tools like MailChimp also provide analytics (e.g., how many people opened the newsletter, how many clicked on the links, what time of day people read the newsletter). These data could be used formatively for students to change their content and modes of delivery to accommodate their audience.

- **Email an Expert:** There are few people who can't be contacted via email. What better way than to have students email an expert in the field they are studying, and maybe even get a response. A few years ago, I was designing a workshop on the topic of the SAMR model for technology integration (e.g., Substitution, Augmentation, Modification, Redefinition), and thought I would ask the father of the SAMR model, Ruben R. Puentedura. I never imagined he would reply, let alone provide feedback (Figure 1.8).

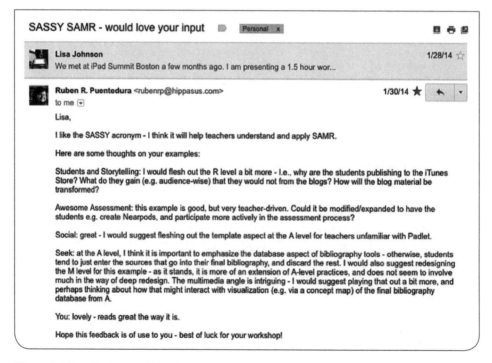

Figure 1.8 Email an Expert With Dr. Ruben R. Puentedura

While email is an on-ramp to many tools, it is merely a vehicle. Where we drive it, and how we drive it is the most important. If we use email to fuel teaching conflict resolution, problem-solving, empathy, and self-advocacy, then we provide students the opportunity to take these skills and apply them to email, life's circumstances, and whatever communication tools they encounter in the future.

Chapter Resources

Email Etiquette Preparation Inventory Assessment

I tend to get easily distracted when I have to digest large portions of new information. I find clipping out the high points and topics from that bulk of information helps me better assimilate and apply that information without being overwhelmed. To that end, I have extracted the main points and action items to support you while you mull over email etiquette in your classroom:

☐ What are the reasons my students need an email?

☐ How will I facilitate the discussion of email etiquette and best practices of communication with my students?

☐ What activities will I use to provide students opportunities to practice email in authentic ways?

Share your answers using the hashtag #cultivatecomm.

My Students' Self-Assessment Checklist

This checklist can be used as a pre- and post-assessment. It is merely here to provide a way to determine what you think your students know and how you have impacted their strength of communication through the information shared in this chapter:

☐ My students can compose an email designed for a variety of audiences that elicits a clear response.

☐ My students can troubleshoot sending large attachments and a variety of file types.

☐ My students know how to decipher and avoid spam and phishing scams.

☐ My students understand the difference between personal and professional communications and can craft clear communications for a variety of audiences.

☐ My students can use email as a vehicle for proactive self-advocacy, anticipating the needs of others, and problem-solving.

Additional Resources and Reading

- Email Etiquette Communication Catcher (found in Appendix B and on https://resources.corwin.com/cultivatingcomm)
- Suggested Reading and Resources (www.pinterest.com/techchef4u/email-ettiquette)

References

Are they really ready to work? (2006). Retrieved from http://www.p21.org/storage/documents/FINAL_REPORT_PDF09-29-06.pdf

HistoryFix. (1999). *Writingfix.com.* Retrieved 1 March, 2016, from http://writingfix.com/wac/Writing_Across_Curriculum_RAFTS_Soc_Studies.htm

Notes

Industry Insights

What communication skills do you wish you had learned in high school or college that would have better prepared you for your profession/career?

Listening: "The art of listening and better professional conversational skills."

—Judy Jacomino (Makeup and Hair Artist)

Influence: "I wish I had learned counseling strategies and how to effect behavior change in others. Just having the knowledge is not enough to help someone—you have to be able to present it in a way that they can understand. Also, I wish I had known better how to communicate with people at different organizational levels."

—Kati Ohlmeyer (MS, RDN, LD)

Empathy and collaborative skills: "Thinking before speaking! It took a lot of work to ensure that my emotions were in check prior to firing off a response....Another skill which I feel is overlooked is empathy. So many young people entering the workforce have difficulty looking beyond themselves, the 'how is this affecting me' mentality, rather than seeing a situation from all points of view."

—Jacob Hanson (Managing Partner With PR With Panache)

Code switching: "Code switching....Engineers speak different than marketing, than design."

—Efrain Velez (Senior Designer)

Perspective: "To always put myself in the recipient's shoes before communicating. Is what I have to say relevant to this person? Is the action I want them to take readily apparent? Am I using the best method (email, phone, in person) given the situation?"

—Kristy Peters (Principal at Litigation Finance Company)

"I wish I had learned how to consider things from the other person's perspective and structure all communication with that in mind. What's in it for them? What do they care about?"

—Danny Johnson (Owner of Real Estate Software Development Company)

Handling critical conversations: "It would have been greatly helpful if I was taught how to properly handle critical conversations while under a great deal of stress."

—Justin Hammond (Cloud Networks Engineer)

Collaborating remotely: "A good deal of work today requires collaboration with other people who you may never see face to face. Developing the ability to work under that model will be critical for a number of careers."

—James Peters (VP New Market Initiatives, Online Legal Services)

Connecting on a personal level: "While I learned presentation skills in high school and college, I don't think my education focused enough on the importance of connecting on an emotional or personal level. While less important in school, navigating the gap between the two in business can be quite complicated."

—James Peters (VP New Market Initiatives, Online Legal Services)

CHAPTER 2

Collaboration and Positive Interdependence

Communicating with peers to think about and through ideas, challenges, and processes

"A real team: a small cast of people recruited for their complementary skills, not their meshing personalities, who hold one another accountable, and who have common purpose and a sense of urgency."

—Marie Gilot (Journalist and Director of CUNY J+ workshops)

Think back to a time when you were a student and you had to work in a group. If you were like me, then most likely this was a source of frustration for you . . . but not for the reason that you might think. As I started to reflect on writing this chapter and my "collaborative" academic experiences, I realized it was not my distaste for collaborative work but the lack of these skills being part of my student vernacular that caused my displeasure for the activity. When I was asked to be in a group, very rarely were the groups strategically formed and beyond that no parameters or norms were set for behavior or interdependence. In fact, most collaborative experiences were simply group projects, and very rarely productive collaboration. As you can imagine, this led to my Type A perfectionist self grabbing the reigns and essentially doing the vast majority of the project solo.

This lack of a positive tableau followed me into college and even my career. Many teachers teach how they were taught or draw from their own learning experiences, so having a framework for productive group work was quite foreign to me. Over the years I haven't lost my strong opinions or Type A personality, but I have had opportunities to see how proactive planning and instructional ground work in the area of collaboration can really impact the productivity, engagement, and efficacy of the group as a whole.

Why Is Collaboration a Necessary Skill for College and Career Readiness?

I feel like this is probably the most rhetorical question of them all. Ultimately, productive collaboration is a by-product of effective communication. As mentioned in the introduction, Collaboration and Team Building specifically was the third highest valued skill and competency under Communication and Critical Thinking (AMA, 2012). Another study depicted in Figure 2.1 found not only the same skills important, but also most difficult to find in applicants ("Millennial Branding Student Employment Gap Study," 2012)

"We hire for hard skills. We fire for soft skills. The ability to interact and communicate with others or behave ethically and take responsibility for things tends to be where people tend to break down."

—Rick Stevens *(Senior Vice President of HR, The Boeing Corporation)*

I think we can all agree that collaboration is a soft skill that lays the foundation for success in almost any field. But, have you ever considered the impact of not having that soft skill in your repertoire?

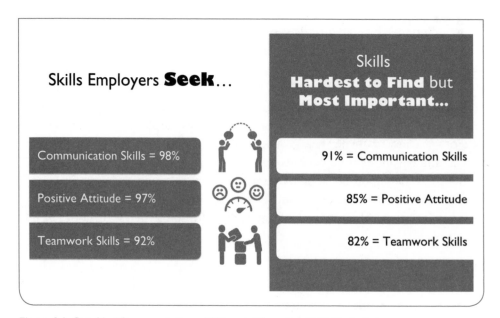

Figure 2.1 Graphical Representation of Millennial Branding 2012 Study Data

Figure 2.2 Graphical Representation of Rick Stevens' Quote

Think about it. People are hired for their certificates and certifications, but those soft skills of inability to work in a group, be resilient, take critical feedback, or problem-solve often break them. Additionally, communication is not just oral and written, but it also includes nonverbal and listening skills that can be embedded within collaborative groups.

What Is Collaborative Learning?

Collaboration, Group Work, Cooperative Learning, Peer-to-Peer Learning . . . call it what you will. Whether students are learning with peers or from peers, they are essentially navigating social relationships within the context of the classroom. For the purpose of this chapter, let's focus on what strategies we can employ to facilitate productive groups that by design culminate in perspectives and products that are greater than what could have been achieved individually. For me the question is less about deciphering labels and more about determining what learning experiences are positively impacted and developed through having students work together and how to set the groundwork for those experiences. I doubt many companies and industry professionals quibble over the distinction between cooperative or collaborative teams. At best, they might give them quirky titles like Innovation Partners or Creativity Catalysts.

Collaborative learning, much like the other six topics in this book, is not only a college and career readiness skill but

> *"The smartest person in the room is the room itself: the network that joins the people and ideas in the room, and connects to those outside of it."*
>
> **—David Weinberger** *(Author)*

a life and learning readiness building block that goes far beyond think-pair-share. Much like email sets the stage for communication with clear messaging and literacy, collaboration sets students up for essential academic scenarios like peer editing, online discussions, and group projects and labs. While we have addressed what can happen when the skill is not developed and present, we have not taken into consideration the benefits nurturing this skill has for our students. Did you know that just observing someone else's actions through a complex task is enough for our brains to map that experience (Ferlazzo, 2012), that collaborative learning fosters resiliency and self-advocacy (Davis, 2012), or that collaboration fuels creative risk-taking and courage (Gregory, 2016)? What is even more interesting is the research on social-emotional learning, which has found that both intrapersonal skills such as self-regulation and goal perseverance and interpersonal skills such as the ability to collaborate are direct factors to complement academic achievement in predicting student success (West, 2016).

When executed and incorporated effectively and with high fidelity, collaborative learning can help students develop and determine their signature strengths or core competencies, identify ideal working and learning processes, and foster a community of peers grounded on trust, empathy, and shared goals.

How Can I Set the Stage for Positive Collaboration and Interdependence?

Take a moment and think about a group you were in that did not function optimally and consider the elements at play that contributed to its less-than-premium results. Now think about a group that you work with in which you feel positive interdependence? What strategies or components does this group have that the other didn't? What elements and processes does this group employ that the other group didn't? I imagine you might have said clear guidelines for work, value and trust within its participants, and honesty. If you ask the *Harvard Business Review*, they will tell you that positive interdependence can only be fostered if it is contained (or "can-tained" as depicted in Figure 2.3) by crucial skills like appreciation of others and the ability to productively and creatively resolve conflicts ("Eight Ways to Build Collaborative Teams," 2007).

So, with positive elements and processes on your mind, I decided to focus on strategies that are employed in actual high-functioning creative teams. After all, if salaried employees and industry professionals utilize these strategies within their companies and teams, I thought they might be worth a gander. For the purpose of this book and the classroom, I distilled the activities shared to ones that focus on

Figure 2.3 Graphical Representation of *Harvard Business Review* Collaboration Tips

Source: https://hbr.org/2007/11/eight-ways-to-build-collaborative-teams

determining and valuing signature strengths, deciphering ideal working processes, delineating norms, and establishing a community through common ground, empathy, and trust. I also only included activities for each section that were fairly low or minimal risk on the social anxiety scale.

The rest of the chapter delineates several activities to cultivate and structure positive interdependence within groups and provides a variety of handouts to be used in conjunction with these strategies. All of the handouts can be found on the companion site https://resources.corwin.com/cultivatingcomm. The first step is setting norms. This can be done as a class or within groups, but should be done early on in the academic year and revisited often.

What are our norms? Norms can be drafted for discussion groups or even groups formed to work on a long-term project. Norms are not rules delineated by a teacher; rather they are a collection of tenets that are generated by the group or class and then agreed to. Remember "Conversations Before Contracts" in Chapter 1. Students will naturally have more buy-in when they delineate these themselves.

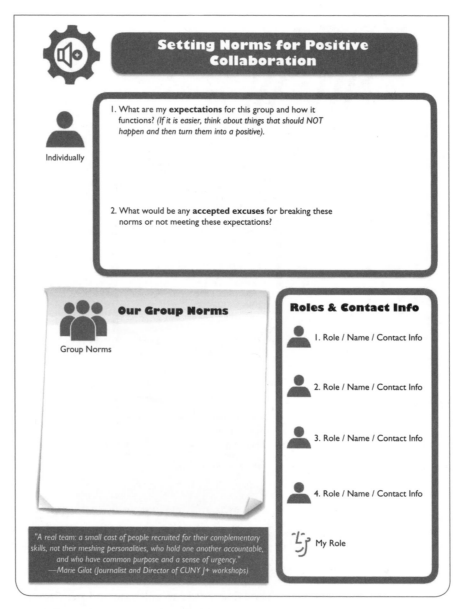

Figure 2.4 Setting Norms for Positive Collaboration Guide

Available for download at **https://resources.corwin.com/cultivatingcomm**

Have each student fill out the top section of the "Setting Norms for Positive Collaboration" handout in Figure 2.4. Once these norms have been group-sourced and adopted by students, make sure that they are reviewed each time groups meet to ensure that expectations are met. The handout in Figure 2.4 can also be stored in student binders or folders to serve as a visual reminder for each student as they work in their groups. As this particular norm process may lean more heavily to the humanities side, I have also included an example of what some positive norms could look like in a mathematics class as well (Figure 2.5).

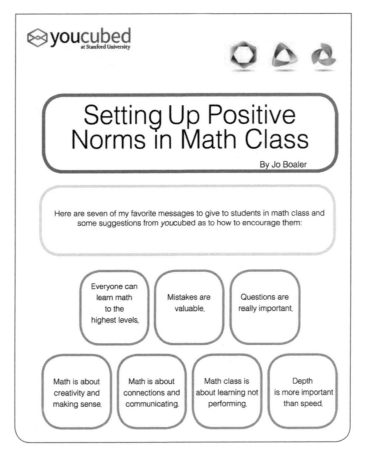

Figure 2.5 Setting Up Positive Norms in Math Class by Jo Boaler

Source: Jo Boaler, http://www.youcubed.org/wp-content/uploads/Positive-Classroom-Norms2.pdf

In my own experience, norms were typically set for me so I had no knowledge about how to actually facilitate or initiate a process like this. One way to develop these norms is to tear a page out of the design thinking handbook and go analog with sticky notes. Each member can generate expectations they have for the group's behavior (e.g., no devices, arrive on time, one person speaks at a time, be respectful). A general rule of thumb is one norm per sticky note. One way to ensure that these norms are shared amongst the group is to structure this activity to be individually generated for a few minutes, and then collected and organized by the group. This way the group or class can see reoccurring ideas as well as some outliers that may not have been thought of. The guide in Figure 2.6 has been provided to use in conjunction with Figure 2.4 to support you and your students with this process. The handout also serves as a model of how visual cues can be utilized to guide group tasks.

I have also used this very same sticky note ideation model to identify best practices for professional development. The picture in Figure 2.7 showcases an ideation exercise I facilitated with my fellow colleagues to develop consensus on the components and experiences that needed to be in place every time we delivered professional development.

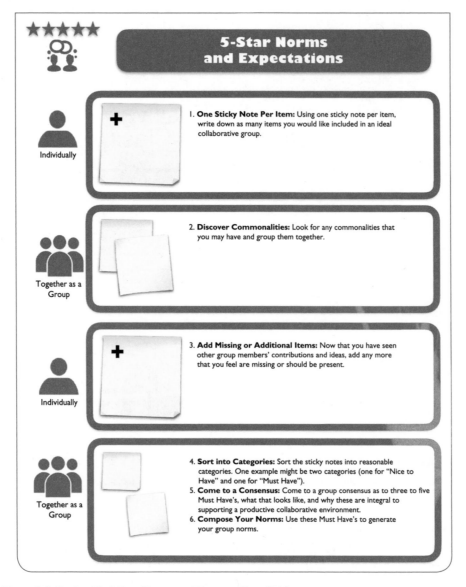

Figure 2.6 Setting Up 5-Star Norms and Expectations Guide

Available for download at **https://resources.corwin.com/cultivatingcomm**

Once the norms have been brainstormed, organized, and agreed to, students can use this information to complete the group norm section of Figure 2.4. If students need additional support or direction, have them turn over their paper, and use a stem like "Each time we meet we should . . . because . . ." or "Things I Need/Want/Expect from my Team Members are . . ." to spark additional thoughts or discussion. If students are setting group norms for collaborative projects, they may want to go one step further and create a social contract that contains more detailed information and specifics of when and where people will meet, and how often they will meet. They could even delineate what the expectations and deadlines are for each individual.

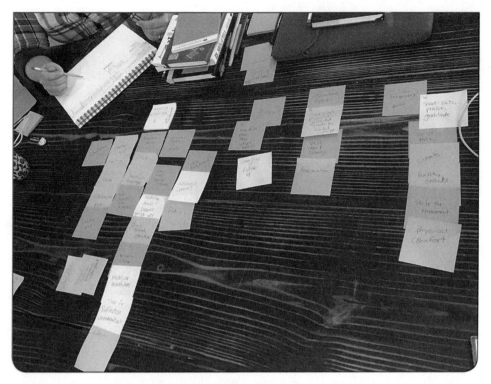

Figure 2.7 Facilitating Ideal Professional Development Setting and Strategies With Sticky Notes

How Do We Build a Community?

This is one I struggled with a bit as a learner simply because many of the strategies can be seen as a waste of time at surface value. However, I can tell you that the people I spend more time with and get to know beyond just the work ecosphere are the people I tend to be more productively effective with. Think about the group of co-workers you may have traveled with to an away game or attended an out of state (or city) professional development with. Yes, you most likely talked about your students and your classroom, but you also talked about your own children or hobbies. In finding these personal connections and commonalities, you have built empathy and trust. But what does this actually look like in the context of a classroom? Below are three activities that can support setting up the foundation for effective communication:

> *"No significant learning can occur without a significant relationship."*
>
> **—James Comer** *(Maurice Falk Professor of Child Psychiatry at the Yale Child Study Center)*

- **Taking Sides:** This is a tried and true activity that allows students to see similarities and differences between their group members as well as begin to think deeply about how they function and work best. It is as simple as the teacher calling out two benign choices and students moving to the side of the room (not the middle—they have to make a choice) that corresponds with the choice they identify with most. I participated in a version of this at SXSWEDU this year. A few of my favorites were coffee or tea, sloth or hummingbird, outside or inside, think to speak or speak to think. What I loved about this activity is it forces safe risk-taking in making choices and provides an opportunity to then discuss why students chose a particular side and what that meant to them within their groups. This not only allowed students to gain a better perspective of working styles and preferences but also facilitated some insight into their own process and environment as well (Ryder & Deutscher, 2016). A few more that could be added to the mix is Prezi or PPT, text or call, selfie or groupie, pencil or pen, etc.

- **Survey Swap:** This activity can be used to teach sensitive topics whether it be politics or even gender related. Have students take an anonymous survey of their views on a topic of your choice and then trade surveys three times. Once the survey has been traded, each student represents the results on the survey they now possess by standing at an Agree, Disagree, or Not Sure table. After the teacher calls out a statement represented on the survey, students move to the Agree, Disagree, or Not Sure table based on what is written on their swapped survey. This activity not only forces students to represent other's opinions, but also challenges their own perspective. Oftentimes our students' sphere of influence is small and narrowly connected to parents or a group of like-minded friends. Challenging these perspectives provides an opportunity to shift perceptions and increase social awareness (Crabill & Floresta, 2016).

- **Role Playing:** As educators, we have to prepare our students with the tools to communicate effectively in the most ideal and less-than-ideal scenarios. Personally, I am very anti-confrontational, so I have often erred on the side of not addressing issues only to have them become bigger issues. One way to facilitate and anticipate how to handle scuffles within a group is to role play them up front. This particular idea has been adapted from an article by Tara Duggan, an expert in knowledge management, on Workplace Communication Exercises (Duggan, n.d.). Her article suggests role playing several scenarios and then offers certain styles of communication that would be needed to resolve the issue (e.g., assertive or meek, direct or indirect, individualistic or team focused). A more expanded version of the five communication styles (e.g., assertive, aggressive, passive-aggressive, submissive, and manipulative) from Claire Newton is included in the chapter resources. The easiest way to do this with students may be to select a few students, provide them with a role and a scenario, and support them with role playing. Another option would be to have students work in small groups and with a variety of scenarios and then share out to the class how they resolved the issues and receive feedback on those solutions from their peers and the teacher.

Additional activities and improvisational strategies can be discovered at http://improvencyclopedia.org. The adapted versions of the Survey Swap activity mentioned above can be found at http://teachingsensitivetopics.weebly.com/resources

.html. While we will not always be blessed in our career with groups of people that function at high levels of productive collaboration, at the very least it is important for us as individuals to be able to be empathetic to other's perspectives and to challenge our own ideas to work fluidly across boundaries. More on critical thinking and perspective evaluation (e.g., our own and other's) can be found in Chapter 6, "Social Media," and Chapter 7, "Curation."

> *"We don't learn from experience . . . we learn from reflecting on experience."*
>
> **—John Dewey** *(Educational Reformer, Psychologist, and Philosopher)*

Thinking About the Other Side of the Coin

Individually

Taking Sides

1. **Individually:** Choose three scenarios/labels that you feel you identify with.

2. **Individually:** What do they mean to you in the context of your school work, your personality, or your relationships with friends or family?

With a Partner

3. **With a Partner:** Find someone that chose one of the same scenarios/labels that you selected. What do those labels mean to them?

4. **With a Partner:** Find someone that chose a different scenario/label than you and discuss what those labels mean and how they defined them.

5. **With a Partner:** Do labels define a person or do people define (or identify with) labels?

Together as a Group

Role Playing

1. **Together with your group:** Choose a scenario you would like to role play.

2. **Together with your group:** Select one person in your group to represent the person with the problem, another to take a side and resolve the issue using a specific style of communication, and one more to facilitate the process.

3. **Together with your group:** Evaluate the effectiveness of the resolution reached and the communication style utilized.

Possible Scenarios

- Group member not pulling weight
- Group member late to meetings
- Group member work subpar
- Group member out of town
- Group member had a death in the family

Possible Styles

- Assertive or Meek
- Direct or Indirect
- Individualistic or Team Focused
- Lean In or Lean Out
- Realistic or Pessimistic

Figure 2.8 Thinking About the Other Side of the Coin

Available for download at **https://resources.corwin.com/cultivatingcomm**

No matter what strategies you employ, remind students to revisit their group or class norms before they get started as honest conversations are built on these permissions. The most important thing to remember is that these activities aren't nearly as powerful if they aren't combined with a discussion and reflection component. To meet this need, I have developed a handout, "Thinking About the Other Side of the Coin," shown in Figure 2.8 on the previous page. This handout can be found on the companion website to facilitate these types of discussions.

How Do We Support Students With Determining Their Signature Strengths and Core Competencies?

Too often we assign groups and roles within the groups without taking into consideration students' strengths and weaknesses. Think about the last time you were assigned a role that was a mismatch. While I have an eye for detail and love being creative and generating instructional materials, I abhor and struggle with keeping deadlines and managing minutia. Fortunately, recently I have been paired with someone that excels in doing just that. Please know that I am not saying that every student needs to do only what they are good at within the group or that they cannot improve certain weaknesses with repeated experiences to improve that skill. What I am saying is that if students are already hesitant to work in a group and they have been slated with a task or role they are not comfortable with or feel they are not good at, they already have two strikes against them. What you might not realize is that people who are seen as the best sources of information and most adept collaborators tend to also have the lowest engagement ("Collaborative Overload," 2016). Honoring students' signature strengths while building the core competency of effective collaboration within all team members is essential for students to not reach collaborative overload.

So how do we set up not only the group but each individual group member for success? First we have to determine what types of roles are necessary within the group. If the group is generating a product that will need to be presented, then roles might be digital designer, orator, project manager, etc. An example of this might be a project-based learning model that utilizes different teams ranging from public relations and research to executive board and advertising to produce a comprehensive environmental cause campaign. In this case, students self-select teams based on roles similar to actual careers with each team contributing to the overall efficacy of the campaign. Ultimately, if students can choose their role and know that their role and attributions to the team are valued, they are set up to be successful. One way teachers can mitigate role and personality disconnect is using a Myers-Brigg personality tests. A teacher could use these tests with students before displaying the roles and then let students sign up for groups based on their results from the personality test.

So what do we do with students who may not know what they do best or what their signature strengths are? That's where *Caffeine for the Creative Team: 150 Exercises to Inspire Group Innovation* by Stefan Murnaw and Wendy Lee Oldfield and *The Decision Book* by Mikael Krogerus and Roman Tschäppeler come in super handy.

The former is designed to spark creativity in teams of industry professionals but can be easily distilled for the classroom to support students with being self-aware.

The latter is a collection of 50 models for strategic decision making that are not intended to provide answers, but to ask questions to allow students to delve into self-discovery. Following are a few of my favorites adapted for secondary students:

> *"The students have to be shown that every project can have some aspect that inspires them, even if the whole does not, You have to show them how to find that inspiration and tap it."*
>
> —**Eric Chimenti** *(Chapman University Graphic Design Program)*

- **Seed Packet** adapted from the "I Grew a Whole Crop of Interns" activity in *Caffeine for the Creative Team: 150 Exercises to Inspire Group Innovation*: This idea entails having students look at the roles for a project and determine what characteristics the "seeds" (students) should have to grow successfully. These could be specific to the role (e.g., creative, task oriented, good with people) or could be external factors that need to be in place to get a good crop (e.g., honest feedback, time to think, autonomy).

- **The Flow Model** adapted from *The Decision Book:* The U.S. psychologist Mihaly Csikszentmihalyi determined five things people who are happy and in "flow" exhibit or possess (e.g., intense focus, choice, neither under- or overchallenged, clear objectives, and immediate feedback; Figure 2.9). The Flow Model has two axes and ranks challenges against your abilities. Students who lack the

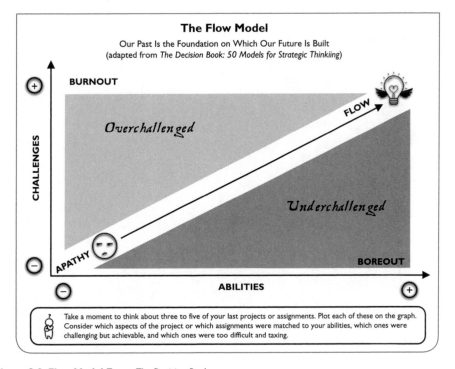

Figure 2.9 Flow Model From *The Decision Book*

Source: Adapted from Krogerus & Tschäppeler (2012)

ability to complete more challenging tasks get burned out and students who have the ability but are provided with unchallenging activities become bored. The idea is similar to Vygotsky's zone of proximal development. The important take-away from this model is for students to be self-aware of what tasks are challenging and what abilities they currently possess. For a slightly different perspective on students' strengths over time and discovery of natural talents, take a gander at Gay Hendricks and his four activity buckets: The Zone of Incompetence, The Zone of Competence, The Zone of Excellence, and The Zone of Genius. Personally identifying these is a significant tool for students to leverage their innate skills to wield powerful contributions to the group.

- **The Uffe Elbaek Model** adapted from *The Decision Book:* This activity is great for those students who are more analytical and visual. Intended to be a public opinion barometer, it has the ability to create a snapshot of you as you are now. The Uffe Elbaek model is similar to the "Taking Sides" activity as both force students to pick between two qualifiers. Where this model stretches students is that it offers a spectrum (e.g., each option on an axis has 10 points to give so if you choose an 8 on Global then you would plot a 2 on Local) rather than a black and white choice (e.g., Global or Local). The most important part of this activity is simply visualizing how we see ourselves, others, and how others' see us and knowing that all of those perspectives can be in flux. I was so enamored with this activity that I actually completed it myself and have revisited it several times (Figure 2.10) and have included a black line master on the companion site to use with students. I also made a few notes about how I interpreted my initial results.

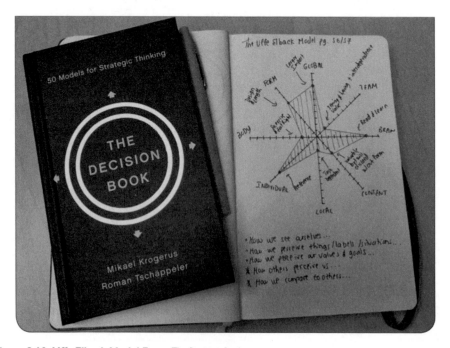

Figure 2.10 Uffe Elbaek Model From *The Decision Book*

Source: Adapted from Krogerus & Tschäppeler (2012)

- **Rock Star Bios** adapted from the "We're On a Mission . . . From the Production Manager" in *Caffeine for the Creative Team: 150 Exercises to Inspire Group Innovation*. Imagine a student group as a rock star union. Each one comes with a rich biographical history and signature skills that play into making the group legendary. In this scenario students determine what instruments they play and write a biography for themselves. This approach plays with both determining signature strengths, but also crafting positive group interplay and dynamics. Once the bios are crafted, students can reconvene with their group, share, and form a band name. This activity (see Figure 2.11) could also

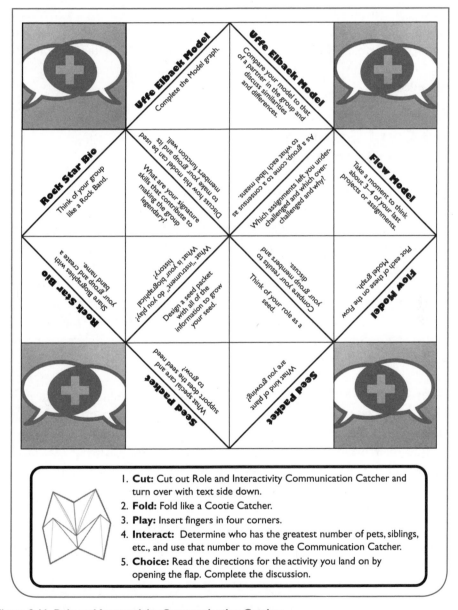

1. **Cut:** Cut out Role and Interactivity Communication Catcher and turn over with text side down.
2. **Fold:** Fold like a Cootie Catcher.
3. **Play:** Insert fingers in four corners.
4. **Interact:** Determine who has the greatest number of pets, siblings, etc., and use that number to move the Communication Catcher.
5. **Choice:** Read the directions for the activity you land on by opening the flap. Complete the discussion.

Figure 2.11 **Role and Interactivity Communication Catcher**

Available for download at **https://resources.corwin.com/cultivatingcomm**

be paired with developing a biography section in Chapter 5 on digital portfolios and resumes.

Not sure if it is the novelty, the kinesthetic nature, or the increase in dopamine, but kids love games. While you can definitely assign any one of the four activities delineated earlier, you can also cleverly orchestrate choice by using the Communication Catcher provided in Figure 2.11. Ultimately whether these activities are utilized individually with students prior to group formations or used after groups are formed to further solidify chosen or designated roles, I hope they will provide a foundation for discovering student strengths and delineating specific expectations within roles.

How Can I Ensure and Measure Ongoing Collaboration?

Laying the groundwork for positive interdependence is key. Collaboration should be a visible skill and strategy no different from multiplying or handwriting. Something that needs to be taught, modeled, and practiced. The more practice that students receive with this skill, the more successful these interactions will be. But no one practices in a bubble. We don't repeat a skill over and over without formative feedback, and we don't practice skills like language in isolation. Let's assume we now have collaborative groups that have found common ground and individuals within these groups who understand their roles and can articulate their signature strengths and optimal learning and work environments. How do we ensure that these groups continue to flourish and function?

- **Glows and Grows:** This is an easy activity to have students do at the end of the class period to tweeze out reflections and reinforce the norms. Essentially each student in the group talks about one thing they could have done better during their meetings or time together (e.g., ignored text, put off calculus homework till next period, not interrupted Ian, contributed more during a discussion) and then shares one glow for another person in the group. Perhaps Ian did a great job of actively participating in the planning or Fiona took the reigns on keeping everyone on task. Recognizing positive contributions and acknowledging these within the group ensures a climate of gratitude and responsibility.

- **Keep/Change/Delete:** While Glows and Grows focuses more on personal strengths and opportunities for growth, the idea of Keep/Change/Delete is helpful for the overall working processes of a group or project. The idea is similar in format to a KWL chart (e.g., What you KNOW, What you WANT to know, and What you want to LEARN) with three columns and could easily be adapted to a Keep/Change/Improve model that is further delineated in the teacher challenge section. The group reflects on how they worked together, what worked, what didn't work, what could be improved, and what may not be needed moving forward.

- **KANBANS:** A strategy that Toyota employs to prevent production bottlenecks can be easily adapted to not only keeping groups flowing but also ensuring that all contributions are visible. This strategy is a visual mind map that can be distilled to three columns (To Do, Doing, Done). Whether achieved with a piece of paper and sticky notes, a dry erase board, or an online tool like Trello, the idea is simple. Each group creates a to-do list of all of the tasks that need to be completed and then assigns each one to an individual. By making this process visible, student accountability is easier to track and manage . . . especially when students have to complete an independent or group rubric.

- **Independent and Group Rubrics:** A more formal (and summative) approach to the processes featured above is to use a Collaboration Self-Assessment tool (2011) like the one generated by St. Cloud State University. The Buck Institute for Education also has a Collaboration Rubric for PBL for Grades 6–12. Examples of these are linked off the companion site.

What Curricular Collaborative Tasks and Activities Can Groups Do?

So I have groups and I know how to evaluate them. But, what does this actually look like in a core content area or traditional learning ecosystem? As types of projects will be further delineated in Chapter 4, "Student Publishing and Projects," I thought it best to hone in on collaborative discussions, brainstorming, and problem-solving. After all, groups formed in the workplace are not only to create a product or complete a project, but also to brainstorm and problem-solve solutions. While all of the activities delineated above nurture and grow healthy collaborative groups, what kind of learning and critical content conversations can be yielded from this harvest? Many of the following tasks can be adapted across the curriculum:

- **Collaborative Agendas:** I have sat through many a meeting that goes awry without a tentative agenda and at the same time frequently referenced old meeting agendas for notes. I have also spoken to many a manager who has lamented that their employees are not equipped with the ability to craft agendas, run meetings, or provide concise project updates effectively or efficiently. This may seem simple enough but teaching students to prioritize what they want to accomplish and summarize conversations and ideas to reference later when they meet with a group or even when they do student conferences with a teacher is a vitally essential communication skill.

- **Group Quizzes:** In no profession that I know of do people work independently to tackle problems and address misconceptions in isolation. For some reason this phenomenon is only seen in the realm of education. Recently I have started seeing an insurgence of collaborative quizzing. Students are strategically put in groups of four. Each student takes their own quiz but the group only receives one grade for the quiz, which incentivizes sharing of information and strategies as well as addressing misconceptions. It forces students who want to "set the curve" to slow down their thinking and pace themselves to work with others on the team. It also provides a safer environment for students to ask questions as they tend to be more comfortable speaking with their peers than a teacher. The idea of group quizzes puts the collective understanding of the group above the individual achievement of one. While students still have to take the tests individually, this idea scaffolds understanding and peer interactions to form symbiotic problem-solvers and foster group accountability.

- **Flipped Literature Circles:** Read a book and discuss it. This is the age-old premise for literature circles. With the influx of technology and accessibility to mobile devices, students don't necessarily have to be in the same room to achieve thoughtful discourse. In fact, through tools like Quip, Google Docs, and Edmodo, students can post discussions and engage in discourse at any time. One high school English teacher, Melissa Dupre, engages in what I like to refer to as flipped literature circles. Much of the discussion and discourse takes place online, but the analysis and review of said discourse happens in person. There is something to be said about printing out transcripts of discussions and analyzing them face to face rather than asynchronously or online. It is important to remember even in online collaborative spaces that scheduling time to address norms, building community, and determining roles is integral to successful online dialogue. Think about how much more invested and committed you are to someone you have met face to face and then work with online as opposed to someone you may have met through an online course and will most likely never have to interact with again.

- **Problem and Idea Swapping:** This can be achieved simply by swapping papers with a partner in your group and having them solve the next step in a problem, providing the next sentence in an essay, or even posing a question that needs to be answered during a silent brainstorming session. The benefit of an activity like this is that each student is engaged in giving feedback or providing solutions. This idea can even be expanded to swapping roles midway through a project and completing the other person's duties or swapping projects and having another group complete the current group's assignment. While this may seem like cruel and unusual punishment, it forces students to communicate their project timeline and vision effectively and may even open up the final project or problem to some additional creative solutions.

- **Saboteurs, Devil's Advocates, and Provacateurs . . . Oh My:** Just like the best movies have unforeseen plot twists, good discussions and collaborative projects can too. Consider designating a saboteur, devil's advocate, or provacateur as a secret role within one of the activities listed above. His or her job is to either lead the group or the class astray by providing incorrect solutions or hare-brained ideas or to provide alternating viewpoints and considerations. This role forces students to think twice and to be able to justify their thoughts and solutions. Teachers can secretly assign this role by preselecting students within each group to serve. For added fun or torture, teachers can enact the role without telling groups that the saboteur or provacateur will be in play.

- **Collaborating Across Cultures:** Due to the expansion of real-time communication tools, we also have to be cognizant that communication is also communicating across cultures. One way to facilitate this is with collaborative activities that incorporate students from other cultures and geographic regions. PenPal Schools is one tool that has seamlessly organized academic standards around collaborative courses so American students can exchange perspectives on issues such as economy, health care, and immigration with a global counterpart.

- **Brainstorming and Ideation:** Collaborative groups are a fantastic place to sow the seeds of design thinking and visible thinking by having students brainstorm, generate meaningful solutions, and explore ideas. Something to remember about these strategies is that they oftentimes work best like good coffee. Sometimes students need time to percolate and think individually before they engage in brainstorming and ideation activities. In collaborative brainstorming sessions this can be achieved by giving students context about the topic and letting them individually brainstorm prior to the group session. With the thinking routines, this can be as simple as giving students time to think and respond individually before they do so within their group. There are also some phenomenal sites that provide clearly delineated steps and procedures for these types of activities:

    ○ Stanford University's Institute of Design: http://dschool.stanford.edu/use-our-methods

    ○ Ideo's Design Kit Methods: www.designkit.org/methods

    ○ Ideos' Design Thinking for Educators: www.designthinkingforeducators.com

    ○ Harvard's Graduate School of Education Project Zero Visible Thinking Routines: www.pz.harvard.edu/projects/visible-thinking

    All of these links are also available on the companion website.

It may seem odd to end a chapter on collaboration and group work without addressing how groups are formed, how often groups meet, how long groups stay together, and what the ideal size of a group is. If I am being totally honest I don't think there is a right or wrong answer to any of these. What I will say is that if your goal is to have high-functioning collaborative groups, sizing them at four to five, providing some flexibility and autonomy for how they are formed, and allowing them to stay together for 4–6 weeks at a time will most likely be an effective equation. Developing good groups is the subject of many other books, while positive interdependence and devising mutually acceptable conventions seems to be only prevalent within some college publications and leading industries. If we are truly going to impact our students, we have to extend our queries beyond the standard educational resources and consider the validity of sources like colleges and careers. To be successful with the upcoming chapters that involve group projects, peer editing, and social media, students have to be able to listen, construct high-functioning groups, resolve conflicts, and be able to evaluate and acknowledge perspectives that may differ from their own to be able to be self-aware and communicate effectively. It is my hope that this chapter sets and solidifies the groundwork for the next five chapters.

Chapter Resources

Collaboration and Positive Interdependence Preparation Inventory Assessment

- ☐ What are the benefits of collaborative learning for my students?
- ☐ How will I define collaborative learning and work?
- ☐ What activities will I utilize to support my students with setting norms?
- ☐ What norms do I feel like need to be essential in devising a social contract?
- ☐ What community-building activities will I integrate into setting the groundwork for positive interdependence?
- ☐ What strategies and activities will I use to support students and their groups with identifying signature strengths and assigning roles?
- ☐ How can I blend the activities in this chapter with some of the suggested activities in the upcoming chapters (e.g., persuasive writing, portfolios, biographies, resumes)?
- ☐ What types of formative and summative assessments will I use to ensure positive interdependence, group accountability, and overall effectiveness of collaborative groups?
- ☐ What types of curricular tasks and activities will my groups tackle?
- ☐ What types of tools and strategies will I incorporate to support brainstorming and ideation?
- ☐ How will I address the nuts and bolts of group logistics (e.g., size of group, frequency with which groups work, and duration of time groups stay together)?

Share your answers using the hashtag #cultivatecomm.

My Students' Self-Assessment Checklist

☐ My students can set norms and expectations within any group setting.

☐ My students can articulate their own ideas comfortably and show empathy for other students' perspectives and points of view.

☐ My students can determine their own signature strength and advocate for specific roles.

☐ My students can express what hard and soft skills need to be in place for them to be successful within their role and their group.

☐ My students can assess the effectiveness of their own (and their peers') participation and involvement within the group.

☐ My students can translate these skills to other group settings (e.g., assessment, brainstorming, ideation) and in other classes.

Additional Resources and Reading

- Setting Norms for Positive Collaboration Handout (found on https://resources .corwin.com/cultivatingcomm)

- Thinking About the Other Side of the Coin Handout (found on https://resources .corwin.com/cultivatingcomm)

- Role and Interactivity Communication Catcher (found in Appendix B and on https://resources.corwin.com/cultivatingcomm)

- 5 Stars Norms and Expectations Handout (found on https://resources.corwin .com/cultivatingcomm)

- Flow Model Black Line Master (found on https://resources.corwin.com/ cultivatingcomm)

- The Uffe Elbaek Model (found on https://resources.corwin.com/cultivatingcomm)

- 5 Stars and Senses Collaborative Environment Handout (found on https:// resources.corwin.com/cultivatingcomm)

- St. Cloud University's Self-Assessment Tool (found on https://resources.corwin .com/cultivatingcomm)

- Suggested Reading and Resources (www.pinterest.com/techchef4u/collabora tion-and-positive-interdependence)

References

American Management Association (AMA). (2012). Critical skills survey, conducted December 2012. Retrieved from http://www.amanet.org/training/promotions/ AMA-2012-Critical-Skills-Survey.aspx

Collaboration Self-Assessment tool. (2011). *St. Cloud State University.* Retrieved March 16, 2016, from https://www.stcloudstate.edu/oce/_files/documents/coteaching/CollaborationtoolCSAT.pdf

Collaborative overload. (2016). *Harvard Business Review.* Retrieved 7 July 2016, from https://hbr.org/2016/01/collaborative-overload

Crabill, E., & Floresta, J. (2016). *Teaching sensitive topics.* Presentation, SXSWEDU 2016 in Austin, TX.

Davis, M. (2012). How collaborative learning leads to student success. *Edutopia.* Retrieved March 16, 2016, from http://www.edutopia.org/stw-collaborative-learning-college-prep

Duggan, T. (n.d.). Workplace communication exercises. *Smallbusiness.chron.com.* Retrieved May 12, 2016, from http://smallbusiness.chron.com/workplace-communication-exercises-10942.html

Eight ways to build collaborative teams. (2007). *Harvard Business Review.* Retrieved July 7, 2016, from https://hbr.org/2007/11/eight-ways-to-build-collaborative-teams

Ferlazzo, L. (2012). Response: Working smarter, not harder, with neuroscience in the classroom. *Education* Week—Classroom Q&A with Larry Ferlazzo. Retrieved March 16, 2016, from http://blogs.edweek.org/teachers/classroom_qa_with_larry_ferlazzo/2012/10/response_working_smarter_not_harder_with_neuroscience_in_the_classroom.html

Gregory, D. (2016). *Shut your monkey.* Cincinnati, OH: HOW Books.

Krogerus, M., & Tschäppeler, R. (2012). *The decision book: 50 models for strategic thinking.* New York, NY: W. W. Norton.

Millennial Branding Student Employment Gap Study. (2012). *Millennialbranding.com.* Retrieved October 12, 2016, from http://millennialbranding.com/2012/millennial-branding-student-employment-gap-study

Mumaw, S., & Oldfield, W. L. (2009). *Caffeine for the creative team: 150 exercises to inspire group innovation.* Cincinnati, OH: HOW Books.

Ryder, D., & Deutscher, E. (2016). *Improv + An Innovative Mindset.* Presentation, SXSWEDU 2016 in Austin, TX.

West, M. (2016). Should non-cognitive skills be included in school accountability systems? Preliminary evidence from California's CORE districts. The Brookings Institution. Retrieved March 19, 2016, from http://www.brookings.edu/research/reports/2016/03/17-non-cognitive-skills-school-accountability-california-core-west

Notes

_____

_____

_____

_____

_____

_____

_____

_____

_____

_____

_____

_____

_____

_____

_____

_____

_____

_____

_____

_____

_____

_____

_____

_____

_____

_____

_____

_____

Industry Insights

How do you ensure that teams are productive, work well together, and meet deadlines? Explain.

Value individual expertise and common group goals: "In the workplace, each team member brings his or her own unique skills and background to the table. Valuing others' expertise and communicating that you are working toward a common goal will bring about superior outcomes."

—Kati Ohlmeyer (MS, RDN, LD)

Mutually agreed-upon deadlines, goals, and action steps: "I set deadlines that we agree on, with action steps and timelines for each step. My team lives in 12 different time zones, from India to California, so everything is done electronically. We use Uberconference for meetings and share screens so that we are literally 'on the same page' when conferencing."

—Cyndee Perkins (App Development Marketing Content Writer and Franchise Consultant)

Set individual and group agendas: "I have weekly team meetings and individual. When I meet with each team member individually, *they* set the agenda. When I meet with the entire team, we collaboratively set the agenda, and I prioritize the items based on urgency of what needs to be done! I've also worked closely with colleagues to share productivity strategies."

—Andrew Gardner (VP Professional Learning at BrainPOP)

Set sprints and know team strengths: "We use 90-day 'sprints,' in which our teams identify what our goals are for the next 90 days, and discuss strategy around achieving those. Additionally, we require all team members to take both a strengthsfinder and Kolbe Assessment upon joining our team. This provides real insight into how each of our team members works."

—Jacob Hanson (Managing Partner With PR With Panache)

Regular deliverable check ins: "I generally allow teams a lot of freedom on a day-to-day basis with regularly scheduled check ins with set deliverables to ensure some progress."

—James Peters (VP New Market Initiatives, Online Legal Services)

Leadership and decisiveness: "Teamwork can be tricky when you have to balance so many voices. I think it works best when everyone is able to share, but it is balanced by strong leadership who knows when to say *when* and make a decision that they stand by and the team can get behind. Too much time is wasted dithering."

—Kristy Peters (Principal at Litigation Finance Company)

CHAPTER 3

Visual Literacy and Presentation Skills

Communicating with peers and educators through visuals, multimedia, oracy, and nonverbal skills to share an idea, process, or learning

"Now maybe some of you guys are trying to convey your idea, and it wasn't adopted; it was rejected and some other mediocre or average idea was adopted. And the only difference between those two is in the way it was communicated. Because if you communicate an idea in a way that resonates, change will happen, and you can change the world."

—Nancy Duarte (Author and Principal at Duarte Inc.)

I want you to think of a presentation you sat through that was incredibly interesting, informative, and insightful. It could be a TEDTalk you watched, a keynote, a professional development session, or even a student presentation. What stood out about the presenter and the presentation? Was it the visuals, the demeanor and presence of the speaker, or the compelling content? Odds are it was a carefully concocted combination of the three.

Too often when we mention presentation skills, people get fixated on the idea of slide design and lose sight of the topic as a multifaceted approach to communicating an idea. Moreover, the same secret sauce of presentation skills is so versatile that it can be served with several other instructional dishes and sampled across the variety of communications endeavors highlighted throughout this book.

So with that in mind, before we dive head first into presentation skills, I want to front-load you with the need for visual literacy, a component of presentation skills.

Why Is Visual Literacy So Integral for My Students?

To appreciate this era of proliferation of information, technology, and imagery, we must consider the positive implications visual literacy could have on our own instruction and student comprehension. Case in point: a revised student handout. Figure 3.1 shows two versions of a support resource for teaching how to tackle an expository writing piece in the context of a state exam. Take a look at the two documents. Which one could you digest and internalize the quickest? Which one will help you remember the content over time?

If the goal of the handout on the left was to truly provide a step-by-step guide for students that could be easily reviewed and replicated on an exam, then there might be a disconnect between intent and reality. People learn more from the pairing of visuals and texts (Walker-Ford, 2014). Think about it. When visuals and text are paired together, we have more information to rapidly decode the content and proceed with comprehension, delivery, and transmittal to others. Moreover, students who engage in multisensory environments that blend text, images, video, etc. "always had much more accurate recall of the information than the students who only heard or read the information" (Gallo, 2014). With that in mind, visual literacy becomes less of a nice-to-know and more of an impetus to providing content and instructional resources that best meet the diverse needs of our students.

If that example didn't quite persuade you, here is another. Growing up as a Gen Xer, I remember the days of what I refer to as the information famine. As a student and a child, I was naturally curious and hungry for knowledge and information. Early on, there was no direct line to Google or the Internet, just parents' answers and opinions and a home Funk and Wagnall's encyclopedia set. With so little information available and very little technology in existence to disseminate that info, much of slide design focused on large bits of text on a slide as that was the easiest way to communicate the information. Flash forward two decades and there is a perpetual waterfall of information available from a variety of sources. Now, with the avail-

Expository Writing

Imagine it is the day of the STAAR English I test, and you are given the following prompt for one of the expository essays:

Read the information in the box below.

Jane Austen (1775–1817) and Franz Kafka (1883–1924) are considered great writers. Their books continue to sell, and they are widely read and studied in schools everywhere. Neither of them, however, received much recognition while they were alive.

Should people do things only to be recognized? Think carefully about this question.

Write an essay explaining whether a person must always be acknowledged in order to have accomplished something.

1. The first thing you need to do is figure out what the prompt is. There is a lot of extraneous information provided; look at the part that begins with **"Write an essay explaining . . ."** That is the prompt, and only that!
   a. For example, in this prompt, only look at the part that says "Write an essay explaining whether a person must always be acknowledged in order to have accomplished something."

2. Turn the prompt into a question.
   a. In this example, the question would be "Must a person always be acknowledged in order to have accomplished something?"

3. Brainstorm what example(s) you can use to answer this question.
   a. Remember, it is best to use your own personal examples.
   b. You should only have one or two examples (three MAX). This should be plenty if you provide enough detail! Make your example into a story!
   c. In this case, think about a time when you did something you were proud of but didn't get recognized for.

4. Pre-write about your example. This will also help you come up with your thesis.

5. Construct a thesis. This is the cornerstone of your essay!
   a. Your thesis will be the answer to the question you created from the prompt.
   b. For example, your thesis for this prompt would be something like "A person does not have to be acknowledged in order to have accomplished something."

6. Then you can write!

Before

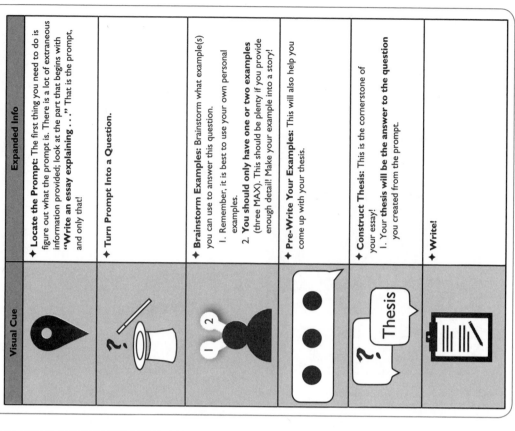

Visual Cue	Expanded Info
	✦ **Locate the Prompt:** The first thing you need to do is figure out what the prompt is. There is a lot of extraneous information provided; look at the part that begins with **"Write an essay explaining . . ."** That is the prompt, and only that!
	✦ **Turn Prompt Into a Question.**
	✦ **Brainstorm Examples:** Brainstorm what example(s) you can use to answer this question. 1. Remember, it is best to use your own personal examples. 2. **You should only have one or two examples** (three MAX). This should be plenty if you provide enough detail! Make your example into a story!
	✦ **Pre-Write Your Examples:** This will also help you come up with your thesis.
	✦ **Construct Thesis:** This is the cornerstone of your essay! 1. **Your thesis will be the answer to the question** you created from the prompt.
	✦ **Write!**

After

Figure 3.1 Expository Text Handout Revision

ability of information, we are not only moving beyond the need for copious amounts of text on a slide, but also adopting the practice of conveying content through visuals to improve both comprehension and retention. This juxtaposition of the growth of information and the reimagination of text on slides is visualized in Figure 3.2.

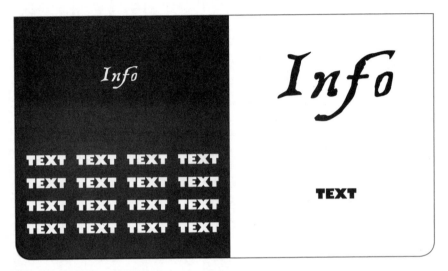

Figure 3.2 Information/Text Compare and Contrast

Why Are Presentation Skills Important for My Students?

Perhaps our students are not trying to change the world with their presentations as Nancy Duarte alluded to in the chapter-opening quote, but they are trying to convey a topic effectively or persuade their peers to accept their point of view on a particular novel or political issue. I have had the opportunity of observing years of student and educator presentations in both the classroom and at conferences all over the world, and what I can tell you is that most presentations fall into two categories:

• Fantastic ideas with poor communication and/or visuals

• Fantastic communication and/or visuals with mediocre ideas

At some point in time, most of us have sat through what can only be deemed as "death by PowerPoint." Many times we dismiss this as an issue with PowerPoint as a presentation tool, but in reality, it is an epidemic of lack of knowledge of visual literacy, which seeps into presentation skills. I recently attended a regional conference where a professor was disseminating truly valuable information on copyrights and appropriate use. Unfortunately, the 8-point font on his slides in an auditorium that easily sat 1,000 educators made it very difficult to make connections between what he was saying and what was displayed on the slide.

While this topic is truly near and dear to my heart, it is not just a passion project of mine. Effective communication via a variety of media and formats is a pillar of the ISTE Nets ("Standards for students," 2016). And, more specifically, oral presentation skills are threaded throughout the Common Core State Standards as early as kindergarten. For example, CCSS.ELA—Literacy.SL.K.6: "Speak audibly and express thoughts, feelings, and ideas clearly." These standards are expanded upon later in the upper grades (National Governors Association Center for Best Practices and Council of Chief State School Officers, 2010). Presentation skills are not just about speaking clearly—they are about crafting a story that effectively feeds the information to the audience through visuals, text, and body language.

What Are the Three Elements of Presentation Skills?

The first thing to know about visual literacy and presentation skills is that they are just that—skills—and they are not innate to students. They have to be taught.

There are many greats in the business and speaking industry who have paved the way: Nancy Duarte, Guy Kawasaki, Carmine Gallo, Garr Reynolds, Akash Karia, and Seth Godin. As the intent of this book is to equip students with college and career-ready communication skills, it makes more sense to draw inspiration and craft educational best practices from the models and mentors who excel with this skill set rather than to draw from our current reality in educational presentations. The best practices shared in this chapter are either a blend of research and direct observations or drawn directly from people who excel at visual communication in the real world.

Nancy Duarte, author of *Resonate: Present Visual Stories that Transform Audiences* and *slide:ology: The Art and Science of Creating Great Presentations,* uses the three-legged stool as a model for illustrating the three pillars of a presentation: visual presentation, content, and delivery. Some students can prepare exemplary content but can't effectively convey this content in presentation form. Other students use the smoke and mirrors of visuals to mask insufficient and unorganized content. Neither is successful because one needs all three legs of the stool. If one of the legs is wobbly, the whole presentation will fall flat. In Figure 3.3, I have adapted Nancy's stool model to a tripod with a few expansions.

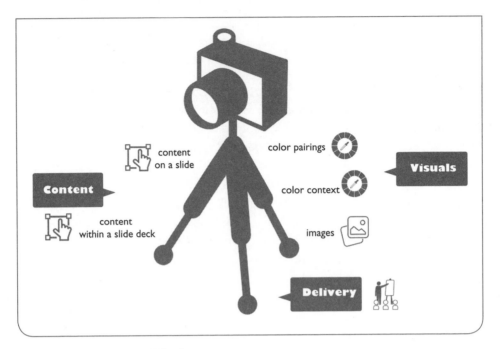

Figure 3.3 Presentation as a Tripod

Source: Adapted from Nancy Duarte's Three-Legged Stool Model (2015), https://alexrister1.wordpress.com/tag/three-legged-stool

Figure 3.4 Presenting Slide Design to Middle School Students

CULTIVATING COMMUNICATION IN THE CLASSROOM

Many teachers and students have asked me to present on this three-pronged skill set. This has allowed me to not only polish the content but also iterate the resources. When I first presented on this topic, it was navigating a few links with students. Now through the act of sharing, interacting with teachers and students, and gathering their feedback, I have crafted additional support resources shared throughout this chapter (Figure 3.4).

What Are Some Best Practices for Drafting a Presentation?

The first thing to remember and to communicate to students is that presentations are writing too, and they share some integral components with other types of writing. When I was in high school, I used to hate writing outlines. In fact, I would write the essay and then retrofit the outline to match the essay. With presentations, I find that to be very difficult. I have to draft some sort of outline prior to opening any piece of presentation software. A fantastic tip I gleaned from Akash Karia's book *How to Design TED Worthy Presentation Slides* is the need to quick-storm, brainstorm an outline or topics, on paper and then storyboard with sticky notes. Sticky notes are beneficial in many ways because they allow you to group and reorganize content, whereas most presentation software immediately forces you into a linear format. Additionally, sticky notes are a good guide for the amount of information that should fit on a slide as they are similar in scale (Karia, 2015).

If you remember the tripod model in Figure 3.3, you will note that I mention three legs. I took that same number and divided the slide deck I built for instructional delivery into three categories. Figure 3.5 serves as a visual outline for the slide deck I share with staff and students. The complete slide deck can be found on the

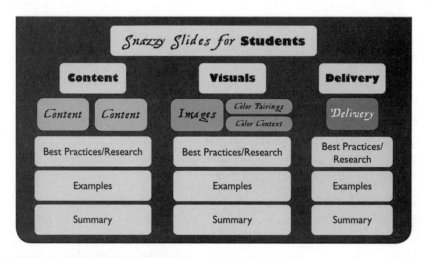

Figure 3.5 Snazzy Slides for Students Outline

companion site. In the Content section, I talk about two types of content (e.g., organizing content within the slide deck as well as on individual slides). Within the Visuals section, we focus on using images and color. Color is then broken into color pairings and color context. Finally, a brief section on delivery, which mainly focuses on ideas that would be typically shared in a speech class, is included. While each section is different, they each offer research-based best practices, examples, and a quick summary.

Content: How Can My Students Effectively Organize Content and Information Throughout Each Stage of the Presentation?

Content is both the body of information to be collected as well as the way that information is communicated on a slide. The Content section questions below focus on getting students to think about how they will organize their content. I enjoyed working with our Curriculum Specialist, Valerie Taylor, to carefully craft these four questions that assist students with organizing the content they plan to share:

Communicating the Organization of Content Within a Slide Deck

- **How do you hook your audience's attention?** *Students are oftentimes given a packet of information or a checklist of topics to cover and include within their presentation.* Suggesting to students to pull out the most interesting pieces of information to lead with is an effective way to capture their peers' attention and set the stage for the rest of the presentation. If students still need additional assistance making decisions on hooks, consider sharing with them the SHARP model (e.g., Stories, Humor, Analogies, References and Quotes, Pictures and Visuals) (Decker, 2012).

- **How do you capture the most important details and information?** *Many times, students are presenting a topic in 3–10 minutes.* Presenting on a topic that has a wide range of information can be daunting. Let students know that they should not present an exhaustive list of information but just the most important details on their topic.

- **What is the best logical order for your information?** *Whether students are working in groups or individually, order is a vital facet of their presentation.* To give them more freedom to make necessary decisions based on theme and flow, students should decide which topics will best lead into another topic within their presentation rather than just presenting topics in chronological order or the order the checklist was written in.

- **How do you leave your peers with an impression?** *"The End" is not an effective way to culminate a presentation.* Suggesting to students to end their presentation with a call to action, thematic quote, open-ended question to ponder, or video that sums up their presentation and provides their peers with something to digest allows students to diversify their use of media and communication.

These four questions should guide students with making decisions on how they will organize the content they will deliver.

Communicating Content on a Slide

Beyond organizing the order and delivery of the content, designing the content on the slides can be a stumbling block for many students. Providing students with a clear-cut list of do's helps them navigate through what is typically a very nebulous and abstract concept. Here are a few industry best practices to get you started.

> *"75+ words is a document: you're not giving a document . . . you're giving a presentation."*
>
> **—Nancy Duarte** *(Author and Principal at Duarte Inc.)*

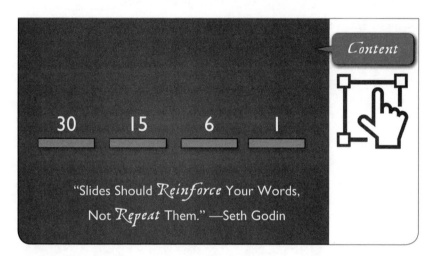

Figure 3.6 Content Guidelines

Some of the best advice you can give a student to visualize the difference between slides and a document is slides are like billboards (Pacini, 2013). The rule of thumb for slide design is that a slide should be able to be understood in 3 seconds or less. If we wrote essays on billboards, people would miss the message and/or get in a wreck trying to read it. Here are a few more guidelines:

- **What font size should I use?** No smaller than 30 (Reynolds, 2013). If students use a smaller font, they will find they can fit more text on the slide, which will not do them any favors when they need to present it. Additionally, most secondary classrooms have 30–35 students. Font smaller than 30 tends to be too hard for your students in the back of the room to see as well.

- **How many words should be on a slide?** No more than 15 (Reynolds, 2013). While this is a recommendation, I think the bigger picture is that while slides are indeed a type of writing, they are not a document. When students place a paragraph of text on a slide, they fall back on their comfort level of simply turning their back to the audience and reading the text, and the audience then loses interest.

- **How many lines of text should be on a slide?** No more than six. When a student uses bullet points and minimal text, these serve as curiosity cues for the audience to whet their palate for what is coming (e.g., note in Figure 3.7 the first bullet only says "Salary." This cue could pique their peers' interest: "I wonder what salary Civil Engineers earn."), while providing enough of a cue to the speaker to be a springboard for expansion. Students can use the speaker's note functionality or use their phone or cue cards as a confidence monitor, which helps them in several ways. It alleviates the stress of memorizing all of the content they plan on presenting, supports the idea that speaker's notes are for their dialogue and slides are for their audience, and also helps them actually think about what they want to say prior to their presentation.

- **How many ideas should be on a slide?** One main idea or message. This can be likened to paragraphs. If there are two main ideas in a paragraph, then there should be two paragraphs. In this case, two slides. While we want students to be concise, we also want students to be effective communicators. Slides are free so encourage students to not be constrained to a limited number of slides when they feel an extra one or four would be better for disseminating their information.

Teaching students to summarize content and pull out the main points is a common instructional task. Think of organizing content on a slide no differently. A great question to ask students is, "Can you eliminate text and still retain meaning?" (Reynolds, 2013). Many times, students are presenting content in a jigsaw fashion

Figure 3.7 Student Slide Example With Phone for Confidence Monitor

with the intent that everyone will need to know the content presented for a test or future assignment. This adds an extra layer of importance. Not only do students need to present information clearly to get their message understood; the content also has to be digested and retained. One way to increase comprehension is to thoughtfully use spacing. In fact, comprehension increases by 20% due to effective white space (Gutierrez, 2014b). A good rule of thumb is the body of text should be no more than 25%–40% of the slide (Gutierrez, 2014b).

I recommend always showing students examples of good slide design. It is very difficult to teach visual literacy and slide design and not show exemplars. Facts and figures are fine, but students need visual examples to scaffold their learning. Rather than recreate the wheel, I was able to locate a few that I use to share with students (which are also embedded in the slide deck on the companion site).

Figure 3.8 shows a standard information slide and then provides three ways to improve it. The first is to vertically group the three pieces of information into columns and then assign a visual cue to each. The second is more traditional in nature but has trimmed down some of the text as well as provided clear sub-headings. The last is more visual in nature and uses a large image as a backdrop with the text on top of the image. None of the three revisions are wrong or right; they appeal to personal preferences. I ask students, "Which one appeals to you, and which one is easier to glean the information from?" Then I encourage them to organize their content and design slides that mimic these. Interestingly enough, the vast majority of students prefer the first and the last over the middle, yet an overwhelming majority of students initially present with slides that look like the middle one.

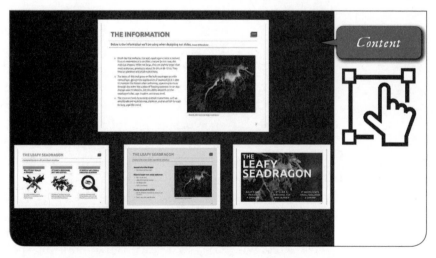

Figure 3.8 "Five Killer Ways to Design the Same Slide" by Crispy Presentations

Source: Adapted from Crispy Presentations,
http://www.slideshare.net/CrispyPresentations/five-killer-ways-to-design-the-same-slide

Figure 3.9 depicts the original slide (at the top) I was given for a GPA presentation to parents and how I divided that slide that really had three main points into three unique slides (at the bottom). While some of the transition includes paring down text, the other updates include a unique spin on color blocking and adding visual icons and color to draw the audience in.

Figure 3.9 Updating a Text-Heavy Slide Using Color Blocking and Icons

Source: Original slide content drafted by Melissa Dupre and Natalie Cannon

I will tell you that any student (or staff member) I have seen present with a paragraph on the slide will always turn away from the audience or their peers and read the slide—every time.

"Slides are to lead, not read. They should paraphrase and anchor what's coming out of your mouth. Because people can read faster than you talk, if you put too much detail on the slide, the audience will read ahead of you and not listen to what you're saying."

—Guy Kawasaki
(Evangelist and Author)

Another reminder to students is that if both they and their slides say the same thing, one of them is not needed. Ultimately, slide design is a very specific skill set and type of communication that relies on visuals, similar to the layout of a billboard. While the actual organization and visual display of a slide can be subjective in nature, sharing concrete examples on a visual design spectrum tends to be the most helpful for students.

Purposeful and strategic repetition and predictability of content is also important to both the speaker and the audience. Using similar slide design when you are talking about similar types of content serves as a visual cue to both the speaker and the audience. English teachers think of this as visual anaphora. The "I Have a Dream" speech is an example of anaphora as Martin Luther King uses repetition of text for emphasis. The slides in Figure 3.10 are all examples of sharing research statistics and draw upon purposeful repetition of content and visual patterns.

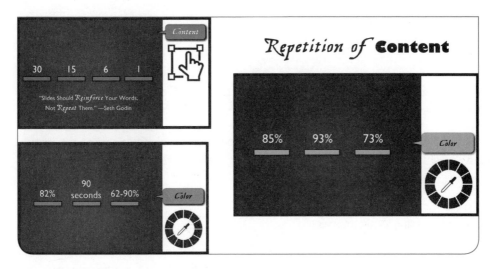

Figure 3.10 Examples of Repetition of Content in Slides

A popular slide design layout happens to be color blocking, pairing contrasting colors in juxtaposed rectangles, as seen in Figure 3.11. This instantly signals that we will be talking about two things and most likely those things will be a comparison or a contrast of two similar topics. This effect is easily created in any slide design software with a filled shape that takes up half the slide. Google Slides has added this element to many of their presentation templates. Four additional examples using this technique can be found in Figure P.1, Figures 2.1 and 2.2, and Figure 7.7.

Figure 3.11 Examples of Color Blocking in Slides

Of all the tips I shared with students, this one seemed to end up incorporated the most in student presentations.

Visuals: How Can My Students Effectively Communicate With Visuals (e.g., Images and Icons) and Color?

We briefly touched on the research behind pairing visuals with text at the beginning of this chapter. Using visuals and color is an integral part to comprehension and information processing.

Communicating With Images

Take a look at Figure 3.12. The slide on the left essentially states that almost 100% of California is experiencing drought. However, the use of a stock background and no image leaves me less than moved. Compare your initial response to the slide on the right that uses an image and a simple graph to convey the same bit of information. Pairing an image with a possibly unfamiliar word such as *drought* is also helpful for students that benefit from the dual-coding of text and image.

> *"The language of the 21st century includes images like never before."*
>
> —**Garr Reynolds** *(Author and Professor at Kyoto University of Foreign Studies)*

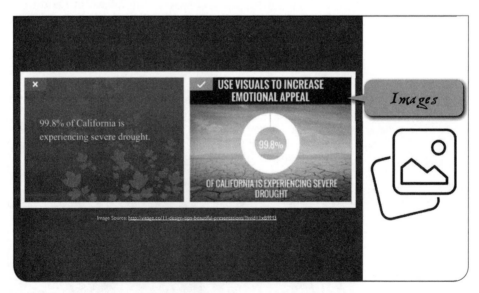

Figure 3.12 "11 Design Tips for Beautiful Presentations" by Katy French (2014)

Source: Adapted from Katy French, http://visage.co/11-design-tips-beautiful-presentations

Take a look at Figure 3.13. The slide on top uses a series of text-heavy bullets. The two slides on the bottom build curiosity by separating the question from the answer, including an original image, and replacing the wordy bullets with easily recognizable icons.

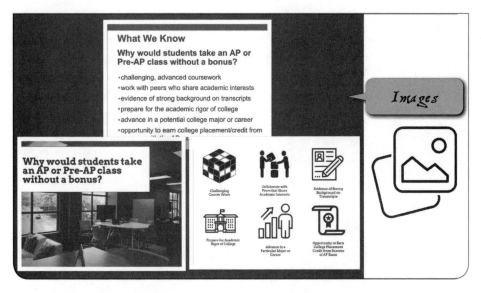

Figure 3.13 Updating a Text-Heavy Slide Using Visuals and Icons

While I could write another chapter on finding images and visuals, I feel like teaching students to craft their own story and meaning is far more of a powerful learning tool and lesson. Many students have access to a camera whether on their phone or with a school-provided device. Just like we can speak about a photograph for minutes without any text description, original images are far more personal and relevant than random stock images scoured from Google:

- **Science Labs:** Picture a student in a science classroom—they could take snapshots of the materials and photos along the way to document their learning and present their findings as a visual lab report.

- **Math:** A student presenting his or her findings on a math problem could take photos of their charts and graphs or different ways his or her peers solved a problem.

- **Geography:** Students presenting a lesson on geography could take screenshots from Google Earth and Maps to include within their presentation.

- **English:** Perhaps students are writing about tone or creating a presentation on best practices for working in groups. This might actually be the perfect time to take original stock images. Guy Kawasaki (pictured in Figure 3.14) famously takes stock images, which are essentially staged images intended to capture real and casual/natural moments. These are not only fun to do but provide a fantastic visual representation for words, actions, and ideas. I had the opportunity to meet Guy Kawasaki at SXSWEDU last year and participated in the stock photo phenomenon.

Though I realize there are times where students need to use nonoriginal photos within their presentations, especially if they need historical or current images, there are just as many times if not more when original images would work better. Students can also use images as metaphors or symbols. This makes staging and taking their

Figure 3.14 Staged Stock Photo of Lisa Johnson and Guy Kawasaki at SXSWEDU 2015

own photos more personally linked to their learning. I've started staging my own photos with my Lego Minifigures (remember, I have two boys; see Figure 3.15). In fact, Figure 3.17 on page 61 citing color psychology layered on Matchbox cars is actually from my son's room and collection. He likes to organize his cars in ROYGBIV order, which worked as a perfect hook for illustrating that piece of information.

While I am not advocating everyone nab the nearest Barbie or Lego figure to craft a presentation, I can definitely tell you that original images almost always make better presentations.

If you are not quite down with using Minifigures, another option is to have students snap shot random images with their devices throughout the year and save them to a shared folder. This way, students essentially have an in-house image gallery to choose from. One of my favorite pairings is art and literacy. Oftentimes, students have to photograph their art for portfolios or submissions. Can you imagine how the power and potential of providing this art in a collaborative folder that other students could access could impact learning and creativity? Now students could use their peers' art to inspire their own writing or poetry or even springboard a mathematics problem. The opportunities are endless when we collaborate across content areas and amongst our peers. More information on protecting original images can be found in Chapter 4 on student publishing.

"Creatively adding *Quotes* to your presentation breaks up the slides nicely and gives your *Audience...* a *Mental Break*." —Carmine Gallo

Original Image by Lisa Johnson

Figure 3.15 Lego Minifigure Original Photo Paired With a Quote in Keynote

Communicating With Icons

You might have been wondering about some of the icons used in the slides and hand-outs above and throughout this book. Icons are the new clipart. They are simple and do not detract from the message. When used deliberately, icons can add meaning and organization to a slide. In Figure 3.16, the student used four icons to structure the four steps she planned to describe in her presentation. When she got to the slide that further delineated that step, she used the same icon. This made the presentation easy to follow. If you return to Figures P.2 and 2.1 and flip ahead to 7.1, you will notice that icons can also be used with data, graphs, and fractions to make them easier to compre-hend and digest. Icons can be designed using an app like Assembly or found on sites like Canva and the Noun Project.

Locating images and icons to represent content might be a difficult skill at first, especially if students are searching for images that might be more abstract and symbolic in nature. A fun entry point to selecting the best image would be a game of Apples to Apples, which forces students to assign the best photo to a given word and justify their selection. Another easy and fun way to practice this art is to start with a PechaFlickr. The site will generate an auto advancing slide deck of random images based on a search term. This would be a great way to practice communicat-ing a coherent idea using images, poetry, or even rhyming. As it does draw images from Flickr, you will want to make sure Flickr is unblocked in your district. I hav-en't encountered drastically inappropriate images populated from Flickr, but I have noted a few questionable ones, so I advise a teacher test run of this before using it within a classroom construct.

Figure 3.16 Student Example of Using Icons

Communicating With Color

Most students and adults don't consider the deliberate use of color. However, there is a fair amount of research to support its impact. Adding color to a technical document improved recall of that information by 82% ("The Big Bang Theory of Colors," 2014). The next time you walk into a clothing store or bookstore, pay attention to what books and items you are naturally drawn to. Do you notice any patterns or trends? "Research reveals people make a subconscious judgment about a person, environment, or product within 90 seconds of initial viewing and that between 62% and 90% of that assessment is based on color alone" (WebpageFX Team, 2013). So how can students utilize this research to be better architects of information? Soon students start realizing that each element of their presentation from content and text to images and color is not decoration but purposeful and strategic.

Color can actually be broken down into two sections: color pairings (or color clashing) and color context. Color clashing or pairings is pretty simple to explain and can be summed up by *Presentation Zen*, "Do no harm with color" (Reynolds, 2013). Essentially don't let color take over or confuse the content.

Slide Background Color: If students are presenting their content with the lights off (especially in an auditorium), then they will probably want to choose black slides as these fatigue the audience's eyes less. An easy way to remember this is to think of the ending credits in a theater; they are typically white text scrolling on a black background. Conversely, if students are presenting in a classroom with the lights on, then a white slide is perfectly fine.

Color Clashing: Color clashing might get a little too much into design for most students, but several students were tickled pink to learn about sites like colorhunt .co that provide possible color pairings and HTML color codes that will pull the exact colors from an image so they can be matched in a presentation's text or graphics using the Color Picker. Keynote, Google Slides, and PPT should all offer this functionality as well.

Contextual color or color psychology can be readily discovered by just Googling "psychology of color" and will result in a plethora of infographics and statistics. Rather than have them dive down a potential rabbit hole, simply share with students that colors have meaning and using color deliberately can capture the audience's attention and even promote discussion. How deep you get into color psychology with your students should depend on their age group, interest, and the nature of the presentation. I shared more in-depth information about color psychology with students who were in career, technology, and economics classes and were presenting products, business plans, etc. Students presenting typical classroom information received the "just the facts" serving size.

Color Psychology: When delivering this content to secondary students, I mentioned (Morton, 2010, 2016):

- Red is the color of extremes and is used to display passion, danger, and even violence. It also stimulates attention to detail (Zandan, 2016) and boosts appetite and increases heart rate ("Color and How Its Cultural Associations Affect Our Mood," 2016).

- Blue is associated with loyalty, authority, and trust, is considered an appetite suppressant ("Color & Appetite Matters," 2016), and lowers blood pressure ("Seeing Red and Mellow Yellow: The Science of Why Color Affects Our Mood," 2011).

- Yellow is used to grab the audience's attention and highlight key points. It has also been found to boost mental activity and memory (Zandan, 2016). It is also the color of happiness and optimism.

- Green promotes discussion (Zandan, 2016) and is often used by eco-friendly companies.

- Purple is said to stimulate creativity as it is a rare color found in nature.

These colors also have impact on learning design. For example, blue is a calming color that can be used when something might appear to be too complicated. Contrastingly, orange is a color that can be used to prevent boredom (Gutierrez, 2014a).

A good rule of thumb is to keep your color scheme consistent with the theme and tone of its presentation. After sharing this information with a group of students preparing a TEDTalk like presentation on a topic of research, they chose to use red to present statistics on violence in relationships and then shifted to the use of blue to represent positive and calming ways to combat the issue of violence in relationships.

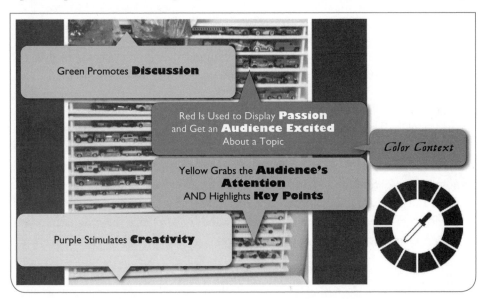

Figure 3.17 Color Psychology Basics (using original image of miniature cars organized by color: ROYGBIV)

Source: http://www.quantifiedcommunications.com/blog/color-psychology-what-colors-make-great-presentations

Delivery: How Can My Students Effectively Deliver Content?

So that leaves us with delivery. Delivery includes the verbal and nonverbal cues that we use to deliver content. While most of our students aren't training to be TED Speakers or keynoters, I hope we can all agree that effective communication skills will serve them well no matter what career path they follow. A London-based public school values oracy, the ability to speak well, so highly that they weave it through every class and lesson. They even created an oracy framework that captures student's progression from Apprentice to Expert in four categories (e.g., Physical, Linguistic, Cognitive, and Emotional-Social). These opportunities for repeated oracy and public speaking not only increase students' future employability ("Oracy in the Classroom: Strategies for Effective Talk," 2016) but also increase development of the language areas in the brain (Gallo, 2014).

Here are a few things for students to keep in mind:

- **Eye Contact:** If you are facing the screen or reading your slides, not only will people lose interest, but they will also not be able to hear you.

- **Body Movement and Positions:** Most polished speakers do not stand in one spot the entire presentation. If they only stand on the left side of the room, then the people on the right side of the room might start tuning out. Rather, they pace with purpose, poise, and passion. I have also noticed that students have a problem figuring out where to put their hands. Carmine Gallo (2014) recommends:

    Picture your power sphere as a circle that runs from the top of your eyes, out to the tips of your outstretched hands, down to your belly button, and back up to your eyes again. Try to keep your gestures (and eye gaze) in this zone. Hands that hang below your navel lack energy and "confidence."

A great way to show best practices for this skill is to have students watch TEDTalks. Additionally, if students are delivering a speech, poetry, or even a persuasive paper, enlisting some insight from *The Emotion Thesaurus* might be helpful. While intended as a writer's guide to character expression, the book provides verbal and nonverbal cues through physical body signals for 75 emotions ranging from amazement and gratitude to indifference and regret. Whether used as a guide for students to incorporate them into their own presentations or recognize these signals in their audience, this tool is a handy quick reference.

> *"The verbal equivalent of a highlighter is to raise or lower the volume of your voice, change the speed at which you deliver the words, and/or set aside the key word or phrase with a pause before or after voicing it."*
>
> **—Carmine Gallo**
> *(Keynote Speaker, Author, and Former CBS 2 Correspondent)*

- **Volume:** Making students aware of their natural volume and how to augment it in a variety of social situations and environments (small, large, crowded, empty, inside, and outside) is a simple but effective skill.

- **Speed:** Students should be reminded to speak at a pace that people can understand them. The Goldilocks of speed is 165 words per minute (Gallo,

2014). While I doubt many students are going to time themselves, I do think this provides a nice guideline.

- **Confidence Monitor:** I have presented countless times over the past decade and I still use a confidence monitor. This is essentially my speaker notes. I don't read them, but they are there if I need them. Most presentation software will offer the ability to see both your slide and your speaker notes at the same time. An alternative for software that doesn't is note cards or notes displayed on a mobile device. An example of this can be found in Figure 3.7.

- **Connection Between Talk and Slides:** While we have laid the framework for slides having more of a visual component, what students say is even more important. If students are using more visual slides, there will be less text on the slide, which means students will need to really know their content, what they plan on saying, and how they actually say it. They will need to know what to say when an image, icon, or slide appears. It also helps if students practice verbal transitions between slides. While I have delivered countless presentations and slide decks, I still get nervous especially when the topic is more of a speech. One trick I have started using is that of visual bread crumbs. I purposefully use transitions and icons to guide me. If everything is on the slide at once, then it is harder to know what to say first, but if you build slides with a combination of guiding visuals or icons and transitions, it eases the tension and helps with flow.

For ISTE's 1 in 3, each speaker has 3 minutes to conversationally share a story. While my first slide (see Figure 3.18) may seem like a collage of images, Figure 3.19 depicts that it was in fact a carefully timed and organized visual map.

Figure 3.18 Connection Between Talk and Slides at ISTE 1 in 3 (1 Story in 3 Minutes)

Slide Action	SAY
Picture of Me and Think Back ...	"Think back to your high school days ... What formats of communication did you have? I remember ..."
Envelope Icon Appears	"Hand-written letters"
Computer Icon Appears	"AOL chat rooms and ..."
Pager Icon Appears	"Pagers."
Picture of Boy Appears	"Now my son has no idea what a corded telephone is. He thinks it is when his phone is charging. He lives in a world of ..."
Wi-Fi Icon Appears	"Constant Wi-Fi"
Emoticon Appears	"Emoticons ..."

Figure 3.19 Table That Depicts Slide Action and Speech Featured in Slide in Figure 3.18

While I am not advocating that every slide deck and student presentation needs to be this polished and timed, elements of the visual bread crumb trail technique are helpful to connecting a student's message with slides and alleviating the stress of memorizing speaker's notes word for word. Figure 3.21 also provides an example of this.

- **Audience Participation:** I know we have all sat through a lecture where at one point we felt like we might fall asleep or were at the very least so bored we began to check our phones, or even worse. check out completely. Conversely, I am sure you remember a speaker or a teacher who really got you excited about a topic through audience participation. Recently, I was in Wichita for a Magnet School Conference, and Toni Robinson from Discovery was the keynote for the day. She spoke on purpose, passion, and possibility and incorporated several audience challenges. She started with having the audience picture someone or something that they were passionate about, locate an image on their phone that they are passionate about, then come up with three content area connections for the photo, and finally share that information with their elbow partner. You could tell that the audience was internalizing the information by acting on it, and they were definitely engaged. Cathy Hunt's iPadpalooza keynote is another fantastic example. She passed out sheets of white paper and then posted an image of Jackson Pollock's *Blue Poles* on the screen. She had us then fold the paper to look like the art, feel the crumpled lines in our papers, and even stand and move our arms and body to mimic the blue poles depicted in the art. I may not remember everything she said in that 90-minute keynote, but I can tell you that I have no problem recalling that experience because I was actively engaged rather than a passive party.

Another method of audience participation might be an ongoing back channel of questions and thoughts using something like Todays Meet. Kahoot and Nearpod are also great tools that allow a speaker to interact with the audience by gleaning real-time feedback. With both of these apps, the speaker can poll the audience and then share a slide that is relevant to the answer. Carl Hooker uses this method with parent trainings. He will ask parents about their thoughts on screen time and then provide follow-up slides that answer the question and provide additional support.

What Tools and Applications Can Be Used in Conjunction With Student Presentations?

Presentations are typically one of the most device-neutral tasks you can ask a student to complete, as there are so many types of software and apps available. Some apps just allow for traditional slides, others offer an audio narration that ultimately produces a video, others create a multimedia scrolling website, and even others offer a suite of creative common copyright-free images embedded within the tool. As tools and features are constantly updated, I have opted to provide a full list of suggested presentation tools on the companion site https://resources.corwin.com/cultivatingcomm.

Beyond Sharing These Resources, How Can I Model Best Practices in My Instruction?

One of the easiest ways to impact change in our students is to model it through the tools we use. Luiz Bravim teaches AP World History and could have easily presented innumerable pieces of data, but felt that nothing conveyed the changes in the labor system better than a single image of children as young as 6 working in decrepit conditions without safety precautions or parental supervision. He even reported that there was no need to do any reviews or previous learned material for the test essays because the image had such lasting power. Since then, he has continued to include bold imagery in his instructional lectures.

Another way to model this information is to use a "Steal My Slide Design" slide at the end of your own slide decks. This approach I borrowed from Adam Bellow (Figure 3.20). I have now started adding a key to the end of my presentation so there is no mystery beyond the design or the visual choices.

Help! I Have a Few More Questions About Presentation Skills and Visual Literacy!

I have presented these best practices and standards to secondary students and educators across the world. And I am often met with four questions that I wanted to address:

- **What if students are not comfortable with public speaking?** Many times we have students that are uncomfortable with speaking in front of the class. One way to alleviate this stress is to jigsaw the presentation process. Rather than

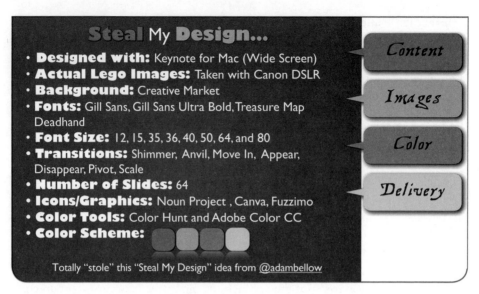

Figure 3.20 "Steal My Design" Slide to Illustrate Design Choices for Students

have each student present his or her content in front of a class of 30–36, set up a presentation satellite cafe. This could look like five students being the stationary presenter and the rest of the class being the satellite around them. This alleviates the stress of presenting in front of a large group and also provides them practice as students get to present the same content 3–4 times to different groups in a more personal setting. Having students save slides as images and narrate over them to create a movie may also alleviate some of the stress associated with public speaking. Another option is teaching students a little trick. No matter how many keynotes I do, I am still terrified every time I take the stage. Margot Leitman, author of *Long Story Short: The Only Storytelling Guide You'll Ever Know*, offers a simple idea of narrowing information down to product words, which essentially creates a set list. I have tailored this technique for slide design. The idea is to remember a series of key words rather than everything you plan to say . . . in this case I pick one key word per slide (Figure 3.21) and then that word is a trigger for everything else I plan to say.

- **How can I grade a presentation when all of the content and text isn't on the slides?** We have to remember that presentations are for the student's learning and not for our ease of grading. As presentations become more and more visual, they will be harder to grade if we are just hoping to check boxes. A solution to this concern might be the Slide Doc. Slide Docs are defined as "a visual document, developed in presentation software, that is intended to be read and referenced instead of projected" (Duarte, 2015). Slide Docs are essentially visual essays designed in slide software. They utilize all of the best practices and research from this chapter but they are not meant to be delivered; they are intended to be distributed, not presented. More information about this type of visual communication can be found at www.duarte.com/slidedocs. Another

Figure 3.21 Examples of Word Set Lists

spin on the slide doc is the slide deck book, which is a method of using slide software to create a textbook. This also gets students familiar with all of the nuances to textbooks such as tables, pull quotes, key terms, discussion questions, etc. Ditch that Textbook featured three middle school history student examples from Matthew Mcfarlane's class using Google Slides. If you are looking to grade presentations much like you would an essay and the slides are not meant to be presented, this is a simple alternative.

- **How long does this take?** This is more in reference to student slide presentations and less about teaching students these skills, which typically takes one class period. Let's be fair. Presentations can suck classroom time. We have to be cognizant of when a full class presentation makes sense and when that information can be divulged in a different format. The idea of jigsawing content is very popular. Teachers have a lot of material to cover and little time to cover it, so splitting the content between groups and presenting in a jigsawed fashion seems to be a go-to method for solving this dilemma. Sometimes, a self-paced jigsaw presentation might be a better alternative. In this case, students or student groups create a presentation on a section of the content. Then this information is made accessible to all students, typically through a link on the class website. Every student can then visit each link and read through the information asynchronously. By using this self-directed format and providing the content as a link, this allows students to take their time to digest the content and review at their pace.

Ultimately, we have to ask ourselves when we assign a presentation as a project if the content is best disseminated through slides and an oral presentation or if the content would be best digested through alternative means. Chapter 4 dives deeper into other types of projects beyond slides.

Additionally, what I found when initially presenting this information to secondary students was that it was often the first time they had ever been told to present in such a way. Providing time for students to reflect on this novel type of communication as well as to make decisions on how they might use it in their own upcoming presentations are integral pieces to see development in the way they craft and present content in the future. To support the brainstorming and planning of a presentation using the tips and best practices shared in this chapter, a Presentation Planner Communication Catcher has also been included, shown in Figure 3.22.

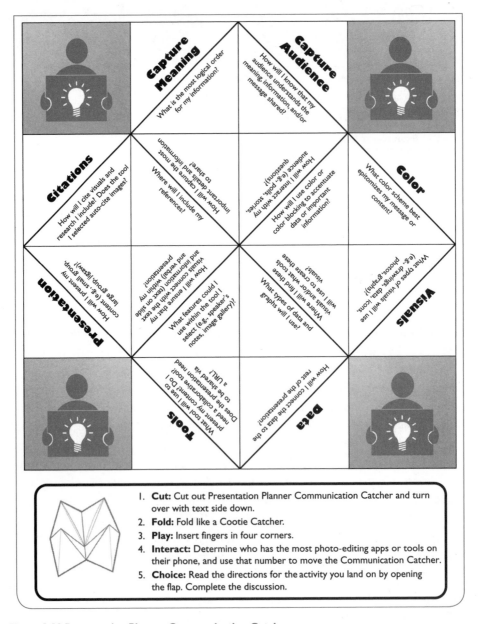

1. **Cut:** Cut out Presentation Planner Communication Catcher and turn over with text side down.
2. **Fold:** Fold like a Cootie Catcher.
3. **Play:** Insert fingers in four corners.
4. **Interact:** Determine who has the most photo-editing apps or tools on their phone, and use that number to move the Communication Catcher.
5. **Choice:** Read the directions for the activity you land on by opening the flap. Complete the discussion.

Figure 3.22 Presentation Planner Communication Catcher

Available for download at **https://resources.corwin.com/cultivatingcomm**

Presentation Skills
Preparation Inventory Assessment

- ☐ Why are visual literacy and presentation skills important for my students?
- ☐ How do these skills apply to other areas of communication, instruction, and writing?
- ☐ How will these skills benefit my students' comprehension and retention of content?
- ☐ How will I teach and disseminate these best practices for visual communication and presentations to my students?
- ☐ How can I support my students with organizing the content for and on their slides?
- ☐ How can I support my students with slides that use images and color purposefully?
- ☐ How will I support my students with delivering their content?
- ☐ What type of audience participation could I model and/or encourage in my classroom?
- ☐ What tools have I used in the past for student presentations?
- ☐ What presentation tools would I like to explore and share with my students?
- ☐ How could I integrate assignments that use students' original images?
- ☐ What other questions do I have about presentation skills and visual communication?
- ☐ Which support resources will I use with my students?

Share your answers using the hashtag #cultivatecomm.

My Students' Self-Assessment Checklist

- ☐ My students can organize content so it is interesting, informative, and memorable for their peers.
- ☐ My students can effectively select, locate, and integrate images and icons as visual cues that complement their content.
- ☐ My students can use color with purpose.
- ☐ My students can select the best application to deliver their content.

Additional Resources and Reading

- Presentation Planner Communication Catcher (found in Appendix B and on https://resources.corwin.com/cultivatingcomm)

- Suggested List of Presentation Tools (found on https://resources.corwin.com/cultivatingcomm)

- Student Presentation Planning Guide (found on https://resources.corwin.com/cultivatingcomm)

- Presentation Student Note-Taking Guide (found on https://resources.corwin.com/cultivatingcomm)

- 3 Infographics: "The Secrets of Slide Design for Students," "Slide Design Hacks for Secondary Students," and "The Dos and Don'ts of Slide Design for Students" (www.slideshare.net/lisajohnson)

- Canva's Design School and Blog (https://designschool.canva.com)

- 35+ Canva Lesson Plans (https://designschool.canva.com/teaching-materials)

- Suggested Reading and Resources (www.pinterest.com/techchef4u/visual-literacy-and-presentation-skills)

References

The Big Bang theory of colors. (2014). Designmantic. *Slideshare.net.* Retrieved from http://www.slideshare.net/DesignMantic/the-big-bang-theory-of-colors

Color & appetite matters. (2016). *Colormatters.com.* Retrieved October 24, 2016, from http://www.colormatters.com/color-and-the-body/color-and-appetite-matters

Color and how its cultural associations affect our mood. (2016). *Psychologistworld.com.* Retrieved October 24, 2016, from https://www.psychologistworld.com/perception/color.php

Crispy Presentations. (2014). Five killer ways to design the same slide. *Slideshare.net.* Retrieved from http://www.slideshare.net/CrispyPresentations/five-killer-ways-to-design-the-same-slide

Decker, K. (2012). Airline-inspired analogies. *Decker.com.* Retrieved October 25, 2016, from https://decker.com/blog/airline-inspired-analogies

Duarte, N. (2015). Slidedocs. Retrieved January 24, 2016, from http://www.duarte.com/slidedocs

French, K. (2014). 11 design tips for beautiful presentations. Retrieved October 1, 2015, from https://visage.co/11-design-tips-beautiful-presentations

Gallo, C. (2014). *Talk like TED.* New York, NY: St. Martin's Griffin.

Gutierrez, K. (2014a). 6 ways color psychology can be used to design effective eLearning. *Info.shiftelearning.com*. Retrieved January 24, 2016, from http://info.shiftelearning.com/blog/bid/348188/6-Ways-Color-Psychology-Can-Be-Used-to-Design-Effective-eLearning

Gutierrez, K. (2014b). A 7-step typography lesson for first-time eLearning developers. *Info.shiftelearning.com*. Retrieved January 24, 2016, from http://info.shiftelearning.com/blog/bid/353234/A-7-Step-Typography-Lesson-for-First-time-eLearning-Developers

Karia, A. (2015). *How to design TED-worthy presentation slides* (3rd ed.). CreateSpace Independent Publishing Platform.

Morton, J. (2010). Why color matters. *Colorcom.com*. Retrieved January 24, 2016, from http://www.colorcom.com/research/why-color-matters

Morton, J. (2016). Explore Colors. *Colormatters.com*. Retrieved October 24, 2016, from https://www.colormatters.com/color-symbolism/the-meanings-of-colors

National Governors Association Center for Best Practices and Council of Chief State School Officers. (2010). *Common Core State Standards initiative*. Retrieved from www.corestandards.org.

Oracy in the classroom: Strategies for effective talk. (2016). *Edutopia*. Retrieved October 25, 2016, from https://www.edutopia.org/practice/oracy-classroom-strategies-effective-talk

Pacini, A. (2013). 5 Simple ways to design slides like billboards. *Echopresentations.blogspot.com*. Retrieved October 25, 2016, from http://echopresentations.blogspot.com/2013/11/slides-are-like-billboards-design-like.html

Reynolds, G. (2013). *Presentation Zen Design: Simple design principles and techniques to enhance your presentations* (2nd ed.) (Graphic Design & Visual Communication Courses). Berkeley, CA: New Riders Publishing.

Seeing red and mellow yellow: The science of why color affects our mood. (2011). *The Huffington Post*. Retrieved October 24, 2016, from http://www.huffingtonpost.com/2011/11/27/how-color-affects-our-moo_n_1114790.html

Slideshare.net. (2013). 7 tips to beautiful PowerPoint by @ itseugenec. Retrieved January 24, 2016, from http://www.slideshare.net/itseugene/7-tips-to-beautiful-powerpoint-by-itseugenec

Standards for students. (2016). *Iste.org*. Retrieved January 24, 2016, from http://www.iste.org/standards/ISTE-standards/standards-for-students

Walker-Ford, M. (2014). 10 reasons why you must use visual content as part of your marketing strategy. *Red Website Design Blog*. Retrieved October 25, 2016, from https://blog.red-website-design.co.uk/2014/05/21/10-reasons-why-you-must-use-visual-content-as-part-of-your-marketing-strategy

WebpageFX Team. (2013). Psychology of color: The meaning behind what we see [Infographic]. *WebpageFX Blog*. N.p. Retrieved from http://www.webpagefx.com/blog/web-design/psychology-of-color-infographic/

Zandan, N. (2016). Color psychology—What colors make great presentations? *Quantifiedcommunications.com*. Retrieved October 24, 2016, from http://www.quantifiedcommunications.com/blog/color-psychology-what-colors-make-great-presentations

CHAPTER 4

Student Publishing and Projects

Communicating with an authentic audience through the application of curricular knowledge and construction of content understanding to create a digital or learning artifact

"The principle goal of education in the schools should be creating men and women who are capable of doing new things, not simply repeating what other generations have done."

—Jean Piaget (Child Development Clinical Psychologist)

U p until now, we have addressed email etiquette and self-advocacy, foundational skills for productive group work, and visual literacy. At face value, projects are simply a way to construct content understanding through a learning artifact. In a highly competitive world seeking creative problem-solvers, trifold poster boards and age-old legacy projects may not be the best way to prepare our students for a world of information surplus and a workforce that thrives on transferable skills.

Communication has very real roots within projects and publishing as students have to be able to clearly and effectively communicate their ideas and learning across a wide variety of media formats and be able to choose the best media format for their content. While communication may be the most neglected of the C's, it is the easiest to combine with other C's. A recent *Scientific American* article purported three qualifiers that had to be present in creative work: *original, meaningful,* and *surprising.* The article goes on to delineate meaningful as the ability to "satisfy some utility function, or provide a new interpretation" (Kaufman, 2016). If you are a *Shark Tank* junkie like myself, then this probably doesn't come as a surprise to you. While I realize that we are not trying to craft entrepreneurs and patent holders with our curricular content, we are also not in the business of cranking out a one-size-fits-all conveyor belt student either. So how can we provide opportunities for our students to flex their communication and creativity muscles without losing sight of our standards? Rather than quoting the myriad of platitudes on creativity or appealing to your sense of entrepreneurial pop culture television, there is one study that I found that clearly examines the need for connecting creativity to college and career readiness. In fact, this study of 1,000 college-educated and full-time salaried employees found that 78% felt creativity was important to their current career, and 71% found it should be taught as a course. But wait . . . there's more! Eighty-five percent felt it was critical for problem-solving, but 32% did not feel comfortable thinking creatively at work (*Creativity and Education,* 2012).

There are so many opportunities for creative thinking in our daily course work and many of them have been sprinkled throughout each chapter of this book. For this chapter, I sought to drill down to student projects and publishing. While the two words "projects" and "publishing" have been combined in this chapter, they really do mean two very different things. Students can complete a project without publishing it, and publishing can mean a variety of different things to different people and is not limited to simply publishing to a walled garden of student examples or sharing on social media. I think the real question is not, "What do these words mean?" but, "How can I use projects and publishing to facilitate opportunities to utilize the 4 C's with core content in an authentic way?"

The three A's of *autonomy, authentic audience,* and *appropriate use* provide a real framework for projects and publishing in this new era of innovation. These three elements can sometimes seem cliché. Do we know what these words really mean? And how do we know we are really accomplishing all three? I feel a little like Inigo Montoya in *The Princess Bride,* "You keep using [these words], [but] I do not think it means what you think it means." We talk about autonomy, but not through the lens of college and career-ready opportunities and tasks. We talk about authentic audiences, but many times only in the sense of online publishing, not through the context of peers and purpose. We talk about appropriate use but we really don't enforce it, and we don't talk at all about protecting students' artifacts beyond a do-not-publish list. So let's take a backstage pass to explore the behind-the-scenes elements of projects and publishing that need to be center stage.

How Can I Provide Autonomy and Choice Within a Project?

When we think of autonomy and choice, we oftentimes think of it in narrow terms. Autonomy and choice are not simply allowing students to choose a different tool to achieve the same outcome. It is the intentional practice of valuing agency over task. It is being given the *why* and allowing students to determine the *how* and the *what* on their own so they become independent thinkers and decision makers. Teachers can provide the standards and the rationale for an assignment (the *why*), but students still have the freedom to choose the ways they express their understanding (the *how*), and with what formats and tools (the *what*). Figure 4.1 adapts Simon Sinek's Golden Circle to illustrate how projects can have both teacher-provided and student-driven elements.

So what does this look like? Let me paint a picture (pun intended). Melinda Darrow's art history students are studying color theory. Rather than assigning them to all do a PowerPoint on the psychology of color for each individual color, the teacher allows students to choose their area of study (the *how*) and their delivery method (the *what*). One student chooses to do a movie analysis of the use of color and shares the videos with students, while pausing them and pointing out which elements he discovered. One student chooses to research the stroop effect and another the historical context and impact of the color gold. One plays with the impact of color choice and swaps complementary colors in paintings and even grayscales famous paintings to visualize the impact on meaning that the absence of color has. Another creates a themed crayon box and renames each color to represent famous paintings (e.g., *Starry Night* yellow, *Blue Dog* blue, *Scream* orange). And yet another uses color to illustrate the impact it has on small spaces by redesigning a studio apartment. It may not surprise you

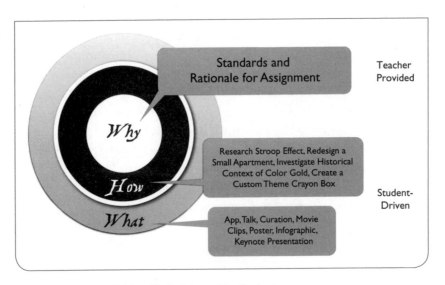

Figure 4.1 Simon Sinek's Golden Circle Adapted for Projects

that every student was totally interested and engaged in their own topic as well as the topics of others. Why? Students were allowed to connect to their curiosities and choose the area of study that interested them *and* no one presented the same topic the same way. The reality is that the cookie cutter model of projects and disposable assignments only

> *"If you assign a project and get back 30 of the exact same thing, that's not a project, that's a recipe."*
>
> —**Chris Lehmann** *(Author and Founding Principal of the Science Leadership Academy)*

exists in schools. It would be a massive waste of company resources to assign the same portion of the same project to each of their staff members and expect very similar results.

While juniors and seniors might be able to navigate this very open-ended individual research project, underclassmen and middle schoolers might need more scaffolding. One way to provide additional intervention and support is to use idea assignments. Natalie Cannon, a secondary Latin teacher, uses this framework in her Latin class during the Masada project. Students can choose any area of study involving Masada (e.g., clothing, food, fashion, politics, armor), but they have to determine the viability of their topic first. Essentially, they do preliminary research on their top three ideas and begin to eliminate topics that they find have limited information, or they don't feel as excited about anymore (e.g., "I didn't find much information on apothecary sets, and the more I studied Roman cooking, the more interested I became in the topic."). The final project should be something that is the most interesting to them and has the least roadblocks to discovering content and support for. This is a project that I have seen year after year, and it still fascinates me and the students.

> *"This is the only time I have ever had students explore deeper into someone else's research like they have been doing. They are clicking through the links and reading the websites, they are watching the long videos that they only previewed in class due to time limits, and they are really looking at the pictures/art/examples that students are including!"*
>
> —**Natalie Cannon** *(HS Latin Teacher)*

One of my favorite examples was a student who was fascinated with ancient Roman pantomime and decided to create an actor's suitcase with real masks and then use those masks to act out a performance, which she videotaped and added to the suitcase on a flash drive (Figure 4.2).

Some students opted to research the medicinal herbs or cuisine of the time and bring in samples, others constructed models of war machinery, and a few even used Minecraft to design models of what historical venues looked like at that time.

So perhaps this type of freeform project is not your pace, but you are looking to diversify what students can do with the content and provide opportunities for

autonomy. Let's consider exploring different types of content formats through the
context of career readiness. What about
an infographic, a press release, an online
game, or a Q&A session with an author or
industry leader in the field? We only have
to look at sites like Hubspot, Buzzfeed,
and Mashable to get a feel for what types
of media and content formats companies
and businesses are generating.

The project ideas in Figure 4.3 are just
a few. If we look at project types in specific career fields, we will find even more
interesting and nontraditional formats like
advertorials, show bibles, beat sheets, and
decision trees. So here are a few ideas to
whet your appetite and expand your content realm:

**Figure 4.2 Actor's Suitcase and
Pantomine Performance (on flash drive)**

Source: http://www.edutopia.org/blog/students-need-pd-
too-lisa-johnson

- **Netflix Beat Sheets and Story Bibles:** How amazing would it be to create
  a pilot episode for a book or historical event? A beat sheet provides an easy
  framework to plan an episode. A story bible is the legend for the locations,
  character bios, and the theme and style that is used when the show gets picked
  up to ensure consistency across the episodes and series. Sample beat sheets
  can be found at jamigold.com, and SavetheCat.com offers 100+ screenwriting
  beat sheets from popular movies ranging from *Avatar* and *Aladdin* to *Pride
  and Prejudice* and *The Hunger Games*. These resources serve as great models to
  springboard a nontraditional project like this.

- **Freebies, Templates, and Guides:** Everyone loves free downloads and goodies,
  and more and more sites, companies, and blogs are offering free downloadable
  content. Students would have to research what the audience would be for their
  product as well as what type of content and templates consumers in that market
  would like to use and then develop a free deliverable that could be offered on a
  website. I have created free graphic organizer templates to be used in conjunction with the online sticky-note note tool Padlet, and Ryan Read cooks up app
  dice to support student-driven creation (Figure 4.4 on page 78). In fact, the app
  dice have become so popular that Seesaw, a digital portfolio tool, asked him to
  create a custom set for a conference and now offer it on their site. As part of
  an environmental project mentioned in Chapter 2, students were required to
  create a mini education lesson that could be delivered to elementary students.
  As a parent of two elementary boys, I suggested including some sort of handout or guide that would go home with students after the lesson. Something
  that included what they learned, what questions parents should ask, and how

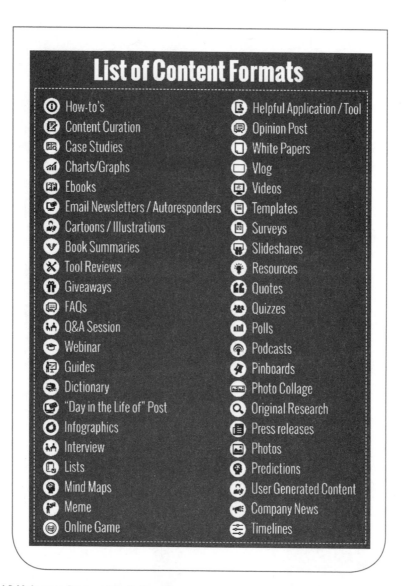

Figure 4.3 Hubspots Content Marketing Plan

Source: Justin McGill at LeadFuze, http://blog.hubspot.com/marketing/content-marketing-plan

we could extend the lessons at home, like finding places to recycle batteries or where to find drought-resistant plants for the backyard.

- **Advertorials:** Back in the olden days of 2011, this might have been considered native advertising or even sponsored content. The idea is fairly simple: content that is meant to look like an article or editorial and oftentimes reads like one, but is a paid advertisement. Lena Dunham's character in *Girls* actually gets hired in Season 3 to write this type of content. Adding a little flavor to your sales copy has now infiltrated sites like Woot and even Etsy. Figure 4.5 is an example of some advertorial style content I wrote for the home button stud earrings I sell on Etsy. I wouldn't so easily dismiss this idea, though, as the idea of buying an item with a story doesn't feel so far removed from reality. In fact, advertorials can

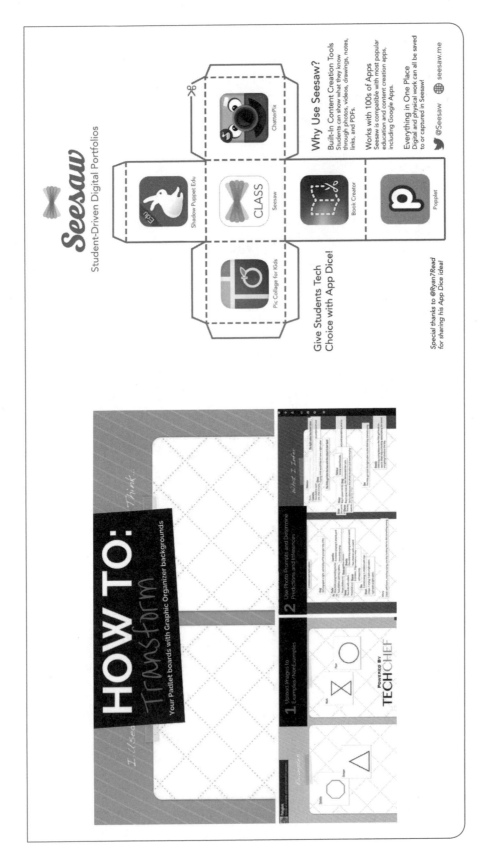

Figure 4.4 Freebies and Guides (Left are graphic organizer backgrounds to be used in conjunction with Padlet online sticky-note tool; right is a custom app dice to be used to drive digital portfolios.)

There's no place like home . . . and no fashion statement more quirky than wearing home button studs on your lobes.

DO wear these studs when you want to be reminded of your favorite iDevice and the power it has for transforming how you connect with the world.

DON'T wear these earrings in hope that they will be an instant command center for your life—sadly, they cannot reset your mood or your day.

TechChef hopes these Do's and Don'ts answer most of the questions regarding this chic-geek piece. Now you can fashionably wear these exclusive one-of-kind earrings well-informed.

Figure 4.5 Etsy Advertorial for Chic Geek Home Button Stud Earrings

be easily adapted to sales copy or information on a jar of sweet tea, cola-flavored kombucha, or even a restaurant's menu. This persuasive type of personal writing has even seeped into the real estate market. In fact, a colleague of mine recently sold her home and was asked to write a letter to entice prospective buyers (e.g., "I have enjoyed many an afternoon sipping sweet tea under the oak in the backyard . . . the nearby park was just a jaunt and my boys loved the tire swing and monkey bars . . ."). Oddly enough, this type of communication isn't just used to persuade people to buy things, but it is also used to persuade people to let you buy things. In fact, my husband and I were recently asked to write a personal letter detailing why we wanted to rent a VRBO (Vacation Rentals By Owner) facility.

- **Listicles:** "10 Things Every Teacher Should Know" or "12 Frightening Truths." The list–article mashup is interesting because it blends lists and explanations from a variety of sources in a clever way that approaches curation. More info on Listicles is provided in Chapter 7, "Curation."

- **Decision Trees:** These are flowcharts that are used in research and analysis to predict outcomes and make decisions. They can also be a process that students are familiar with (e.g., study tips, finding good books on Amazon). Figure 4.6 highlights an example of a table of information that I transformed for staff into a decision tree. Both formats are essentially the same bit of information, but the decision tree uses visuals and a flowchart to easily support the process. While decision trees essentially simplify a complex decision or process, I will tell you from firsthand experience that creating something to simplify a process or decision is actually very time-consuming and requires a fair amount of knowledge about the audience and all of the possible outcomes and entry points. One of the most popular pieces of media that thrives on decision trees is the "Choose Your Own Adventure" book. In fact, this idea is so sticky that even modern day authors play with it. Ryan North has adapted both *Romeo and Juliet* and *Hamlet* as choosable path adventures with *To Be or Not to Be* and *Romeo and/or Juliet: A Chooseable-Path Adventure*. The worldwide Minecraft sensation has even created Minecraft: Story Mode that employs the tools of

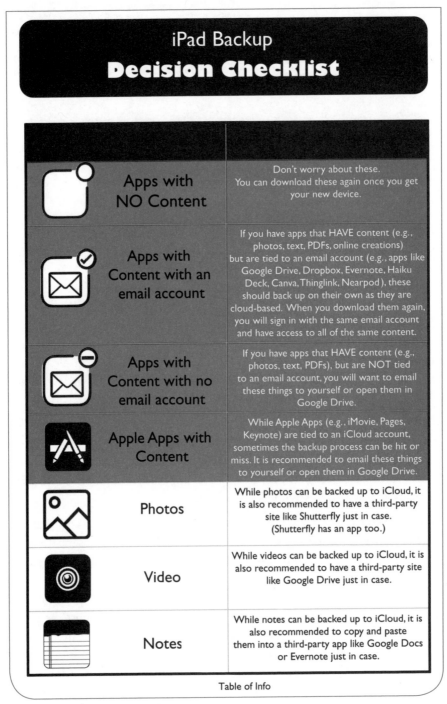

iPad Backup **Decision Checklist**	
Apps with NO Content	Don't worry about these. You can download these again once you get your new device.
Apps with Content with an email account	If you have apps that HAVE content (e.g., photos, text, PDFs, online creations) but are tied to an email account (e.g., apps like Google Drive, Dropbox, Evernote, Haiku Deck, Canva, Thinglink, Nearpod), these should back up on their own as they are cloud-based. When you download them again, you will sign in with the same email account and have access to all of the same content.
Apps with Content with no email account	If you have apps that HAVE content (e.g., photos, text, PDFs), but are NOT tied to an email account, you will want to email these things to yourself or open them in Google Drive.
Apple Apps with Content	While Apple Apps (e.g., iMovie, Pages, Keynote) are tied to an iCloud account, sometimes the backup process can be hit or miss. It is recommended to email these things to yourself or open them in Google Drive.
Photos	While photos can be backed up to iCloud, it is also recommended to have a third-party site like Shutterfly just in case. (Shutterfly has an app too.)
Video	While videos can be backed up to iCloud, it is also recommended to have a third-party site like Google Drive just in case.
Notes	While notes can be backed up to iCloud, it is also recommended to copy and paste them into a third-party app like Google Docs or Evernote just in case.
Table of Info	

Figure 4.6a Table for iPad Backups

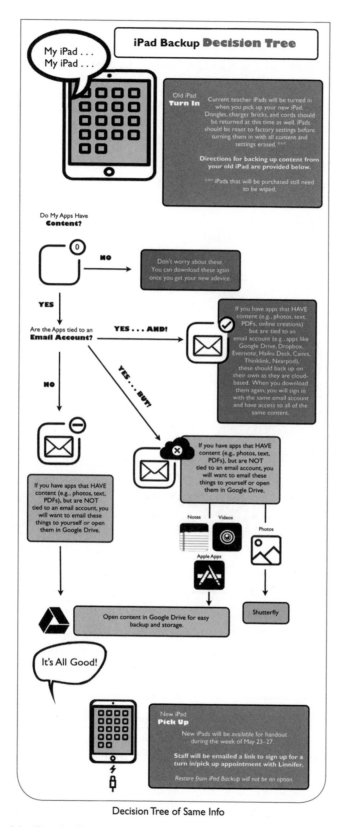

Decision Tree of Same Info

Figure 4.6b Decision Tree for iPad Backups

the choose-your-own-adventure platform. This idea could easily be adapted to plotting out possible or even improbable scenarios for a historical figure or event or mapping out the scientific method in a lab or even multiple ways to solve a complex math problem.

- **Custom and Original Visualizations:** While one may just discount these as infographics, I challenge you to think about visualizations as a way to facilitate and clarify the comprehension of content or ideas. An example of an updated visualization is shared at the beginning of Chapter 3. This idea doesn't have to be a full-blown infographic or handout though. Sometimes it can be as simple as a flowchart. In Figure 4.7, I took three written directions that have proven to be confusing for students and massaged them a bit with shapes, icons, and arrows. I wasn't sure how teachers and students would react, but I felt very validated to find out that this was one of the first years in over a decade that this process made sense to students.

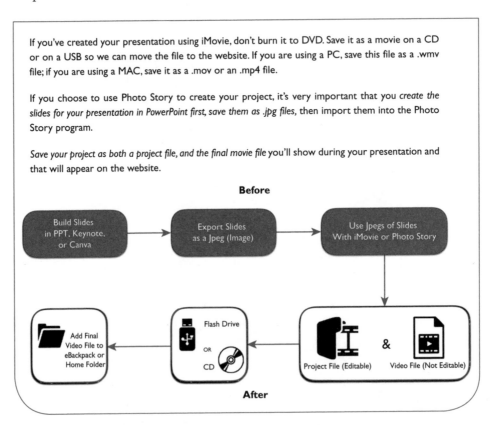

Figure 4.7 Revised Process for Vietnam Memorial Project Mentioned Later in This Chapter

Interestingly enough, what I have been doing for my own teachers is actually a paid profession, as seen in Figure 4.8. In this example, a bare bones flowchart of tips and steps for selling a home has been reimagined to create a clear and concise one-page visual summary. If you are interested in more of Todd's work, check out his site and his Pinterest boards. He also does one-page visual summaries of books.

CULTIVATING COMMUNICATION IN THE CLASSROOM

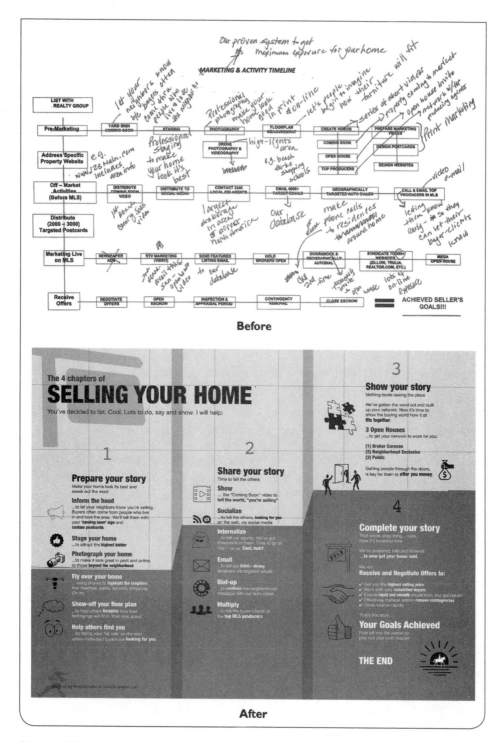

Figure 4.8 Visual-One-Pagers by Todd Clarke

Source: Todd Clarke, http://visualonepagers.com/process

The important thing to remember about autonomy, choice, and legitimacy of content formats is to provide clear rationale and context as to the why and allow students to discover the how and the what. In the bigger picture and context of "the real world," it is less about the types of projects that students choose to create and more about the ability to choose the right media to best suit their content ideas and how they want to clearly and effectively share that information with their classmates and the world.

How Can I Provide an Authentic Audience for Students' Projects and Publishing?

When we think of an authentic audience, many times we envision publishing work online. But that isn't necessarily an authentic audience. Just because something is published online doesn't mean anyone sees it or interacts with it. Yes, an authentic audience means more than just work that only the teacher sees, but I think we can expand the definition even further. In Chapter 2, we talked about working productively and collaborating effectively in teams, and in Chapter 5, we will talk about peer feedback. I can't think of a time in my professional career where I completed a task or a product so my employer could check off that I actually mastered a skill. In a career, an authentic audience is essentially a group of your peers that evaluates your work and/or the audience that the work is designed to support or benefit.

Over my years of observing student presentations and projects, I can tell you that the special magic of authentic audience cannot be defined in narrow terms. Yes, an authentic audience can mean a global audience, but it can also mean an audience of peers or the community, or it could be an audience with a purpose.

Let's first address the audience of community. Too often we assign projects and then don't build in time for students to share those projects with their class. And very rarely do we invite parents into those classrooms to participate in this process and add value to it. My youngest son is not much of a picture taker. In Figure 4.9, the photo on the left shows him posing for mom, and the picture on the right shows him sharing his work with another teacher who came to visit the classroom on publishing day. I realize these pictures are of an elementary-age student, but I

Figure 4.9 The Power of an Authentic Audience Within the Classroom

can tell you time and time again that I see the same thing at the secondary level. When parents and other teachers sit in on project showcases, it sends the message to students that their work matters in a way that is very different than what their peers can offer.

Peers, other campuses, and local and national entities can offer a tangible authenticity and purpose to our students' work that publishing online alone may not. Below are some examples:

- **International Entities:** The Memory Project is an example of a service project. High school students make portraits for kids in orphanages around the world. Students design a portrait based on a photo of the child. The portraits are then delivered to the orphanages, and then the children will have a memento created just for them. But the experience doesn't end there. The students that created the portraits receive a video of the art being delivered to all of the children in the orphanages. I am not ashamed to say that I have watched this video several times and each and every time have cried at how much these portraits matter to the children receiving them.

- **National Entities:** The high school Vietnam Memorial project is by far my favorite. I can't think of a more authentic audience for this project than our Vietnam veterans. Students do primary research and contact families and friends of these individuals and then create a memorial video for their selected soldier, which is added to the school's online wall and shared with the living family members and friends of that veteran. Memorial projects are such a great way to intertwine empathy and purpose with research and multiple literacies. This could be adapted to local police officers killed in the line of duty or even victims of terrorism or tragedy.

- **Local Entities:** Our community is an untapped but welcoming opportunity for authentic partnerships.

  ○ **Harry Ransom Student Blog:** One of our students mentored with the Harry Ransom Center and then was allowed to write a piece about her findings on the collection. As she was presenting her mentorship project, the thing that came up over and over was her pride to have her work actually published on the Harry Ransom site alongside other professionals. This project is discussed further in Chapter 7 on curation.

  ○ **American Sign Language (ASL):** A few years ago we partnered with the Texas School for the Deaf. High school ASL students created an original children's book using the Book Creator app, gathered original art illustrations from first graders at Texas School for the Deaf, and then compiled it all. Each page included the elementary students' original illustrations and a high school ASL student signing different portions of the text included in the book. The finished product was then shared with the TSD elementary students.

- **Other Campuses**:
  - ○ **MAPS:** The project involved students focusing on self-awareness of their own test-taking and time-management skills, interviewing upper elementary students about their own study and organization habits, and then creating a children's instructional book to foster these skills in upper elementary.

- **Cross-Design Within Our Own Campus:** There are so many opportunities to partner with another department or class on the campus.
  - ○ **Design Projects for Using Maker Parts:** Drama students can request particular set elements and the engineering and technology classes can build and 3D print them or wire them.
  - ○ **ASL and Computer Science:** One ASL student also enrolled in a computer science course had some freedom as to what his coding project would be. He saw a need for a finger-spelling app that was not juvenile or flash based and decided to code the tool within his computer science class. He used the current ASL class as his product testers and even had a fellow student serve as a hand model for the app. Three years later, all of our ASL students still use this app.

- **Intra-Campus Publications:** Many secondary campuses have literary magazines and newspapers. Don't assume that people already know about the good work your students are doing in the classroom. In the case of the ASL student, I actually submitted that as a lead to the school newspaper for another student reporter to cover as a story. Also keep in mind that just because your students aren't on the newspaper or literary magazine that they can't have their work included in those publications. I visited with two students writing expository pieces on sensitive topics that were phenomenal. I suggested that they be submitted to the newspaper. At the mere prospects of the publication, the students became visibly interested and excited. While students who are not enrolled in the journalism class don't typically write for the paper, it wasn't that they couldn't . . . just that no one had really asked to before.

These opportunities are not necessarily hard to find, but they do require a little work and planning. Know that the work and planning that goes into this is nothing compared to the meaningful experiences that students will have for the rest of their lives. All of these opportunities for an authentic audience can be shared online, but being shared online in of itself does not mean that students have an authentic audience or a strong purpose for their work.

How Can I Ensure Appropriate Use (of Incorporated Elements and Original Ones)?

Let's say that students now have the freedom of choice to delve into choosing the right tool for their project and have opportunities provided for an authentic audience. How do we ensure that we provide a framework for appropriate use, while not squelching autonomy and innovation?

If I had to shine a light on one dark corner of projects and publishing, it would be the blatant disregard for appropriate use of images. Very rarely do I see a student use the permissions section of Google images. We have tools like Turnitin to address plagiarism of written content, but we have nothing in place beyond a reverse image search to address multimedia theft. Is it easy to teach this topic and is there a clear-cut answer for these questions? No and no. In fact, when I was writing this book, I had several questions of my own like, "Do I need permissions for pictures that I take of places or products and apps or tools? Do I need permissions of pictures that I take of people if the subjects are not recognizable?" If people in the industry struggle with copyrights and acceptable use, then just imagine the murky copyright waters we wade in for the classroom.

So how do we teach students to locate appropriate images? The first piece of this is teaching students that just because something is on the Internet does not make it appropriate to use. I would venture to say that the majority of students use Google as their search engine. Teaching the ability to search by license and ability to reuse and reuse with modification is key. This is a feature of most of the G-Suite tools as well as the Google search engine. The sticky wicket of all of this is you are still using someone else's image property and at any point they may decide to change the copyright or usage guidelines and then you are out of compliance. And even if the work is copyright free, most times this still requires the user to properly cite the images. Fortunately, there are a few ways and tools to navigate these murky waters with your students:

- Teach students how to use and navigate the license portion of Google images.
- Use search tools and websites that provide copyright-free images.
- Use tools and apps with Creative Commons images or public domain clipart or icons embedded.
- Have students capture or draw their own images.
- Create an in-house school library of student art, photographs, and illustrations.

Suggested tools for each of these options are linked off of the companion site. So, let's say that students want to draw their own images or at the very least capture their own. And let's say that they also want to publish this work online. This is a realm we don't travel into often, but should.

Misattribution isn't a victimless crime, and in a world of crafting students' digital footprints, work that doesn't lead back to the originator is an issue. When I first started blogging, I posted a picture of my seventh-grade math classroom, where I taught, to illustrate the idea of the flipped classroom. I was proud and honored to find that very same image appeared on a popular educational technology blog until I realized that the image was attributed to someone else and didn't even link back to my site. I added a comment in the thread of the blog to request the image be reattributed, and a few years later it was. I could rest the whole blame on the blogger, but honestly, I didn't know any better at that point how to proactively protect my work either.

If our students are publishing work online, we as educators should be providing a structure to support the attribution and credit of this work. If the image gets pinned or borrowed, how does the originator get discovered and receive recognition? There are two solutions to this rising issue:

- **Clever Watermarks:** This is the easiest entry point for students. If they are publishing an image online that could easily be downloaded, screenshotted, or re-pinned, they should watermark it. This can be achieved in a few ways:

  - **School or Classroom Logo and #:** All schools have a logo of some sort. Consider providing that logo to students and having them add it to the top of their image with the URL of the school. This can be achieved using any slide or collage software. Crafting a specific classroom logo with a class URL is another option. Adding a school hashtag is also useful so when others discover the images and student work, they can follow the hashtag to see other amazing things the school is doing. This is a fantastic way to easily craft and curate a positive message for your school, your students, and the work that you do.

  - **Student Name:** As students enter high school, they may want to start attributing their work directly to themselves with a signature or logo. Refer to the iAm project in Chapter 5 if this is the route you would like to explore with your students.

  - **Quotes or Content:** This is an exceptionally clever way to advertise yourself. Picture your own images with your quotes or a famous quote (cited appropriately of course). This way the images aren't benign in nature—they actually have purposeful content attached to them. This could be a student solving a math problem with the process mapped out on top of the image, an original artwork or painting with a quote by an artist or author that inspired the work, or a science lab with a hypothesis layered over the image. This can be achieved by adding a textbox to an image in slide software and then exporting or saving that slide as an image. Some of my favorite educators and speakers do this (see Figure 4.10). Kevin Honeycutt uses his own images, his quotes, and even posts all of them to a gallery on his site titled "HoneyQuotes," so people can reuse them within their own content and presentations, thus building in a legitimate authentic audience for his images and ideas. I decided we could do the same thing with the Teacher Features in our school and started adding teacher quotes to the images that were used within each blog post.

- **Crafting a Visual Style:** Creating a visual style takes time and practice. If students are building a portfolio to share with colleges or a future career, crafting a visual style is helpful and will set them apart from the fold. In fact, each one of these individuals has such a distinct visual style that their work can be

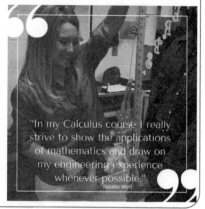

Kevin Honeycutt @kevinhoneycutt

Natalie Wyll (calculus teacher featured on high school principal blog)

Figure 4.10 Examples of Clever Watermarks

recognized and easily attributed back to them. Figure 4.11 shows seven examples of how this could be achieved:

- ○ **Amy Burvall:** Amy Burvall has a distinct color palette of black, pink, and white and uses the Paper by FiftyThree app to create her own slides and quotes.

- ○ **Lisa Johnson:** I use a mix of selfies using Photo Booth app and Keynote to add a personal touch.

- ○ **Kasey Bell:** Kasey Bell uses an avatar and a specific font and format from Canva to achieve her signature style.

- ○ **Jennifer Gonzalez:** Jennifer Gonzalez, better known as "Cult of Pedagogy," has an iconic style that blends the simplicity of grayscale drawings with a splash of color and topped with witty titles and a unique font, using MS Paint.

- ○ **Ross Cooper:** Ross Cooper is a prolific blogger. Each blog header graphic has an image or icon, a thought provoking question or title, and his Twitter handle and website URL.

- ○ **Sylvia Duckworth:** Sylvia Duckworth uses Paper by FiftyThree and oftentimes a yellow banner and listicle approach blended with a whimsical cartoon style. Her sketches have become so popular that she recently published 100 of them in a publication titled *Sketchnotes for Educators: 100 Inspiring Illustrations for Lifelong Learners*.

- ○ **Brad Ovenell-Carter:** Brad is also a wizard with Paper by FiftyThree and has a very distinct style and color palette that he uses with his sketch notes. So popular indeed that he was asked to be the sole illustrator for the book *Blended Leadership: Six Simple Beliefs for Leading Online and Off*.

Whether students are sharing their original artwork, drawings, or images, we want to protect them from misattribution and ensure that their work is credited to them. It may seem like there is a slanted focus on image protection over other types of media. It is simply due to the fact that images are one of the most prevalent types of content published beyond text and videos. There are multiple sites that check for text plagiarism, and video plagiarism is somewhat difficult as one would have to screen record over it or download it using a third-party site. While text and video plagiarism have checks and balances or at least a few road blocks in place, I don't want to leave them out of the discussion either. The best and easiest way to protect students' work of any kind or format is through Creative Commons. Students can easily access the site on any device and essentially type in fields to create a license for their own work and how it should and can be used and attributed. Once students type in their parameters, the site produces a text license

> *"Create your own visual style. Let it be unique for yourself . . . and yet identifiable for others."*
>
> **—Orson Welles**
> *(Actor, Director, Writer, and Producer)*

Amy Burvall @amyburvall

Lisa Johnson @TechChef4u

Kasey Bell @shakeuplearning

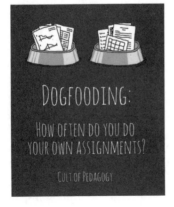

Jennifer Gonzalez @cultofpedagogy

Ross Cooper @rosscoops31

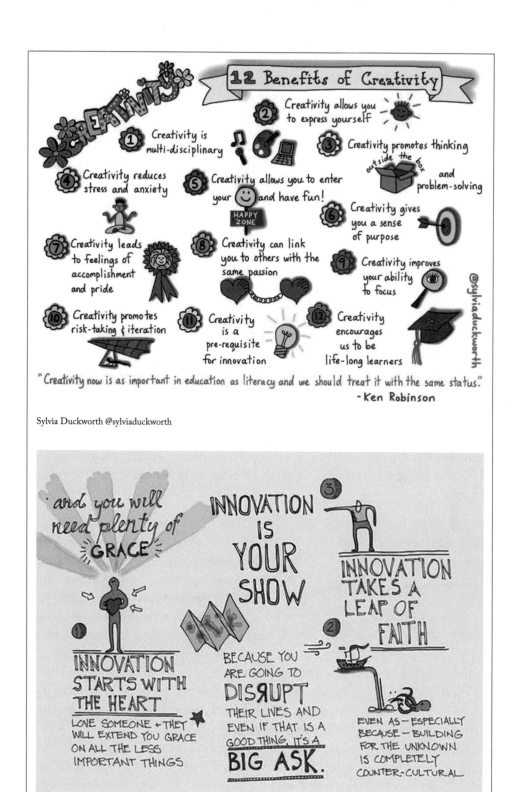

Sylvia Duckworth @sylviaduckworth

Brad Ovenell-Carter @braddo

Figure 4.11 Examples of Visual Style

that can be copied and pasted into any project or content format. If students are publishing blogs or PDFs, it is a good habit to use this citation at the bottom of their posts and creations. If students are publishing videos, adding an image at the end of the video that includes this information is encouraged.

Below is an example of a license for the Slide Design for Students handout I created for some student workshops. The handout is original, but it is also built from a compilation of research shared from a multitude of other sites that I have curated into one place. My intent for the work is that if it is shared, it is shared with the same license and that at no point people can gain commercially from something that I offer for free online and to students.

> *Slide Design for Students by Lisa Johnson is licensed under a Creative Commons Attribution-NonCommercial-ShareAlike 4.0 International License. Based on works at https://pinterest.com/techchef4u/snazzy-slides*

Practicing this skill with students not only protects their own work, but widens their understanding of others' work as well.

How Do I Revise an Existing Project?

You might live within that pocket of innovation in your school that consistently provides opportunities for autonomy, authentic audiences, and appropriate use. Yes, this future exists but is oftentimes not a reality for all of our students.

> *"The future is already here. It's just not very evenly distributed."*
>
> **—William Gibson**
> *(Fiction Novelist and Essayist)*

On the other hand, if you are feeling overwhelmed or need to entirely scrap every project you do with students, stop and breathe. Many of your current projects and perhaps even some that you experienced as a student most likely have elements in place to support these ideals. If I harness my inner student, I am instantly taken back to a time of diorama shoeboxes, coat-hanger mobiles, and sheet protectors. My favorite project was a research assignment where I was assigned a decade and had to design historical fiction journal entries and artifacts. Each entry required me to really delve into the political climate, geographical setting, dialogue, and vernacular of the time period, as well as diet, attire, and relationships of the character from the perspective of that character. At its core was a project that allowed me to research content and then apply that knowledge and understanding to create something that didn't exist before. What it lacked was an authentic and purposeful audience. At no point did I truly receive valuable feedback from my peers about the product. At no point was the product anything more than a grade in a grade book.

Flash forward almost two decades. This type of writing is considered historical fiction and championed by one of my favorite authors, Diana Gabaldon of the Outlander series. Today this assignment could be given an authentic audience by weaving it into a Netflix series pitch, publishing online using a blogging tool, or holding a campus contest for which the winning piece would be performed by the drama department. Yes, we could add some modern-day spins to the project by

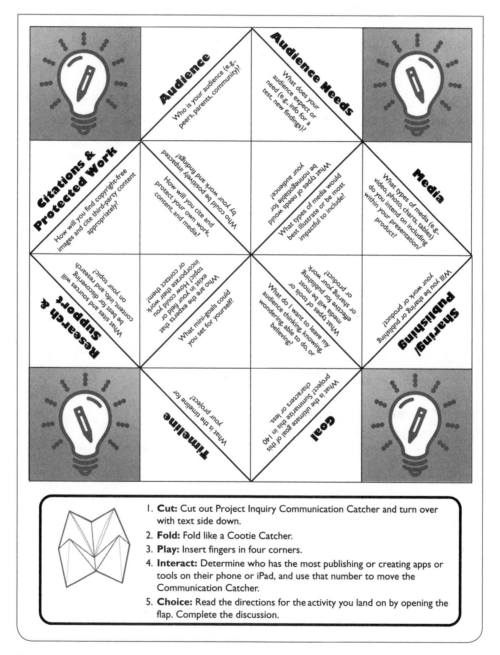

Figure 4.12 Project Inquiry Communication Catcher

Available for download at **https://resources.corwin.com/cultivatingcomm**

asking students to create an Instagram or Snapchat account for students to post their historical fiction snippets to or have them interview current historians for additional insight. But ultimately, this project at its core could still be a relevant task. So before you decide that every project you assign needs to incorporate augmented reality or be scrapped entirely, consider asking yourself four questions:

- Have I provided autonomy within the *why* and the *how* of the project?
- Are my students using content formats that add legitimacy to their work?
- Have I provided an authentic and purposeful audience for my students?
- Are my students able to use images appropriately and protect their own work?

In Chapter 2, we set the groundwork for collaboration that can facilitate both group projects and peer review of individual student assignments. Chapter 3 delved into visual literacy and oral delivery skills through the lens of presentations, which is the most common type of project students are assigned. Chapter 5 will take a hard look at portfolios and the importance of having an academic and professional online presence. The intent of this chapter is to weave creativity, innovation, and independent thinking into the art of communication, while still addressing college and career readiness. Rather than create a Communication Catcher with a variety of tools and projects, I created a Project Inquiry Communication Catcher (Figure 4.12), which ultimately supports students with scaffolded questions to lead them to the right type of audience, content format, and appropriate practices for citation to create an authentic work.

Chapter Resources

Projects and Publishing
Preparation Inventory Assessment

- ☐ What are the benefits of projects and publishing for my students?
- ☐ How will I provide autonomy within a project to allow for choice of how the project is accomplished and what tools are utilized to showcase the learning?
- ☐ What structures and processes will I have in place for idea assignments?
- ☐ What content formats will I suggest to students?
- ☐ What opportunities have I provided or can I utilize for authentic and purposeful publishing at the campus, district, national, and global level?
- ☐ What tools and strategies are in place to ensure students use images appropriately?
- ☐ What tools and strategies are in place to protect and credit students' original work?

☐ How can I revise or revamp existing projects to provide these opportunities for my students?

Share your answers using the hashtag #cultivatecomm.

My Students' Self-Assessment Checklist

☐ My students can determine an area of study that is of interest and can be easily researched.

☐ My students can select a tool and method of content delivery that is most appropriate for their area of study.

☐ My students can publish and provide purposeful content for a variety of authentic audiences.

☐ My students can navigate the process of selecting appropriately licensed images using a variety of tools.

☐ My students can protect their own work and images using a variety of methods and tools.

Additional Resources and Reading

- Project Inquiry Communication Catcher (found in Appendix B and on https://resources.corwin.com/cultivatingcomm)

- Suggested List of Project Tools (found on https://resources.corwin.com/cultivatingcomm)

- Suggested List of Copyright and Creative Commons Tools (found on https://resources.corwin.com/cultivatingcomm)

- Curated Boards of Sample Student Projects (found on https://resources.corwin.com/cultivatingcomm)

- Suggested Reading and Resources (found on www.pinterest.com/techchef4u/student-projects-publishing-and-copyrights)

References

Creativity and Education: Why It Matters. (2012). Retrieved July 13, 2016, from http://www.adobe.com/aboutadobe/pressroom/pdfs/Adobe_Creativity_and_Education_Why_It_Matters_study.pdf

Kaufman, S. (2016). Creativity is much more than 10,000 hours of deliberate practice. Scientific American Blog Network. Retrieved 16 October 2016, from https://blogs.scientificamerican.com/beautiful-minds/creativity-is-much-more-than-10-000-hours-of-deliberate-practice

Industry Insights

What are the most persuasive things you look for in a resume and interview to hire an applicant? Explain.

Experience: "Experience in this field of work is the most important—how many different clients has the person had the chance to work with."

—Judy Jacomino (Makeup and Hair Artist)

Passion: "People that show passion for software development by having side projects outside of work."

—Danny Johnson (Owner of Real Estate Software Development Company)

Cultural fit and interpersonal skills: "We can train someone [that has] basic skills to excel at the work we do; however, the ability to work with a team toward a common goal is something that often times takes too long to teach for our small business. Because we are a services-based firm, it is essential that we be able to communicate effectively, politely, and efficiently."

—Jacob Hanson (Managing Partner With PR With Panache)

Proactive about learning: "The resume must have relevant skills, but during the interview process the applicant must be able to show genuine capability of being proactive about learning and being wrong."

—Justin Hammond (Cloud Networks Engineer)

Clear communication: "From the resumes that I see come across my desk, I think resume writing and communicating more professionally could be improved upon. Especially those who are attending a trade school or those receiving a more nontraditional education."

—Melissa Johnson (VP/CFO in Real Estate)

Attention to detail: "In the job posting we are very specific about how to write the subject line of the email. If people don't follow that direction, I won't even look at their submission. This is like the brown M&M requirement hidden in entertainers' performance riders. If you can't follow that simple direction, how do I know you'll have the attention to detail necessary for this position?"

—Andrew Gardner (VP Professional Learning at BrainPOP)

Evidence of cohesive direction: "A persuasive cover letter that explains why they would be a good fit and how their experience dovetails even if it didn't jump out at me when I first looked at their resume."

—Kristy Peters (Principal at Litigation Finance Company)

Collaboration: "I look for candidates who have worked in unique, collaborative environments. It's a critical skill set in my work and not one that is often focused on for law students or entry level associates."

—James Peters (VP New Market Initiatives, Online Legal Services)

Empathy and a learner: "The resume simply gives elements about which to have conversations in an interview. It is the way the person talks about himself or herself as a learner and an empathetic individual that informs a hiring decision for us."

—Reshan Richards (Chief Learning Officer at Explain Everything)

CHAPTER 5

Portfolios and Resumes

Communicating with peers and professionals
to collect information and learning artifacts
to reflect on one's own learning to cultivate
self-knowledge and self-advocacy

*"It sounds a little extreme, but in this day and age, if your work isn't online,
it doesn't exist."*

—Austin Kleon (Writer and Artist)

R ecently, I dug through some of the work that my own parents had archived
for me—yellowed pages of short stories and crayon drawings. To be
honest, the stories I had written meant very little to me as I had no memory of them nor my rationale or inspiration behind writing them. I would assume
many of you reading this have similar artifacts and limited stories of your own
learning. Now imagine finding an old high school poem and being able to hear
yourself read the poem, noting the intonations and emotional pauses. Imagine an
image of a handmade Morse code telegraph that you made with your dad for a
third-grade science experiment and a video documentary of your learning process
along the way. At the time that many of us were in school, the technology to properly archive our learning artifacts, outcomes, and processes was either expensive or
not readily available. Sentimental value is not the only reason to archive a variety
of learning artifacts. Real learning happens when we create new neural pathways,
which is done not through telling or doing, but recalling and reflecting (Bungay
Stanier, 2016).

Figure 5.1 Archiving Paper and Pencil Tasks With Digital Tools

"What artifacts do your kids have to prove they attended school and learned? If everything your kids have in their learning and creating resume could be lost in one house fire, maybe they should be encouraged to diversify in their means of sharing."

—Kevin Honeycutt
(Speaker and Author)

Flash forward three decades or so, my kindergarten son brought home his very first "About Me" book with hand-drawn images and text. He sat on my lap and proudly flipped through each page. I noted that how he described the pages and elaborated upon the images was far more than what I could capture with an image alone. Having access to an iPad, I quickly snapshotted the pages and had him narrate over each one to create a video (Figure 5.1). Not only have I captured the essence and nuances of his writing and thought process in a way I couldn't have done with the mere image alone, but I found that including the audio narration was truly beneficial to seeing his articulation evolve over time. It isn't just the enhanced technologies associated with the archival process, but the ease of access and transferability.

What Is a Digital Portfolio?

If learning were just about collecting work or a series of isolated events, then a whole chapter on digital portfolios would hardly be necessary. While digital portfolios are a collection of student work and media (e.g., documents, videos, links, images) that can be viewed electronically, it is more about facilitating the habit of reflection, providing opportunities for iteration, and crafting introspection through purposeful interactions with the products and process of our learning over time.

> *"The ePortfolio is the central and common point for the student experience. It is a reflection of the student as a person undergoing continuous personal development, not just a store of evidence."*
>
> **—Geoff Rebbeck** *(e-Learning Coordinator, Thanet College, quoted in Devlin, 2016)*

Sylvia Rosenthal Tolisano (@langwitches on Twitter) has created a fantastic metaphorical graphic to inform and empower others to embrace the idea of digital portfolios, shown in Figure 5.2. When we view portfolios as a living and ongoing process that serves to synthesize student learning, it is easier to move forward and to consider our classrooms as learning studios where students can flourish through a collection of instructional best practices, including but not limited to the art of reflection.

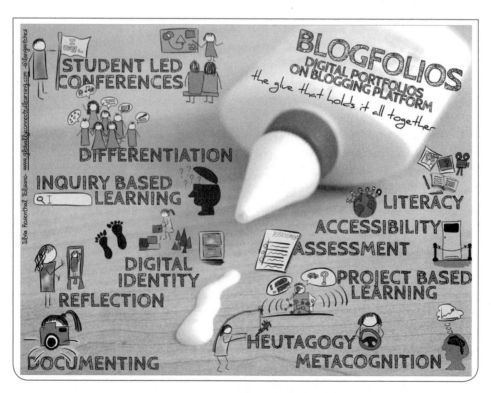

Figure 5.2 "Digital Portfolios: The Glue That Holds It All Together"
Graphic by Silvia Rosenthal Tolisano (@langwitches)

Source: Silvia Rosenthal Tolisano, http://langwitches.org/blog/2015/12/30/top-10-visuals-infographics-on-langwitches

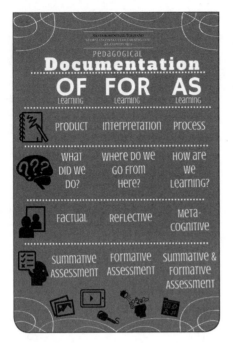

Figure 5.3 "Pedagogical Documentation: OF Learning, FOR Learning, AS Learning" Graphic by Silvia Rosenthal Tolisano (@langwitches)

Source: Silvia Rosenthal Tolisano, http://langwitches.org/blog/2015/12/19/documentation-offoras-learning

Digital portfolios are less about being the glorified equivalent of a digital manila envelope or flash drive and much more about documenting the learning process. Whether we call them ePortfolios, digital portfolios, learning portfolios, scholastic scrapbooks, or even life portfolios, our pedagogy compass must be in tact or we will find ourselves losing sight of our best practices and charting a course to the Castle in the Air where purpose and pedagogy don't always see eye to eye. Once again, Sylvia Tolisano provides a fantastic graphic to help you grapple with the idea of documentation OF, FOR, and AS Learning (Figure 5.3).

Unlike some of the previous chapters, initiating a digital portfolio process with your students can take more time than simply addressing best practices for visual literacy or image copyrights. It is not to say that the elements of the previous chapters won't be interwoven into the fabric of a good portfolio; it is simply that laying the framework for this process can take longer and may require more of a time commitment and perhaps even a pilot or district adoption.

In Chapter 4, we introduced Simon Sinek's (2016) Golden Circle through the lens of letting students choose the how and what of their project (Figure 5.4). If this piqued your interest and you have not heard Simon Sinek's talk about the Golden Circle and starting with *why,* I give you permission to bookmark this page, go watch the 18-minute TEDTalk, and then return to this chapter. Go ahead . . . I promise I won't be offended.

Now that you have a firm understanding of the power of *why* and *how* every new initiative should focus on purpose and vision, rather than simply the *what* (the tools and procedures to complete it), I encourage you to consider your motivations for embarking down the path of digital portfolios rather than jumping on the digital portfolio party boat simply because you hear it is all the rage. You may have had your interests piqued by the idea and are still mulling around the possibilities. If this is you, then you may require some additional insight as to why digital portfolios are a must for your students and their individual needs.

This chapter will not only dive into the rationale for scholastic scrapbooks and portfolios but will support you with the how and the what, as delineated in Figure 5.4, and empart ways that portfolios can be used outside of and beyond the K–12 sector.

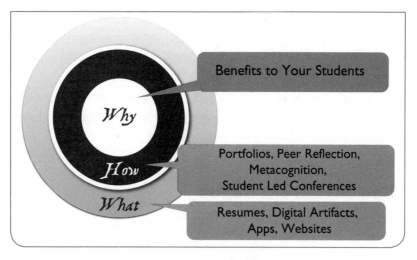

Figure 5.4 Simon Sinek's Golden Circle Adapted for Portfolios

What Challenges Can Digital Portfolios Solve for Me and My Students?

Many times the best tools and initiatives are those that are born from need or that present a solution to a challenge. At one point in time digital portfolios (or electronic portfolios) were a novelty or a nice to have. Through the influx of mobile devices, technology in school, and the transition of paper and pencil tasks to digital assignments and products, it is no surprise that digital portfolios will eventually just be a standard in schools no different than requiring a binder or pencil.

A fair number of elementary schools still send home a folder with student work at the end of the week. In secondary, students may periodically return home with their trifold poster board and working wooden model of a catapult once the project was graded. But this model is quickly fading out of favor. How many job interviews or business meetings start with a professional, a trifold poster board, and puff paint? As more and more schools have adopted technology and tools that allow for student creation, two challenges emerge that have shed light on why this model may be broken:

> *"The reason we've stopped seeing as many articles about ePortfolios is because they've approached standard practice in the education and employment fields."*
>
> —**Elyse Hartman** *(Specializes in Medical Coding Training and Certification)*

- **Challenge 1—Digital Student Projects:** More and more, student products are becoming digital in nature and if not collected or transferred to a tool that students have access to, they will simply be lost, wiped at the end of the year, or dusted off for show in an exclusive teacher folder.

- **Challenge 2—Device Neutrality:** Students now have access to a variety of mobile devices and platforms. It is no longer realistic to expect that they can return home with a CD or flash drive of their work when many families don't even have devices that will provide access to these tools.

The answer to these challenges can be as easy as selecting a web tool that both teachers, students, and parents have access to no matter what device they own at home or use at school.

How Can Digital Portfolios Directly Benefit My Students?

Beyond the basic need of storage and lifelong access to student work, students receive valuable benefits from developing and maintaining a portfolio composed of authentic work. The benefits range from metacognition and digital literacy skills to critical thinking and self-directed learning. Students benefit not only from the product, but from the process too.

Additionally, digital portfolios can be used to address content standards by keeping student work organized by standard or lesson outcome. Including this process within a portfolio allows students to drive and assess their learning, and provides a well-rounded view of student effort and what our students know and can do with evidence-based learning artifacts.

"ePortfolios possess the potential to bridge the conflicting goals (e.g., portfolio-based assessment and standardized assessment) as they combine individual student work with standards–based assessment, while also organizing and indexing student data."

*—***June Ahn** *(Associate Professor at NYU Steinhardt)*

It is important to note that not all digital portfolios are created equal. Once you decide the purpose of digital portfolios for your students, it will be easier to navigate the myriad of platforms available.

What Is the Main Goal of a Digital Portfolio?

Digital portfolios can be beneficial for our students and may even be solid solutions to some of the digital workflow challenges we face in this mobile world. Before you dive deep into the depths of digital portfolio platforms, it is important to discuss how the goals you have for your students correlate with the types of platforms available. We are way past the time when a CD or a flash drive would suffice, so for the purpose of this chapter, we will assume the platforms and tools we are using are accessible via the web.

With that being said, there are really two types of digital portfolios to focus on—(1) *developmental* (sometimes referred to as learning or workspace portfolios), which is used to demonstrate how learners advance and develop over time, or (2) *showcase*, which is a collection of exemplary work. If you are unsure which one of these is the best one to meet your students' needs, consider using a blend of both.

If students are growing with their portfolio year after year then most likely, the resource will include both advancements over time, highlights of quality work, and assessments and reflections along the way. If portfolios are meant to travel with a student from year to year, then coordinating decisions about vertical alignment and consistency of expectations will help make these repositories of learning effectual in the long run for both students and teachers. For example, our English Department chooses to have students archive at least three writing samples digitally each year using the same platform so students have access to them each year and future teachers do as well.

There is not really a one-size-fits-all option for a portfolio platform and there are a variety of facets to take into consideration. Too many, in fact, to include in this chapter. A complete guide to reviewing portfolio platforms and processes is included on the companion site. Ultimately, the foremost advice is to choose the best tool that meets your instructional goals and your students' creation and sharing needs. The worst thing you can do is adopt a tool without considering your vision and campus goals and then try to retrofit the tool to meet those needs.

What Will Be Included in a Digital Portfolio?

So let's assume now you have reviewed the portfolio platform consideration guide and/or have a platform or tool in mind. Work samples can now be collected and reflected upon. Beyond having students share final products and their reflections, make it a practice to have them add the learning objective for the piece, a brief summary of the task or project, and a summary of the process. Here is a list of what could be included in a digital portfolio:

- Learning objectives/goals/targets
- Task explanations
- Products
- Process
- Student reflections
- Self-assessments
- Peer-assessments
- Achievements

This is really where documentation OF, FOR, and AS Learning (Figure 5.3) are blended into one. Students provide products and work samples OF their learning, formatively interpret those pieces FOR learning, and ultimately reflect on their own process AS learning.

What Is an Easy Entry Point Into Portfolios?

Of all the communication formats delineated within this book, initiating portfolios is by far the most daunting, even with the myriad of support resources online and within this chapter. If you are looking for a way to dip your toe into storing and showcasing student work, here is a simple "start small" plan. I have created a Google Doc Portfolio Index template (Figure 5.5) that combines many of the strategies delineated in this chapter. With this index, students have a standardized yet flexible roadmap to begin collecting all of their digital and learning artifacts in Google Drive. The index also includes learning goals, exemplars, and a space for additional artifacts (which will be helpful when writing resumes their junior and senior year).

To minimize student error and to maximize effectiveness of how the portfolios and the portfolio index would be shared, accessed, and organized, we used a Google Sheets add-on called Doctopus to push out and share a set of folders and a portfolio template to every student. Once these were shared with the student body during our annual iPad Base Camp, the process was seamless to have them add the folders to their Drive, color-code them, and begin completing the reflection portion of their portfolio index.

Any content area Grades K–20 can use a portfolio or a simple index like this one. While the type of content being added and the types of prompts and tasks being

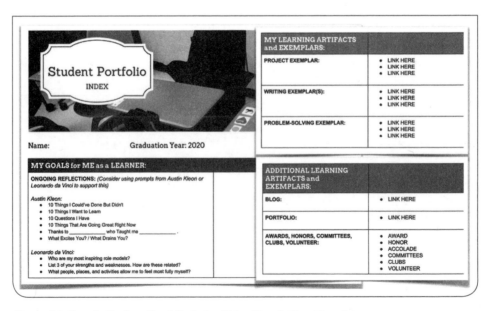

Figure 5.5 Sample Student Portfolio Index Using Google Docs Template

Figure 5.6 Portfolio Station at Freshman iPad Base Camp

utilized may differ, the purpose and process differs very little. Here are some ideas for what digital portfolios might look like in each content area:

- **Language Arts:** Students can include essays, reflections on a novel, or even audio recordings of them reciting an original poem.

- **Social Studies:** Students can include links to a slide deck book on the Revolutionary war, a timeline, current events, or even an infographic of research they did on a region of Europe.

- **Math:** Students can include screenshots of handwritten problems, videos of student explanations using tools like Explain Everything or Screencastify, and even a link or screenshot of a Desmos graph they created.

- **Science:** Students can include lab reports, hypothesis, a Kahoot or Quizlet they built to study for an upcoming chapter, or even ongoing personal health data.

- **Career and Tech Education:** Students could include the file they designed to 3D print their first creation or include screenshots of the program they coded.

- **Fine Arts:** Students can include links to how-to guides they created using Snapguides that narrate their process from materials and an idea to a complete ceramic piece. Students could capture a video of their recital or include images of the sets they built or costumes they designed.

Eventually through the process of cataloging success and learning, students are able to unlock their potential as a lifelong learner, not by amassing content, but by curating their skills and abilities. One thing to keep in mind with any type of curated portfolio is the need for them to remain formative and not summative and to include all of the elements mentioned in the previous chapter (e.g., authentic audience, choice, purpose). Denise Pope, coauthor of *Overloaded and Underprepared: Strategies for Stronger Schools and Healthy Successful Kids,* strongly advocates for the mantra of "voice, choice, revision, and redemption" (Pope, Brown, & Miles, 2015). Keep this in mind when allowing students to choose what work they would like to have included in their portfolio and providing them the opportunity to revise and iterate their work. This idea of continuous improvement also prepares our students to be resilient as they start to view intelligence as a commodity that can be developed and increased rather than a reserve that is static or could be depleted over time. Conversations before Content is needed here as well. If students and teachers see a portfolio as "one more thing," the work and thought processes will be cursory at best. With one-third of college institutions actually requiring one (Hiles, 2016), there is no time like the present to explain how powerful this tool will be in identifying and parlaying their skills to pave future pathways. More fascinating is the research from the National Survey of Student Engagement that found reflective and integrative learning was one of the top six engagement indicators (*Engagement Insights,* 2015).

How Can Students Reflect on Their Learning Journey?

Too often we see portfolios as a reflection on one product or idea rather than a reflection on learning in and of itself. An easy entry point into digital portfolios even before the inception of projects and assignments is open-ended prompts (see Ongoing Reflections section in Figure 5.5), which lead students to really delve into how they think, learn, and process information. Adding these types of questions and prompts not only expands the portfolio beyond the body of curricular work but allows students to truly develop metacognition as they reveal how we learn and think best. Both Austin's and Gelb's reflective prompts are included in the portfolio index and in Figures 5.7 and 5.8.

These types of lists and questions facilitate students with the process of cultivating the habit of extrapolating intrapersonal insight, which will further inform and impact their mindful awareness for directing and driving their own learning.

I have tried several of these myself and have become far more effective and efficient at knowing what works best for me when it comes to structuring daily tasks, tracking a project, or even communicating effectively with others. Leonardo Da Vinci was also an expert at this type of thinking. Michael J. Gelb provides some fantastic self-assessment strategies in his book, *How to Think Like Leonardo da Vinci* (1998). Figure 5.8 shows a few of my favorites.

Oftentimes, we think about self-knowledge in narrow scholastic terms and forget that it encompasses person, task, and strategy variables (TEAL, 2016). Metacognition

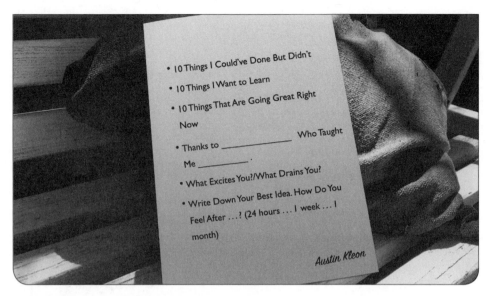

Figure 5.7 Reflective Prompts Gleaned From Austin Kleon's *Steal Like an Artist Journal:*
A Notebook for Creative Kleptomaniacs

Source: Adapted from Kleon (2015)

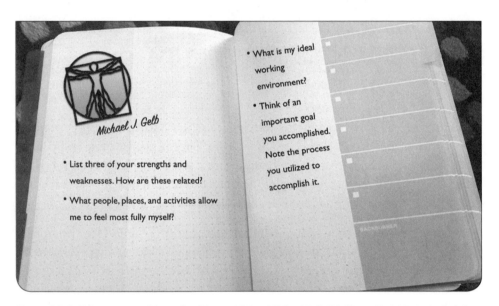

Figure 5.8 Self-Assessment Strategies Gleaned From Michael J. Gelb's *How to Think Like Leonardo da Vinci*

Source: Adapted from Gelb (1998)

is really about leveraging what we know about our *person* and our strengths and weaknesses, understanding the *task* and how it relates to our person (how long it will take us to read or comprehend), and the *strategies* we have to process and make sense of information, tasks, and experiences to be successful in school and beyond. The University of Wisconsin cleverly developed a five-part cycle of self-reflection that revolves around the well-known learning domain classification tool, Bloom's Taxonomy ("Reflection Resources," 2016). The cycle is shown in Figure 5.9.

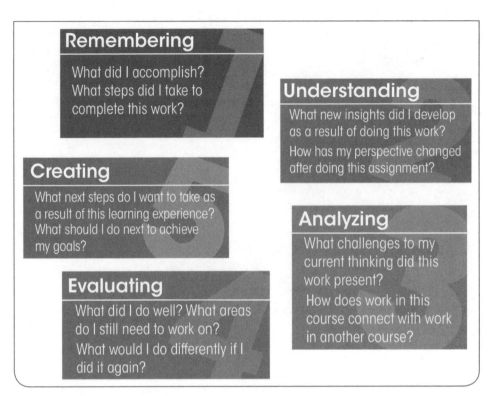

Figure 5.9 "Developmental Reflection Based on a Learning Taxonomy"
Developed by Dr. Carleen Vande Zande

Source: Dr. Carleen Vande Zande, https://www.uwosh.edu/usp/for-faculty-and-staff/resources-for-your-students/eportfolio/reflection-resources

Ultimately, reflection is about asking the right questions rather than proposing the correct answer. Reflection also helps us see a student's first effort not as a failure, but as a first attempt at learning. Oftentimes we complete a project and forget to honor all of the iterations and learning that happened along the way to reach the final piece.

A fantastic example of showcasing iterations is Yasmeen Tizani's HS mentorship portfolio, shown in Figure 5.10. Her Bulb portfolio showcases all three versions of her senior project, which was to create an original learning artifact as a companion to her mentorship experiences. As she mentored with an architect, it seemed natural to create a model. To show the evolution of her process and learning, she included sketches and preliminary models as well.

Learning should be a fluid and living process and reflection is simply, or not so simply, the life blood that informs and drives that process further. Digital portfolios should be a learning outcome that ultimately positively impacts student learning. If done well, the magic sauce of reflection threaded through portfolios cannot only produce happy and healthy students but ones that perform at a high standard. In fact, I revisited Yasmeen's portfolio site a year or so later to use as a model with some of our current students and noticed that not only has she maintained the site, but she started using it in college, too (Figure 5.11)!

Figure 5.10 Yasmeen Tizani's High School Portfolio Using Bulb

Source: Yasmeen Tizani, https://www.bulbapp.com/yasmeen

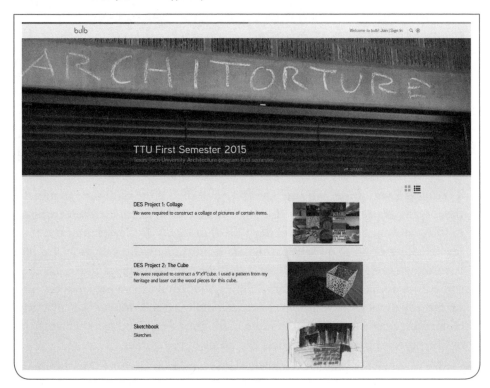

Figure 5.11 Yasmeen Tizani's College Portfolio Using Bulb

Source: Yasmeen Tizani, https://www.bulbapp.com/yasmeen

How Can I Involve Peers in the Iterative Process of Learning?

Chapter 2 focuses on collaboration and positive group interdependence. While students' own reflections on their learning artifacts and processes are valuable, we would miss the mark as educators if we did not provide constructs for students to be able to provide effective feedback to others as well. According to a study on visible learning conducted by John Hattie, student involvement, formative assessment, and effective feedback have a sizable positive impact on student learning (Waack, 2014). Student-led peer conferences are one way to provide students with feedback on their work and ideas.

- **Self-Selected Evaluations:** Students could select one project or piece of work that they choose to have evaluated.

- **Focus on Feedback:** These peer conferences are less about rubrics and checkboxes and more about thoughtful conversations with peers that provide "helpful feedback (that) is goal-referenced; tangible and transparent, actionable; user friendly (specific and personalized); timely; ongoing; and consistent" (Wiggins, 2012). With this in mind, peer conferences should be about conversations, disconfirmation, and error analysis. Imagine a band playing for a producer. Would the band get any better if they were just met with constant praise and empty affirmations? Conversely, imagine showing someone how you solved a complex math problem, and then having them solve the problem correctly without discussing or explaining your own error.

- **Queries That Spark Clarity:** While our brains are wired for desiring clarity and certainty and we live in a culture of instant gratification, we have to support students with the ability to ask questions of their peers that help them develop rather than perform (Bungay Stanier, 2016). One of the most eye-opening quotes I found from *The Coaching Habit* was that when you offer insight, you actually one up yourself, essentially raising your status and lowering theirs.

- **Timing Is Everything:** We also have to know when is the right time to initiate these types of peer discussions. Talking can actually deplete us when engaged in the creative process. Ryan Holiday (2016) in *Ego Is the Enemy* indicates that "even talking aloud to ourselves while we work through difficult problems has been shown to significantly decrease insight and breakthroughs." He notes that sometimes we spend too much time talking about and explaining a project that we actually think we have gotten closer to completing it. I would never advocate eliminating peer conferences, but more highlighting the need to structure them in function and timing to best meet the needs of the learner.

The work in achieving productive collaborative groups in Chapter 2 will support these efforts and will lead to Austin Kleon's adage, "Good work isn't created in a vacuum; (it is) a two-way street, incomplete without feedback."

I think it is important to note the potential of appropriate peer feedback to spark learning and individual progress. By using specific and kind peer feedback at the right time, students can create something that was not just good enough but better than they thought they could possibly do.

> *"Good work isn't created in a vacuum; (it is) a two-way street, incomplete without feedback."*
>
> —**Austin Kleon** *(Artist and Author)*

The Center for High-Quality Student Work is a superb site that delineates specific processes and provides exemplars. If you are looking for a concrete framework for peer formative feedback, I suggest checking out *Harvard Business Review*'s STOP/KEEP/START, Cult of Pedagogy's Single Point Rubric, or Emily Wray's Feedback Model aligned to Bloom's Taxonomy (Figure 5.12). These models are fantastic for looking at a piece of student work.

In Figure 5.13, you will see a Peer Portfolio Communication Catcher that can be used in a variety of fashions to support the body of student work collected. It can serve as a tool to springboard peer reflective conversations of their portfolios and artifacts. One possible pathway would be to have a student share their portfolio and have a group of students ask him or her these questions. Another option would be to have a group of students rotate answering perhaps the same questions about their own portfolios.

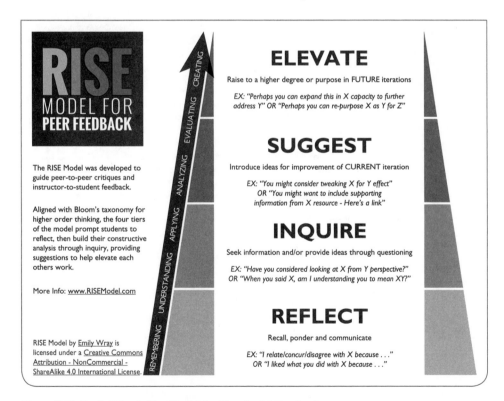

Figure 5.12 Emily Wray's Rise Model for Meaningful Feedback

Source: Emily Wray, http://elwray.squarespace.com/feedback

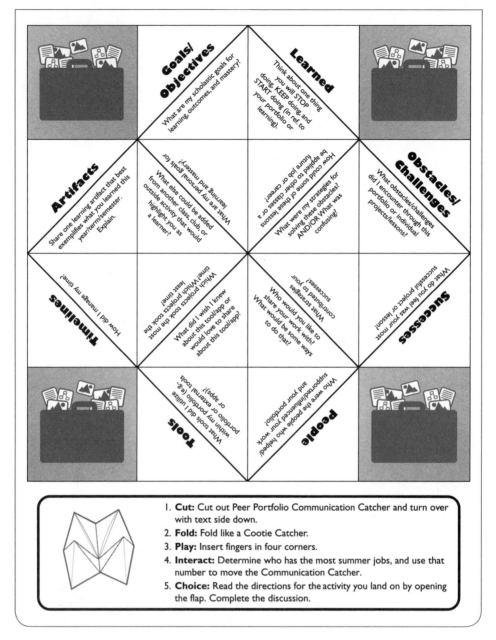

Figure 5.13 Peer Portfolio Communication Catcher

Available for download at https://resources.corwin.com/cultivatingcomm

Whichever option you choose should be a beneficial conversation or learning walk through a student's scholastic scrapbook and allow students to ascertain the skills they need and the direction they need to move forward. These portfolios can also be reviewed by parents or used as a tool to guide student conferences and create pathways for meaningful discourse, work, and progress. The Wildwood World Magnet School (2015) piloted this process and found not only increased levels of engagement with students and parents, but also that teachers didn't feel the need to defend student grades. Wildwood's pilot soon spread to a schoolwide practice that occurred twice a year. While the conferences are typically 10–15 minutes in nature, parents can continue to review and discuss the work beyond the confines of that time slot. If you are considering this approach, the Wildwood World Magnet also has a sample questions document available to support these discussions, and it is also linked off of the companion site.

I think Tim Elmore's quote is fitting as portfolios can be a tool to impact our students for years to come, but they can also be more than that. If we see portfolios for students as escalators to self-awareness and personal growth, and if we see students as our future, then this process is truly beneficial to transform their world and ours.

> *"If we can help this generation move from backpack to briefcase really well, we may transform their world."*
>
> **—Tim Elmore** *(Founder and President of Growing Leaders, via Catalyst Podcast)*

How Can a Portfolio Impact Future Career and College Readiness?

This chapter would not be complete if I didn't touch on the topic of showcase portfolios and resumes. My mother has been in the same job for over 20 years. With the rapid pace of new careers being created and the flux of entrepreneurial and start-up opportunities, the type of career stability that my mom experienced may not be a reality for our students.

We now assign trust and legitimacy to those that have some sort of website or online presence. Think about the last time that you shopped for a photographer, a handy man, or even a doctor. Many of us wouldn't even consider hiring a photographer without seeing their photos and website. I have even selected dentists and doctors based on customer reviews and the images of the facility online.

> *"Students need to know that an employer doesn't always care about the name of the college or high school on their résumé. Employers would rather see the quality and professionalism of the work in their portfolio."*
>
> **—Doug Martin** *(High School Graphic Design Teacher)*

While most middle school students are probably not considering composing a cover letter or resume any time soon, many of our high school students are. Though most large colleges rely on other qualifiers like college admission essays, test scores, class standing, etc., some smaller colleges may request a resume. In addition, many companies have shifted their requirements for employment from traditional qualifiers to soft skills like self-regulation, problem-solving (and problem-finding), and good communication skills. For example, Google has stated that "G.P.A.'s are worthless as a criteria for hiring . . . we found that they don't predict anything" (Friedman, 2014). They rely more on five attributes: general cognitive ability, emergent leadership, intellectual humility, ownership, and expertise.

While not all of these soft skills can be easily documented exclusively through a resume or online portfolio, students can share strong examples of each by curating and crafting their own exemplars.

A few years ago, I had a high school student ask me if there were any good resume templates available. With that one request, I fell deep down the rabbit hole of resumes and online portfolios. All of the information I discovered on that journey has been organized in to one website (www.smore.com/nyex-blended-resumes).

Gone are the days of the one-size-fits-all resume. Resumes and online portfolios are now very individualized and may even allow for some latitude with creativity and format depending on the position. So what does all of this mean for our students? How can we support them with successful college and career-ready strategies? Here is a quick formula:

- **Start Collecting Professional Praise:** I do realize that this may come off a bit strange. Typically, students only collect recommendations when they need them for jobs or colleges rec letters, but it is a good practice to keep positive emails and ask teachers that worked closely with them to offer quotes from time to time. These can also be collected from comments in a portfolio platform as well or gleaned from recommendations and endorsements within tools like LinkedIn. I have kept these and began adding them within my own resume to break up text and to humanly illuminate the skills I am referring to. I have provided an example of this on the companion site.

- **Write a Bio:** Michael Margolis wrote an article for 99 U "The Resume Is Dead, the Bio Is King" and likens a bio to an origin story or superhero back story . . . essentially who you are, how you got to be who you are, your vision for solving a problem, etc. (Margolis, 2011). Using the writing prompts and questions within the chapter can support your students with easily crafting this message. The chapter on social media also serves up a veritable cornucopia of support for this idea of crafting your message, understanding how people perceive you online, and being intentional with the content you share. Being reflective during this process also supports students with writing well-crafted and insightful college admission essays.

- **Build a Basic Resume for the Job You Want:** The resume is not in fact dead; it just doesn't hold the all impactful weight that it once did. Employers will still Google you and make conjectures and judgments about the information they find. However, providing a quick experience summary in a tangible format is still a must have ... at least for now.

- **Build a Showcase Portfolio or Online Profile:** As I mentioned, the student developmental portfolio that you use with your students can be eventually transitioned or transformed into an online showcase portfolio or at the very least provide helpful in creating an online career portfolio. These portfolios can easily be linked to the basic resume.

Communication isn't just building and showcasing your skills on paper, and even online. It is understanding who you are, how you came to be that person, what you want, how you tackle challenges, iterate past failures, and interact with others. It is also leveraging what you know about visual communication to highlight your skills in the best light. We are constantly judged by the format of our communications. Note the before and after of my fellow colleague's resume in Figure 5.14 on the next page. What can and might be assumed about the applicant on the right versus the left? Both highlight the same skills and credentials, but the one on the right says that she is also organized, understands structure, and can be clear and concise.

While I don't want to dive too deep down the well of personal branding, I also don't want to leave you unprepared for moving in any direction you see fit and/or necessary with your students. We talk about branding student images in Chapter 4. While helping students understand their why and their personal flavor may seem trivial, for me as an educator, it was the one thing that helped me understand my voice and how I wanted to share it with others. TechChef4u.com was born because I loved cooking up and creating technology-infused lessons for others that had flavor and an element of whimsy.

I realize that not everyone wants to create a brand, *but* everyone needs to be able to articulate their core competencies, signature strengths, and personality effectively. In this very competitive job market, we have a multitude of highly qualified applicants on paper and sometimes whether it seems fair or not, one person might be chosen over another in an interview simply because you think you might enjoy spending 8 hours a day with them over another. No doubt being able to artfully craft a biography and articulate your brand of you is an effective skill to have in your back pocket. One of my favorite resources for developing student's personal brands within the classroom is "iAm A Brand Called Me" (Figure 5.15). It is developed by fellow Apple Distinguished Educators and is available as both a Google Sites and an iTunes U Course. This incredibly thorough and thought-provoking course is intended for Grades 9–12, but could easily be adapted for a middle school classroom. The iAm resource also includes an "iAm in the classroom" section that illustrates ways students can transfer the skills of life tracks, logos, personal statements, and professional timelines to curricular content in all four core areas while still flexing these core competencies of communication and college and career readiness.

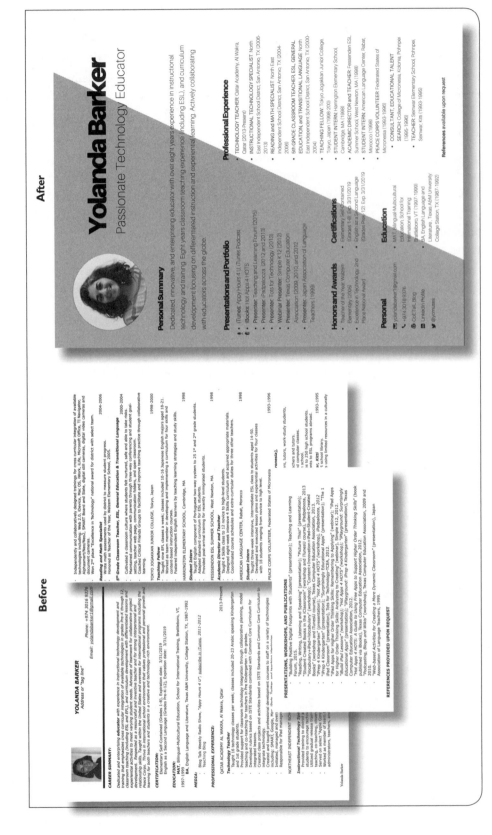

Figure 5.14 Resume Reboot Using Canva Templates

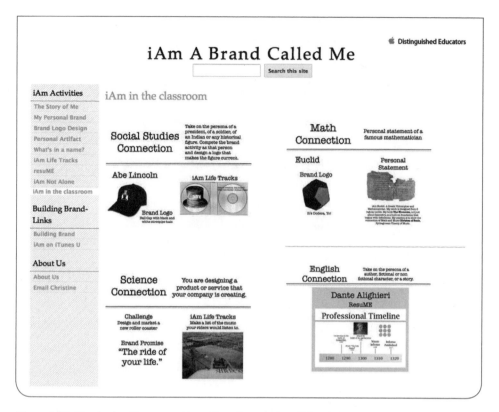

Figure 5.15 iAm in the Classroom Extensions Featured on "iAm A Brand Called Me" Google Site

Source: https://sites.google.com/site/adeiamcollection/my-personal-brand

To help equip and empower students continue to prepare for their futures, here are the four *P*'s that you can use in your classroom:

- **Practice:** Students need practice with a variety of these skill sets. One way to creatively practice the art of building a resume is to have students craft a resume for a fictional or historical character (Figure 5.16). Teachers could even discuss why one character would make a better applicant than another for a particular position or what information would have been helpful to include within that character's resume that could have gotten them the job. Students could create a resume for their dream job. A fantastic question to pose is what characteristics, skills, and experience might be essential for being successful in this line of work?

- **Perceptions:** What is written on a resume and how the resume is written and designed are two very different things. Employers may perceive a resume with misspellings and grammatical errors as careless with no attention to detail. Conversely, a resume that is clear and easy to follow might inform someone that person is organized. We can't control someone's perceptions and judgments of us, but we can strive to use best practices in communication and visual literacy to remove barriers to positive perceptions. This idea of recognizing how others

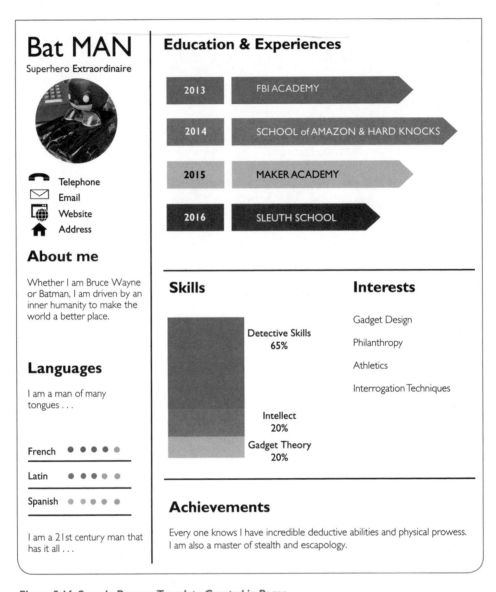

Figure 5.16 Sample Resume Template Created in Pages

perceive us and crafting a positive digital doppelgänger is addressed in further detail in the chapter on social media.

- **Publishing:** The more students publish online, the more familiar they become with these tools and the easier it will be to repurpose their content in the future. Canva offers several resume templates that can be easily edited. Additionally, reviewing all of the formats gives students more insight as to what types of information could be included in a resume and how that information might be displayed. For example, jobs don't have to be listed in the standard description of duties format and linear bullets. Other options might be a horizontal visual timeline (see Figure 5.16). Many of the best practices for visual literacy mentioned in Chapter 3 are also threaded through the development of a resume. If you are looking for a resource for students to support career discovery and research (both education needed and soft skills encouraged) that also exhibits visualizations and career paths, DK's publication *Careers: The Graphic Guide to Finding the Perfect Job for You* is a must have for your class.

- **Peers:** Peers allow us to explore perceptions people have about us before we leave the safety of the playground. Peers also provide us opportunities for feedback and the ability to fine tune our interpersonal skills through collaborative work and discussions.

> *"Technology is just a tool. In terms of getting the kids working together and motivating them, the teacher is the most important."*
>
> —**Bill Gates** *(Author and Cofounder of Microsoft)*

Moving forward . . . we as educators have to remember that while these technologies exist and can impact our students' learning, we play a critical role in this equation.

I realize this chapter was probably like eating a big Italian dinner. You are stuffed with information and probably full of ideas. Though I am not saying you need a midafternoon siesta, I would suggest remembering that while we can do anything suggested in this chapter and this book, we have to remember that it will not be possible to do everything. Spend some time with your team and your administration really prioritizing your entry points and even timeline into portfolios, peer reflections, student-led conferences, and perhaps even resumes. A 2-2-2 model is a great way to help you navigate this process (e.g., two things I plan to do in the next 2 weeks, 2 months, 2 years).

I am in fact of Italian descent, and I have to say that I absolutely love gnocchi, which are dense and filling potato dumplings. While I can't digest more than a bowl at a time, that doesn't mean I don't come back for more . . . a little later. My intent for the resource section below is just that. Once you are done mulling over the content of this chapter, feel free to nibble or consume the challenges and preparation inventory as well as the hand-crafted list of curated resources and suggested readings.

Chapter Resources

Digital Portfolio Preparation Inventory Assessment

☐ What are the reasons my students need a digital portfolio?

☐ What are the direct benefits of a digital portfolio for my students that I want to focus on?

- [ ] What roles will ownership, sharing, feedback, and organization play in the selection of a digital portfolio platform for my students?
- [ ] How often will students add to their portfolio?
- [ ] What portfolio platform will I choose?
- [ ] What training is necessary for myself, my students, and my parents?
- [ ] Will students lead conferences with teachers and parents using their portfolio?
- [ ] What types of descriptions, tasks, and artifacts (e.g., learning objectives/goals/targets, task explanations, products, processes, student reflections, self-assessments, achievements) will be included in student portfolios?
- [ ] Will I use additional writing prompts that inform student's about how they learn best?
- [ ] What type of reflection prompts will students use to evaluate and critique their work and the work of others?
- [ ] How often will peers be involved within providing feedback on digital portfolios?
- [ ] What digital tools will I make available to students or support students with integrating within their digital portfolios?
- [ ] How will I use a portfolio as a springboard for college and career readiness?
- [ ] How can I creatively adapt and incorporate resume, interview, and portfolio skills within my curriculum?

Share your answers using the hashtag #cultivatecomm.

My Students' Self-Assessment Checklist

- [ ] My students can add and organize content in their digital portfolio.
- [ ] My students can reflect on individual artifacts within their portfolio.
- [ ] My students can reflect on their process of learning.
- [ ] My students can provide effective formative feedback to their peers.
- [ ] My students can use communication best practices to craft a bio, resume, showcase portfolio.

Additional Resources and Reading

- Peer Portfolio Communication Catcher (found in Appendix B and on https://resources.corwin.com/cultivatingcomm)
- iAm A Brand Called Me Course (https://itunes.apple.com/us/course/iam-a-brand-called-me/id531749219)

- Sample Professional Resume With Quotes (found on https://resources.corwin
.com/cultivatingcomm)

- Sample Questions for Student-Led Conferences (https://www.edutopia.org/
sites/default/files/resources/edutopia-wildwood-world-magnet-student-
led-conference-question-sheet.pdf)

- ePortfolio Platform Considerations (found on https://resources.corwin.com/
cultivatingcomm)

- Suggested Reading and Resources (https://www.pinterest.com/techchef4u/
digital-portfolios-and-resumes)

References

Bungay Stanier, M. (2016). *The coaching habit: Say less, ask more, and change the way you lead forever.* Toronto, ON: Box of Crayons Press.

Devlin, I. (2016). Exploring the pedagogy of ePortfolios. Learning and Teaching at Navitas. Retrieved October 17, 2016, from http://learningandteaching-navitas.com/exploring-the-pedagogy-of-eportfolios

Engagement insights: Survey findings on the quality of undergraduate education. (2015). Retrieved July 13, 2016, from http://nsse.indiana.edu/NSSE_2015_Results/pdf/NSSE_2015_Annual_Results.pdf

Fagan, K. (2015, May 7). Split image. *ESPN.com.* Retrieved from http://www.espn.com/espn/feature/story/_/id/12833146/instagram-account-university-pennsylvania-runner-showed-only-part-story

Friedman, T. (2014). How to get a job at Google. *Nytimes.com.* Retrieved January 24, 2016, from http://www.nytimes.com/2014/02/23/opinion/sunday/friedman-how-to-get-a-job-at-google.html?_r=1

Gelb, M. (1998). *How to think like Leonardo Da Vinci.* New York, NY: Delacorte Press.

Hiles, H. (2016). Digital portfolios position students for success in the workforce (EdSurge News). *EdSurge.* Retrieved October 18, 2016, from https://www.edsurge.com/news/2016-07-06-digital-portfolios-position-students-for-success-in-the-workforce?utm_content=buffer2ca9c&utm_medium=social&utm_source=facebook.com&utm_campaign=buffer

Holiday, R. (2016). *Ego is the enemy.* New York, NY: Penguin.

Kleon, A. (2015). *The steal like an artist journal: A notebook for creative kleptomaniacs.* New York, NY: Workman Publishing Company.

Margolis, M. (2011). The resume is dead, the bio is king. *99U by Behance.* Retrieved January 24, 2016, from http://99u.com/articles/7025/the-resume-is-dead-the-bio-is-king

Pope, D., Brown, M., & Miles, S. (2015). *Overloaded and underprepared.* San Francisco, CA: Jossey-Bass.

Reflection Resources—University Studies Program. (2016). *Uwosh.edu.* Retrieved 24 January 24, 2016, from https://www.uwosh.edu/usp/for-faculty-and-staff/resources-for-your-students/eportfolio/reflection-resources

Sinek, S. (2016). How great leaders inspire action. *Ted.com*. Retrieved January 24, 2016, from https://www.ted.com/talks/simon_sinek_how_great_leaders_inspire_action?language=en

TEAL: Teaching excellence in adult literacy. (2016). Fact sheet: Metacognitive processes. Retrieved January 24, 2016, from https://teal.ed.gov/tealguide/metacognitive

Waack, S. (2014). *138 influences related to achievement—Hattie effect size list*. Retrieved January 24, 2016, from http://visible-learning.org/hattie-ranking-influences-effect-sizes -learning-achievement

Wiggins, G. (2012). Educational leadership: Feedback for learning—Seven keys to effective feedback. *Ascd.org*. Retrieved January 24, 2016, from http://www.ascd.org/ publications/educational-leadership/sept12/vol70/num01/Seven-Keys-to-Effective -Feedback.aspx

Wildwood IB World Magnet School. (2015). Student-led conferences: Empowerment and ownership. *Edutopia*. Retrieved January 24, 2016, from http://www.edutopia.org/ practice/student-led-conferences-empowerment-and-ownership

Notes

_____

_____

_____

_____

_____

_____

_____

_____

_____

_____

_____

_____

_____

_____

CHAPTER 6

Social Media

Communicating with peers and a global audience online through social media with the ability to be both a critical consumer of content as well as a thoughtful creator and crafter of their digital doppelgänger

"It's okay to live without 100% popularity."

—**Danny Gregory**
(Author and Cofounder of Sketchbook Skool)

The subtitle for this book promises "future-ready skills for secondary students." The five previous chapters address aspects of communication (e.g., email, collaboration, presentations, visual literacy, and student projects and publishing) that, while they have evolved, have been in existence in some form for some time. Yes, technology has changed the formats and importance of these modes, but these topics are not innovative in and of themselves.

Social media, on the other hand, is a relatively new means of communication and has rapidly changed how, when, and with whom we communicate. Just for fun, return to a time before social media and ask yourself what your day, evening, weekend, and communications with friends and family looked like. Juxtapose these thoughts and feelings with what you know about your relationships and your relationship with social media now. When I engaged in this thought exercise, I came up with these seven answers (see Figure 6.1).

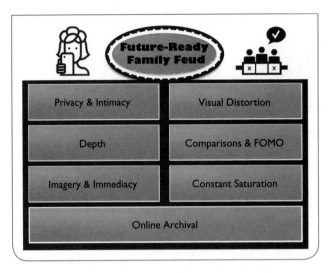

Figure 6.1 Graphical Representation of Social Media Changes Using Family Feud

- **Privacy and Intimacy:** The closest thing I had to group chats in high school was a spiral notebook that would be passed around between my two best friends. Now I can post intimate details of my day or trip to a group of my closest 200 friends and family or even 18,000 people in my professional learning network. Another interesting phenomenon is the level of intimacy that is shared on social media. Not only do we post family photos, but photos of car crashes, funerals, hospital visits, or the possum nuisance one caught in a trap in the back yard. The social etiquette barometer of both privacy and intimacy has definitely received an updated set of calibrations.

- **Depth:** When my friends and I weren't together, we had deep 3-hour conversations on the telephone. Now I find it an inconvenience to talk on the phone and most of my conversations take place in texts or Facebook direct messages. These conversations also tend to be more shallow in nature in comparison with these phone interactions of yesteryear.

- **Imagery and Immediacy:** Without ubiquitous mobile devices, the only way we shared images was drawings, photocopies, or torn pages of magazines and the only way we shared videos was with VHS tapes and DVDs. Now someone can capture and post a selfie or a groupie without batting an eye. Or better yet . . . broadcast live video in a matter of seconds.

- **Visual Distortion:** Before mobile devices and social media filters, the ability to manipulate photographs was time consuming or at the very least required cost-prohibitive software. Now there are no shortage of apps that can change or improve one's appearance. But it isn't just one's appearance that can be distorted. Zilla van den Born proved during a social engineering experiment that we can "filter and manipulate" reality. She fooled her friends and family with photo-editing software and Facebook into thinking she was on a 5-week vacation in

South Asia when in fact she never left her home town of Amsterdam ("Dutch Girl Fakes a 5-Week Vacation," 2014). Sites like Fotoforensics, which can determine how much a photo has been manipulated, and FakeAPhoto, which allows visitors to have a go at determining which photos are real and which have been doctored, have even popped up to wheedle some truth.

- **Comparisons and FOMO (Fear of Missing Out):** Before networking apps, we might have visited with a friend to hear about their new job or thumb through their vacation photo album over a lunch break. Now we are bombarded by success stories and vivid filtered vacation photos (I mean really, think about how many you thumb through before selecting the best one to share) from literally everyone we know (or have known), and we begin to form opinions about ourselves. If someone does report failure, it is typically a funny mishap, not real-life hardships. These comparisons are not only dangerous, but also disabling, as the FOMO (Fear of Missing Out) acronym suggests when it was added in 2013 to the Oxford dictionary. While the idea of the grass is always greener predates this acronym, there is a very real anxiety that plagues our students to be in the know, to worry about what they're not doing, and a pressure to be included ("Do You Know How to Switch Off?" 2012).

- **Constant Saturation:** Secondary grades can be a difficult for anyone. You are awkward and really just making sense of the world and who you are in it. I moved around a lot as a kid. Making friends was difficult for me. My parents fought to make ends meet and to give me a good education so I didn't always have the nicest clothes or that coveted Liz Claiborne handbag. I also wore glasses in an era when geek chic wasn't a thing and had a cleft in my chin which fellow classmates referred to as a "butt chin." Many of us probably shared similar painful experiences . . . but we weren't constantly saturated with them. While I may have thought about them while I was at home, I wasn't constantly berated by them again and again online. Now body shaming and bullying takes a toll on our students' self-esteem, both in school and out of school.

- **Online Archival:** I have ticket stubs and pictures from my youth, but thankfully I don't have the embodiment of my entire secondary education online. I think it is safe to say that most of us can rest easy that the misguided angst and hare-brained decisions of our youth haven't played out online. And if we had a social media account in seventh grade, I can't say that we wouldn't have wanted it scrubbed prior to job hunting or the college application process either. What is even more interesting to ponder is how our own children will feel about having their childhood stories and family mishaps and anecdotes shared with 250 of their parents' closest friends and relatives since they were born. Even the *New York Times* tackled this topic of oversharing and ethics in a piece titled "Why I Decided to Stop Writing About My Children" (Bastos, 2016). This idea of online archival doesn't just impact our current students, but will continue to be a source of focus and possible debate as a whole generation of students reach adolescence and adulthood.

Many of our beliefs and practices are ingrained with our own experiences and the technology (or the lack thereof) of our time. Myspace and LinkedIn launched in 2003, Facebook in 2004, Twitter in 2006, Instagram in 2010, Snapchat and Voxer in 2011, and Periscope in 2015. While these may or may not be the social media accounts that our students use, this type of communication is still in the stages of infancy and is both dangerous and powerful, but not for the reasons you might think.

At some point, we need to stop paying lip service to teaching buzzwords like social media and cyberbullying and start tackling these very real and tough conversations. The underlying foundation of social media is really soft skills and social-emotional learning and teaching these skills can actually improve academic achievement ("New Vision for Education," 2016). Educators often focus on developing students' skills as creators, but where we miss the mark is addressing students as critical consumers of content as well. This chapter seeks to balance the scales of social media and delve into both the creation and consumer aspects of the tool. We can't change what others share online, but we can change how that information and those stories impact us.

How Do We Teach Students to Practice Emotional Hygiene When Consuming Content?

Our digital lives influence our emotional wellness in ways we don't even realize. In fact, some research has even started to find a link between depression and amount of time spent online (Olson, 2016). One could easily dismiss this as too much screen time and forbid these types of interactions, but I think there is a greater underlying issue to these findings and that is the need for teaching students to not only be critical consumers of the information and stories they digest online but also practice good emotional hygiene. There have been multiple articles recently touching on perfect social media lives ending in tragedy. One of the most devastating is the one about Madison Holleran that ESPN covered, titled "Split Image," which details a haunting story of a 19-year-old college student who shared a seemingly happy life of Instagram posts and committed suicide within the same hour she posted a twinkling picture of a park at dusk (Fagan, 2015). If we don't start talking about the difference between lives led on social media and lives led in "real life," these types of tragedies could continue.

"My goal was to prove how common and easy it is to distort reality. Everybody knows that pictures of models are manipulated. But we often overlook the fact that we manipulate reality also in our own lives."

—Zilla van den Born *(Freelance Graphic Designer and Retoucher)*

So how does emotional hygiene connect to communication skills for college and career readiness? I can tell you from first-hand experience that watching someone's highlight reel play out on social media every day, comparing it to your daily blooper reel, and then drawing conclusions about yourself and your value can have damaging effects on communication and productivity. You might even be surprised to know that productivity is actually connected to confidence and "it is our thoughts that drive our actions" (Tate et al., 2015). Oftentimes our communications and actions are based on our assessment of a situation. If our assessments are inaccurate or skewed, our decisions and forthcoming communications could very well be mismatched whether they are online, in email, or in person (Wright, 2016).

One of the best books I have read recently was *FLAWD* by Emily-Anne Rigal. The book is wisdom from a student who was bullied, became a bully, and then not only recovered, but started an antibullying initiative called "We Stop Hate.org" and wrote a book about her lessons learned. One of my favorite metaphors she uses is that of a mask. This is similar to the idea of hats. Everyone wears different hats (e.g., teacher, mom, sister, friend, colleague, mentor, boss), and normally we only wear one at a time so you only get to see one aspect of that person's personality and life. While we may play a role or a part, we are not our masks. What we share online is simply one of these masks, but it is what's behind the mask that matters: how we see ourselves and what characteristics and strengths are needed to play those parts well.

> *"We mistake ourselves for our stories. We have stories, but we are NOT our stories."*
>
> —**Mark Matousek** *(Author)*, as quoted in *FLAWD*

We can't change the existence of this social skewing phenomenon, but we can change the impact through awareness and perspective. In Chapter 2, we set the groundwork for positive interdependence and collaboration. One of the activities, Mirroring Stories, is a fantastic format for getting students to talk about this topic. As these questions are of a more sensitive tone, I thought to adapt this activity with scaffolded questions using an inner circle and outer circle model. For this activity, the outer circle (B in Figure 6.2) would face the inner circle (A in Figure 6.2). Then the outer circle partner (B) would answer a question. The inner circle partner (A) actively listens and then shares their answer to the same question or prompt. Once each pair shared, the outer circle partner shifts to the left or clockwise.

The questions in the Mirroring Masks Mixer activity in Figure 6.3 are scaffolded to start out simply with, "How many masks do you wear a day?" and progress to "What do you wish your family and peers knew about wearing that mask?" If a student doesn't feel comfortable with the prompt, he or she can always reframe their response and address what about that question made them uncomfortable. A version of this inner outer circle activity was used in a SXSWEDU 2016 workshop I attended and can be used to teach a variety of sensitive topics as well (Crabill & Floresta, 2016). Additional support resources can be found on the companion site.

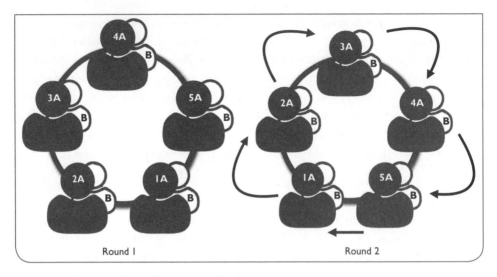

Round 1   Round 2

Figure 6.2 Mirroring Masks Mixer Group Configurations

Most students have an ongoing record of their life's activities. Providing a framework for perspective of this phenomenon though the context of social awareness of their online identity, the roles they play, and the ability to have a critical eye for online social skewing is integral to supporting our students as they grow online, in our classrooms, and in life. This mask activity could also be easily adapted to using with historical and literary figures.

How Do We Teach Students to Be Critical Consumers of Social Media Content?

While I was in the final stages of editing this book, ISTE revised their Standards for Students. The section "Knowledge Constructor" includes the standard, "evaluate the accuracy, perspective, credibility, and relevance of information, media, data, and other resources" which I found exceptionally fitting for this chapter ("Redefining Learning in a Technology-Driven World," 2016). Gone are the days of every house receiving the same newspaper at the same time and digesting the same pieces of news. Now we get our news from Twitter, Facebook, and Feedly, and we only digest what we have selected to receive or what others share with us. In fact, I spoke to one student researching colleges and was surprised to learn that he discovered the institution due to an ad they had posted on YouTube. I am also a little ashamed to admit that I have bought a t-shirt or two that was suggested to me by a Facebook ad.

But do we ever consider what this means to our students as consumers of news and responsible citizens? Tony Wagner addresses this concern of fragmented news sources in his book *Most Likely to Succeed:* "Every citizen selects and controls the news he or she receives, and we all gravitate toward comfortable predictable sources that reflect our own beliefs" (Wagner & Dintersmith, 2015).

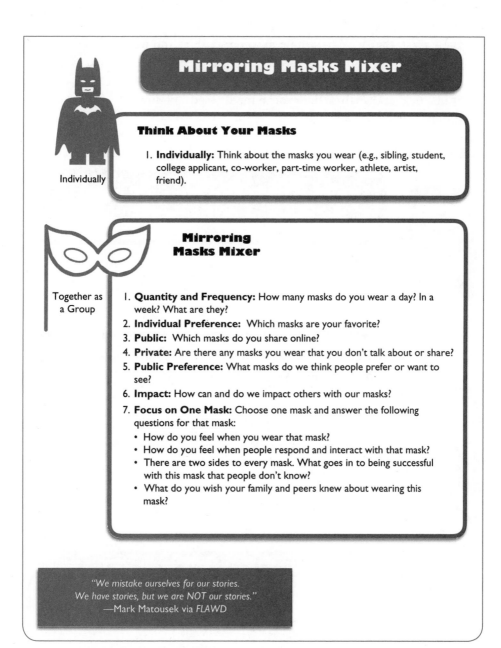

Mirroring Masks Mixer

Think About Your Masks

Individually

1. **Individually:** Think about the masks you wear (e.g., sibling, student, college applicant, co-worker, part-time worker, athlete, artist, friend).

Mirroring Masks Mixer

Together as a Group

1. **Quantity and Frequency:** How many masks do you wear a day? In a week? What are they?
2. **Individual Preference:** Which masks are your favorite?
3. **Public:** Which masks do you share online?
4. **Private:** Are there any masks you wear that you don't talk about or share?
5. **Public Preference:** What masks do we think people prefer or want to see?
6. **Impact:** How can and do we impact others with our masks?
7. **Focus on One Mask:** Choose one mask and answer the following questions for that mask:
   • How do you feel when you wear that mask?
   • How do you feel when people respond and interact with that mask?
   • There are two sides to every mask. What goes in to being successful with this mask that people don't know?
   • What do you wish your family and peers knew about wearing this mask?

*"We mistake ourselves for our stories.
We have stories, but we are NOT our stories."*
—Mark Matousek via *FLAWD*

Figure 6.3 Mirroring Masks Mixer Discussion

Available for download at **https://resources.corwin.com/cultivatingcomm**

Ask yourself, do I use social media as news and legitimate curricular content? The President (@POTUS) and First Lady (@FLOTUS) have Twitter accounts, the White House has an Instagram and Snapchat account, and CNN is on Pinterest. Making students aware of these tools and using them in the classroom is vital to students understanding that they have to engage with multiple forms of news and media. But we can't stop there. Students have to be more than aware that these exist; they have to be able to recognize bias and weed through content to make informed judgments based on facts and evidence. So what could this look like in the classroom? Have students find a popular news feed or industry expert in a field and analyze their social media feeds. Figure 6.4 provides a guide for students' analysis.

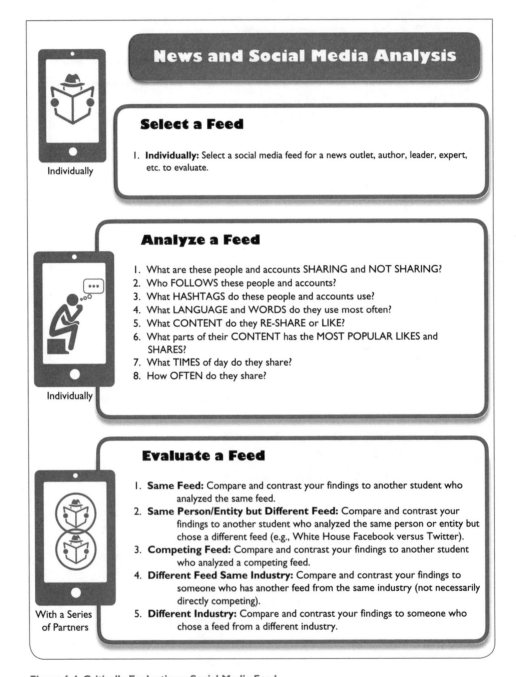

News and Social Media Analysis

Select a Feed

Individually

1. **Individually:** Select a social media feed for a news outlet, author, leader, expert, etc. to evaluate.

Analyze a Feed

Individually

1. What are these people and accounts SHARING and NOT SHARING?
2. Who FOLLOWS these people and accounts?
3. What HASHTAGS do these people and accounts use?
4. What LANGUAGE and WORDS do they use most often?
5. What CONTENT do they RE-SHARE or LIKE?
6. What parts of their CONTENT has the MOST POPULAR LIKES and SHARES?
7. What TIMES of day do they share?
8. How OFTEN do they share?

Evaluate a Feed

With a Series of Partners

1. **Same Feed:** Compare and contrast your findings to another student who analyzed the same feed.
2. **Same Person/Entity but Different Feed:** Compare and contrast your findings to another student who analyzed the same person or entity but chose a different feed (e.g., White House Facebook versus Twitter).
3. **Competing Feed:** Compare and contrast your findings to another student who analyzed a competing feed.
4. **Different Feed Same Industry:** Compare and contrast your findings to someone who has another feed from the same industry (not necessarily directly competing).
5. **Different Industry:** Compare and contrast your findings to someone who chose a feed from a different industry.

Figure 6.4 Critically Evaluating a Social Media Feed

Available for download at **https://resources.corwin.com/cultivatingcomm**

This idea can even be taken a step further by having students find a competing news source or voice on a topic and completing a compare and contrast. This activity brings the Masks Mixer activity full circle as students are not only aware of how their peers skew or shape their digital doppelgänger, but also realize that this is a practice that happens on much greater scale—even in the news we consume.

How Do We Teach Students to Carefully Craft Their Digital Doppelgänger?

But social media isn't just our own perceptions of others and the world around us; it is crafting a positive digital doppelgänger too, which is gently touched on in the activities mentioned above. In 2012, *The Onion* posted an article titled "Report: Every potential 2040 president already unelectable due to Facebook." While *The Onion* is a news satire site, one has to ponder the element of truth in this statement. Headlines like "They Loved Your G.P.A. Then They Saw Your Tweets" are a very real reality (Singer, 2013). And don't ever think that just because you have a limited number of followers that no one is listening. Justine Sacco, a director of corporate communications in the industry of managing imagery and reputation, learned the hard way when she tweeted several offensive tweets to her 170 followers before a flight to Africa and became a very public example of how no audience is too small and how even trained professionals can misuse a tool. By the time she landed she was the number one worldwide trend on Twitter and was fired (Ronson, 2015). And no excuse as an adult will be able to get you out of the damage that one of these misguided posts could cause. Model Dani Mathers learned this the hard way when she posted a naked picture of another woman showering in an LA Fitness locker room and body shamed her with the caption, "If I can't unsee this, then you can't either," to all of her followers on Snapchat. She later apologized and said she didn't know how to use Snapchat and that she only meant to send it to one friend and not all of her followers. The damage was already done—not only did Dani lose her job, delete all of her social media accounts due to the media backlash, and incur banishment from all LA Fitnesses for life, but she also may be facing criminal charges for disseminating private images (Escobar, 2016).

The reality of these stories and headlines is that if adults are making these mistakes, we can't really expect our own students not to either unless we provide them with the proper skills and tools. On the companion website, you'll find a Digital Citizenship Survival Kit that Craig Badura created and I revamped with some interactivity, which you can use with your students. It includes greater detail about each of the objects pictured in Figure 6.5. Using metaphors like this is so valuable in putting the reality and need for these types of skills into perspective for our students.

I revisited this kit and decided to reimagine it for this book through the context of conversations, which prove to be far more integral to impacting change than

Figure 6.5 Craig Badura's Digital Citizenship Survival Kit as an Interactive Guide

Source: Craig Badura, https://www.thinglink.com/scene/449979950884192256

contracts and mandates. Figure 6.6 is a Digital Doppelgänger Communication Catcher to use with students to elicit some deeper conversations about their digital doppelgänger.

How Can I Support Students With Positively Integrating Social Media?

Now that we have addressed how to be both critical consumers of social media and cognizant of the shadow their digital presence casts online, let's discuss opportunities to leverage social media conversations and positive online presence with our students. Most schools block the use of social media, so I realize this might be a sticking point for some. I think this ruling falls much into the same category as not allowing students to have email accounts, and while I realize we can't all be as laissez faire as "Pete the Cat," whose motto is "It's All Good" in the popular children's series, I think there is a lot of good that can come of students using social media purposefully and positively while they are still under our care.

Secondary students are most likely online with or without us. Therefore, it's important that we provide opportunities for crafting and sharing authentic work, as well as teaching how to leverage these tools as a means to communicate and

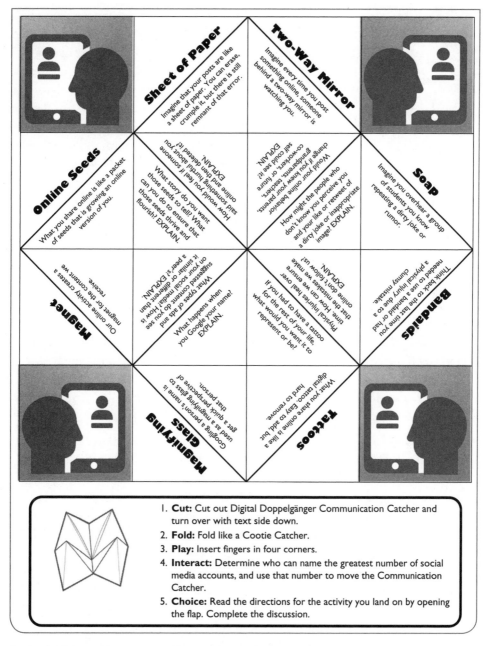

The figure contains the following labeled sections:

Sheet of Paper — Imagine that your posts are like a sheet of paper. You can erase, crumple it, but there is still remnant of that error.

Two-Way Mirror — Imagine every time you post something online, someone behind a two-way mirror is watching you.

Online Seeds — What you share online is like a packet of seeds that is growing an online version of you.

How would you feel if someone online said something hurtful about you and then deleted it? EXPLAIN.

What story do you want those seeds to tell? What can you do to ensure that those seeds thrive and flourish? EXPLAIN.

Would your online behavior change if you knew your parents, co-workers, or future self could see it? EXPLAIN.

How might the people who don't know you perceive you and your like or retweet of a dirty joke or inappropriate image? EXPLAIN.

Soap — Imagine you overhear a group of students you know repeating a dirty joke or rumor.

Magnet — Our online activity creates a magnet for the content we receive.

What types of ads and suggested content do you see on your social media? How is it similar or different than a peer's? EXPLAIN.

What happens when you Google your name? EXPLAIN.

If you had to have a tattoo for the rest of your life, what would you want it to represent or be?

Physical injuries heal over time. How do we ensure that the mistakes we make online don't follow us? EXPLAIN.

Think back to the last time you needed to use a bandaid or had a physical injury due to a clumsy mistake.

Bandaids

Magnifying Glass — Googling a person's name is used as a magnifying glass to get a quick perspective of that person.

What you share online is like a digital tattoo: Easy to add, but hard to remove.

Tattoos

1. **Cut:** Cut out Digital Doppelgänger Communication Catcher and turn over with text side down.
2. **Fold:** Fold like a Cootie Catcher.
3. **Play:** Insert fingers in four corners.
4. **Interact:** Determine who can name the greatest number of social media accounts, and use that number to move the Communication Catcher.
5. **Choice:** Read the directions for the activity you land on by opening the flap. Complete the discussion.

Figure 6.6 Digital Doppelgänger Communication Catcher

Available for download at **https://resources.corwin.com/cultivatingcomm**

gain insight. Furthermore, Googling applicants is a very real practice so teaching students how to communicate appropriately online through both visual and textual media is vital to their success in college, their career, and in life. If you or your school are still hesitant to have students do this through their own social media platforms, consider creating class accounts that can model these types of activities.

The bulk of this chapter may appear like a downer, as I have spent the majority of it highlighting negative media narratives and awareness of how social media impacts us. However, I hope that you see this as more of a hearty steak dinner (sorry, vegetarians) that is an instructionally and pedagogically dense dish. Recently, I paired a steak with a dish of mint watermelon and a tinge of sea salt. I found it to be a surprisingly clever and upbeat way to refresh the palette after said slab of meat. So, I thought you might enjoy some flavorful and effective ways to spruce up using social media with your students that is a little less dramatic. Below are a few examples.

- **Memes for Good:** Memes are prevalent but oftentimes mean or sardonic in nature. In fact, one of the most popular memes is an awkward picture of adolescent Maggie Goldenberger that was captioned "Ermahgerd Gersberms," which quickly spun out of control (King, 2015). While we all share and most likely find these memes amusing, I can't imagine how we would feel if we were unintentionally the subject of one. What if students created positive memes of their own work or images and shared them online? This also provides an opportunity for students to model how to use humor without being demeaning or insulting.

- **That's Good . . . That's Bad:** Carl Hooker published a clever post, "How Modern Technology Could Have Changed These Classic Movies." He mentions how movies like *When Harry Met Sally* and *The Sixth Sense* would be forever changed if Harry and Sally were on Facebook and saw no need to reconnect, or Cole posted selfies with dead people on Instagram to support his claims. Some of my favorite children's books are *That's Good! That's Bad!* and *Fortunately, Unfortunately*. They each explore both sides of a situation, so I thought adapting the premise might be helpful. What if students chose a popular children's book, integrated social media, and proposed how it could have positively or negatively changed the story. For example, what if *Green Eggs and Ham* turned into a stalking or cyberbullying issue. Conversely, what if *Green Eggs and Ham* used the premise of the ALS Ice Bucket Challenge and had people all over the world taking selfies with green eggs and ham to raise awareness and funds for organic chickens? Perhaps a stretch, but what we have to remember is two things: (1) It is far easier to give someone else advice or tell them what they should have done, and (2) social media for our students is omnipresent and for them picturing a world without it is like us imaging a world without running water.

- **Put Social Media to the Test:** We are just gracing the surface of what a connected world means for information and knowledge. One student was researching the pros and cons of paper and digital charting in the medical field. Rather than pulling solely from a cursory Google search, he used his parent's Facebook group of physicians and posed the question. He amassed far more data and anecdata than he could have with an Internet search and through the process learned how valuable tapping into groups of professionals on social networks could be.

- **Stage a Selfie:** Selfies are rampant online. But how often do we take a moment to stop and think about how others perceive the images we share? And how often do we evaluate the identity that we share online through our images? Staging a purposeful selfie is the self-awareness modern-day version of a coat of arms. Imagine students creating a self-portrait where every element of the image is purposeful and deliberate (e.g., setting, color, facial expressions, props). In a world of snap decisions, an online profile pic can impact not only how people perceive you online, but also if people want to be connected to you.

- **Scroll Back:** We post daily and frequently. But do we ever look back? Apps exist to do this in a singular fashion (e.g., what you were doing on this day a year ago or 4 years ago). But have we really thought how to leverage this ability on a greater scale and for more than a random nostalgic whim? Have students pull up any social media feed and scroll back a month, 6 months, a year, etc. Do they feel the same way they did in these posts? How have they changed and grown? Are there any posts they wish they had deleted or at the very least are no longer relevant? This would be a fantastic springboard for a writing assignment as well.

- **Posterize and Vocalize:** Because I am a firm believer in purposeful and authentic tasks and involving students in the discussion, I am especially fond of students creating content. While there are a myriad of posters from Common Sense Media and even Teachers Pay Teachers that echo the "think before you tweet" rhetoric, why not let students design their own campaign, tagline, and commercials? Posters could be displayed around campus and videos aired on the school announcements. This could even be threaded through a health class, tackled as a service project by student council, or a topic for a digital art or multimedia class to design.

- **Take Up a Cause or Post Passions:** Too often we forget that we can use social media for good. Remember the project in Chapter 2 where students chose an environmental campus issue (e.g., creating green spaces on campus for studying or reducing the amount of plastic waste in the cafeteria) and created a campaign to impact it. This is something that provides a real-world context for using social media to impact change. Now think back to Chapter 4 and the idea of authentic audiences and projects with purpose. Whitney Woodard is an example of just that. She had a passion for creating jewelry in high school and decided to use Instagram her senior year to showcase her wares. Flash forward 2 years, and she has a booming social media presence (Figure 6.7) and business. There are many pathways to success.

Figure 6.7 Beaded by W Student Business Utilizing Instagram

Allowing our students to have authentic experiences with both ethical and intellectual engagement is not only vital to their understanding and appropriate use of social media, but to their futures as well. In fact, the Making Caring Common project, a consortium formed by the Harvard Graduate School of Education, is looking to reshape the college admissions process to include more meaningful and authentically chosen endeavors than a laundry list of random extracurriculars ("Turning the Tide," 2016). Just think about the day when the student who holds a patent for a bluetooth remote that controls robots (visit the ChapR.com and follow @ChapResearch on Twitter), the student who self-published a book (*Be.* by Koffi Descoteaux on Amazon), the student who created an Instagram account to sell jewelry to garner funds to travel the world and blog about it (follow @globalgaby on Instagram), and the student who held multiple offices in school are all held to the same standards. It is not to say that any of these are greater or less than each other: some are simply more or less traditional but should carry no less value.

What we create and share (whether it be words, links, or visuals) online is not only a conduit for our communications but also a reflection of how people see us. Being cognizant of this phenomenon is half the battle. The other half is not only putting our best "foot" forward, but also sharing other facets of ourselves such as our work and strengths through these channels. While the mathematical portion of this analogy might be lost, the third half of social media is the ability to use it to communicate purposefully. I can't tell you how many times I connect with professionals via Twitter, Facebook, and LinkedIn and have meaningful two-way conversations and exchanges. Above all, social media should empower students to communicate. And students should be equipped with the tools, lessons, and strategies to let their scholastic social narrative unfold and serve as a positive prologue to their professional career.

Social Media Preparation Inventory Assessment

☐ How does social media impact my students?

☐ How will I teach my students to be critical consumers of personal and global news and social media?

☐ How will I support my students with awareness and strategies for creating a positive social media presence?

☐ What experiences will I provide for my students to use social media in an authentic way?

Share your answers using the hashtag #cultivatecomm.

My Students' Self-Assessment Checklist

☐ My students are aware that social media is only one aspect of a person's life and can be distorted and skewed.

☐ My students are aware of the types of masks (e.g., perspectives and versions) they wear and share online.

☐ My students understand the idea of a digital doppelgänger and have considered the impact their online behavior and preferences have on their real life.

☐ My students can leverage social media to share authentic learning artifacts and stories.

☐ My students are aware of online biases in news and social media.

☐ My students can evaluate and analyze multiple news and social media sources for bias.

Additional Resources and Reading

• Mirroring Masks Mixer (found on https://resources.corwin.com/cultivatingcomm)

• Digital Doppelgänger Communication Catcher (found in Appendix B and on https://resources.corwin.com/cultivatingcomm)

• News and Social Media Analysis (found in Appendix B and on https://resources .corwin.com/cultivatingcomm)

• Suggested Reading and Resources (www.pinterest.com/techchef4u/students -and-social-media)

References

Bastos, E. (2016). Why I decided to stop writing about my children. *Well.* Retrieved October 13, 2016, from http://well.blogs.nytimes.com/2016/07/29/why-i-decided-to -stop-writing-about-my-children/?_r=0

Crabill, E., & Floresta, J. (2016). *Teaching sensitive topics.* Presentation, SXSWEDU 2016 in Austin, TX.

Do you know how to switch off? (2012). *Psychologies.* Retrieved October 13, 2016, from https://www.psychologies.co.uk/self/are-you-on-247.html

Dutch girl fakes a 5-week vacation to South East Asia by posting phoney photos to Facebook. (2014). *PetaPixel.* Retrieved July 19, 2016, from http://petapixel.com/ 2014/09/11/dutch-girl-fakes-5-week-vacation-south-east-asia-posting-phoney -photos-facebook

Escobar, S. (2016). Model who posted a photo of a naked woman at the gym is fired. *Good Housekeeping.* Retrieved July 19, 2016, from http://www.goodhousekeeping.com/beauty/ news/a39410/dani-mathers-body-shaming-gym-photo

King, D. (2015). Ermahgerddon: The untold story of the ermahgerd girl. *Vanity Fair.* Retrieved April 2, 2016, from http://www.vanityfair.com/culture/2015/10/ermahgerd -girl-true-story

New vision for education: Fostering social and emotional learning through technology. (2016). *World Economic Forum.* Retrieved July 18, 2016, from http://www3.weforum.org/ docs/WEF_New_Vision_for_Education.pdf

Olson, S. (2016). All that time on social media can make you depressed. *Medical Daily.* Retrieved March 31, 2016, from http://www.medicaldaily.com/social-media-major -depressive-disorder-mental-health-379396#.VvaT2EVkD0c.twitter

Redefining learning in a technology-driven world: A report to support the adoption of the ISTE Standards for Students. (2016). *Iste.org.* Retrieved July 14, 2016, from http:// www.iste.org/docs/Standards-Resources/iste-standards_students-2016_research-validity -report_final.pdf?sfvrsn=0.0680021527232122

Report: Every potential 2040 president already unelectable due to Facebook. (2012). *Theonion.com.* Retrieved 13 October 2016, from http://www.theonion.com/video/report -every-potential-2040-president-already-unel-27963

Rigal, E.-A., & Demers, J. (2015). *FLAWD: How to stop hating on yourself, others, and the things that make you who you are.* New York, NY: Perigee.

Ronson, J. (2015). How one stupid tweet blew up Justine Sacco's life. *Nytimes.com.* Retrieved April 2, 2016, from http://www.nytimes.com/2015/02/15/magazine/how-one -stupid-tweet-ruined-justine-saccos-life.html

Singer, N. (2013). They loved your G.P.A. Then they saw your tweets. *Nytimes.com.* Retrieved April 2, 2016, from http://www.nytimes.com/2013/11/10/business/they-loved -your-gpa-then-they-saw-your-tweets.html?pagewanted=all&_r=1

Tate, C., McCue, M., Team, T., Tate, C., Rapetskaya, M., Team, T., & Burkeman, O. (2015). Are confident people more productive? *99U by Behance.* Retrieved May 4, 2016, from http://99u.com/articles/52306/are-confident-people-more-productive

Turning the tide: Inspiring concern for others and the common good through college admissions. (2016). *Mcc.gse.harvard.edu.* Retrieved April 2, 2016, from http://mcc.gse .harvard.edu/files/gse-mcc/files/20160120_mcc_ttt_execsummary_interactive.pdf?m= 1453303460

Wagner, T. & Dintersmith, T. (2015). *Most likely to succeed.* New York, NY: Scribner.

Wright, C. (2016). Plan well and execute: Multiple facets key to effective communication. *Nhregister.com.* Retrieved May 4, 2016, from http://www.nhregister.com/opinion/20160430/ plan-well-execute-multiple-facets-key-to-effective-communication

Notes

_____

_____

_____

_____

_____

_____

_____

_____

_____

_____

_____

_____

_____

_____

_____

_____

_____

_____

_____

Industry Insights

If you could give our current middle school or high school students one piece of advice for the future, what would it be?

Learn about people and yourself: "Learn about people and how to communicate (EQ, customer service), which requires learning about yourself."

—Brandon Mitchell (Veterinarian)

Take feedback and persist: "Understand that criticism/feedback is intended to help you improve. In your first 10 years in any profession, you most likely won't be successful right away, so remember to keep a growth mindset, persist, and recognize that failures can make you stronger if you don't interpret and internalize them as criticism of your character."

—Andrew Gardner (VP Professional Learning at BrainPOP)

Don't procrastinate: "Anxiety will always be present as a procrastinator. Take the time needed to do your due diligence for each task asked of you."

—Judy Jacomino (Makeup and Hair Artist)

Be clear and diverse: "Say what you mean, mean what you say, and be able to say it in many ways."

—Efrain Velez (Senior Designer)

Be globally aware: "Students need to have global awareness, an understanding of and appreciation for different cultures. In marketing, for example, an important feature in a product in the UK is not necessarily an important feature in a product in China, or the way that something is presented in one society would not be appropriate in another."

—Cyndee Perkins (App Development Marketing Content Writer and Franchise Consultant)

Follow your intuitions: "Do what you are passionate about and don't be afraid to explore. It's never too late to follow your dreams, but life will be so much more fun if you do it from the get-go instead of doing what you think you're 'supposed to do.' It's your life and you are the one who knows what you want!"

—Kristy Peters (Principal at Litigation Finance Company)

Have the right attitude: "Keep an open mind, be humble, and learn independently. It doesn't matter to us how stellar a resume looks; if the attitude, willingness to learn and work hard, as well as the ability to explore and discover solutions without guidance are not there, the next 40–50 years will be much harder than they need to be."

—Jacob Hanson (Managing Partner With PR With Panache)

Leverage every situation: "If you are in a position where you have no choice or agency, put yourself in problem-solving mode. What is the path to cause the least amount of friction or trouble for others (empathy) while maintaining your own happiness, and possibly using the experience to leverage something in the future?"

—Reshan Richards (Chief Learning Officer at Explain Everything)

CHAPTER 7

Curation

Communicating ideas, learning, and
trends with peers and a global audience
through the process of seeking, distilling,
and making sense of information to be
both a critical consumer of content
as well as a lifelong learner

*"Carefully curated is redundant and implies that there is such a thing
as sloppy curating, which is ridiculous."*

—Colin Brady

Enter the visual time machine that is your brain and set it for a date in
the 1980s or 1990s. Where did you find your ideas and inspirations? For
me, I remember tearing out pages of recipes or crafts and placing them
in individual sheet protectors in a three-ring binder and even organizing them
with tabbed dividers. When Pinterest launched in 2010, I remember getting beta
invites from friends and dismissing it as a tool to find cake ball recipes and room
decor ideas. While there is nothing wrong with these topics, I had another focus
and need. I had just started a job as an Instructional Technology Specialist and
was handed a first-generation iPad. At that point in time, stories and ideas for
using iPads were scarce. Around the same time, I started blogging about my own
experiences with purposefully integrating the device into instructional settings.
I was also scouring the Internet for other teachers doing the same thing. When
I found these teachers and ideas, I didn't want to lose them; I wanted to

essentially tear out gems of inspiration from blogs and websites and put them in sheet protectors. And that's when it really hit me. Pinterest was far more than recipes and do-it-yourself hacks; it was a way I could build my own virtual educational inspiration binder and that's what I started doing. Flash forward 6 years, and the work I did to curate these resources has not only impacted my own learning and journey but over 25,000 others, as boards can have followers. The game changer of online curation tools is twofold, a place to easily locate and organize ideas for ourselves *and* others. Sometimes we take this new technology for granted. But think back 10 . . . nay, 20 years . . . How did you find good teaching ideas, what did you do with them once you did find them, and do you still refer back to these?

As I had my own skewed views of what Pinterest was, people have misconceptions of what curation really is. The idea of curation is not necessarily new or even novel. We have had curators in museums for years that have artfully, thoughtfully, and deliberately organized media around a common theme, idea, or journey. The difference is that the work of curation was done by few and the impact of the curation was only seen by those that had access to it. Now the work of curation is done by many, and the number of people who see it and have access to it is astronomical. In fact, a report in late 2015 estimated the number of active users on Pinterest at 100 million (Smith, 2014). But curation isn't just Pinterest—Netflix, iTunes, and Amazon curate content for users based on behavioral analytics, too.

What Is the Value of Curating for My Students?

There is a very real need for curation. Step back in to that time machine and take a gander at your high school, college, and first year teaching self. Where did you get your information and content, and what types of people and entities were providing and publishing that content? Two major shifts have happened in the past two decades: One is the ability for anyone to create content to put online, and the other is the ability to collect and organize that content. At some point, the sheer volume of information and content online will be so vast and dense that basic searches will not provide suitable or useful results. Basic searches are just analytics and a gamed system of words, hashtags, and search engine optimization. In fact, I have actually started using Pinterest as a search engine over Google because I find that I discover far more accurate results. Even ISTE has revised its student standards to include curation as part of workforce readiness and the "acquisition, construction, and demonstration of knowledge." The report goes on to tout, "finding and sorting content, recognizing patterns and distinctions within sources and organizing content into focused groupings are all skills that require higher-order thinking skills" (*Redefining Learning in a Technology-Driven World*, 2016).

You might remember from the foreword my comment about content being searchable and not necessary to be solely committed to memory. Somewhere there is this misnomer about knowledge that because content is on the Internet and Googleable, there is no need to constantly consume it. Harold Jarche said it best, "Work is learning and learning is work." He refers to a framework of capturing knowledge as Personal Knowledge Mastery (PKM). In Chapter 5, we discussed digital portfolios: Curation for learning is very similar to the portfolio process. The main difference is rather than curating and showcasing your own content, you are distilling, processing, and reflecting on others' ideas through the lens of your own personal learning. CoSchedule, a content marketing tool, offers a ratio of 5:3:2 (5 parts from others, 3 parts from you, and 2 personal from you) and 4:1:1 (4 parts original from you, 1 part from you, and 1 curated from others). If you have ever used the reading strategy text-to-text, text-to-self, and text-to-world, than this idea of making connections and discovering universal themes that resonate with your own experiences to craft a cocktail of comprehension won't be foreign to you (Figure 7.1).

> *"Content curation is the process of sorting through the vast amount of content on the Web and presenting it in a meaningful and organized way around a theme. The work involves sifting, sorting, arranging, and publishing information."*
>
> —**Beth Kanter** *(Trainer and Nonprofit Innovator)* **via CoSchedule**

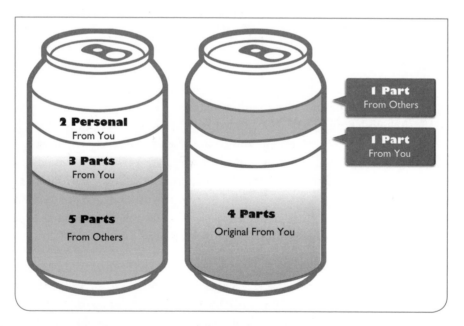

Figure 7.1 Graphical Representation of CoSchedule's "How to Schedule Your Social Media Content Curation for Massive Growth"

Source: CoSchedule (2015), http://www.slideshare.net/coschedule/how-to-schedule-your-social-media-content-curation-for-massive-growth-infographic

Harold shares a slightly different model for this process that I think is also very relevant: Seek, Sense, and Share (Figure 7.2).

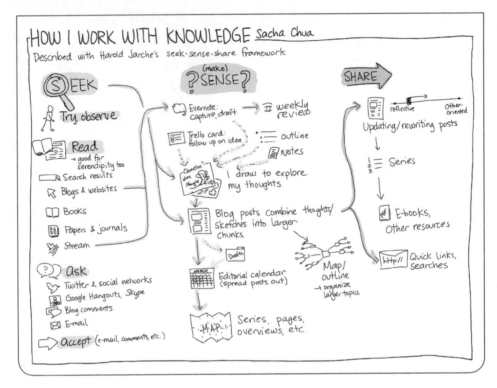

Figure 7.2 How I Work With Knowledge (described with Harold Jarche's Seek-Sense-Share Framework) Sketchnote by Sacha Chua

Source: Sacha Chua, http://sachachua.com/blog/2014/03/describing-personal-knowledge-management-routines-harold-jarches -seek-sense-share-framework

Beyond my affinity for alliteration and structured frameworks, the heart of this model is lifelong learning, reflection, and sharing. I am not misguided enough to think that I gained all of my content and technical knowledge and expertise solely through my own volition. I built a knowledge network early on and continually seek to make sense of trends and issues facing education and the classroom. I benefit from other knowledge experts in the field that sift through and share relevant content. But I didn't stop there, I started to personalize my own learning experiences and revelations and share those as curations as well.

One of the first reasons we curate is to make sense of the learning we have experienced and to archive it for quick retrieval afterwards. What we forget is that when we do this digitally and publicly, this work of curation can have an impactful ripple effect unbeknownst to us. Figure 7.3 depicts an example of a "Sketch-Note TAKE-AWAY" that I created using a photograph of my hand-written notes, Canva (the image frame), and Thinglink (all of the interactive icons layered on top of the image that link to apps, iTunes U courses, TEDTalks, and articles that were mentioned during the session), for my staff after attending iPadpalooza Gold Coast.

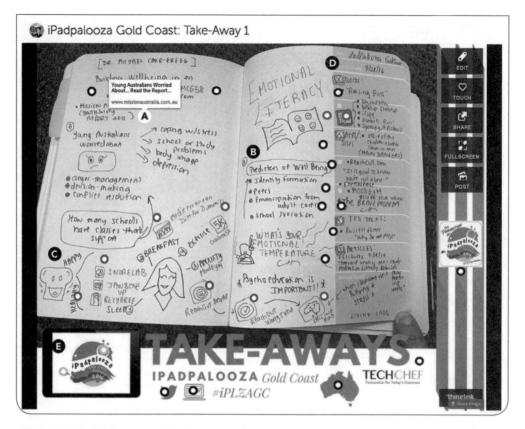

**Figure 7.3 Epic PD Recaps or Take-Aways Are One Way to Curate
Learning From an Event (using a combination of original notes, Canva, and Thinglink)**

Organizing it in a visual manner made it easier to navigate and refer back. What I didn't realize is how publishing this distillation would benefit not only my staff but also other educators all around the world who were not able to attend for lack of funding or geography. In fact, I had an attendee of one of my sessions stop me at the end and tell me the only reason she knew about iPadpalooza events was due to my curations and reflections about my experiences attending.

The process of curation is the very real work that we now do daily to make sense of the content and communications that we are flooded with and experience on a daily basis. To be able to communicate effectively, we have to be able to locate and navigate information and ideas, organize them, make sense, and draw meaning from them. When we begin to blur the lines of social media, online publishing, and curation, we begin to realize that curation is not only for me . . . but we.

How Can I Design Lessons to Explore Curation in the Classroom?

To provide students with multiple opportunities to navigate curation through both authentic and curricular avenues, I compiled eight different activities that can be found on the Curation Communication Catcher in Figure 7.4.

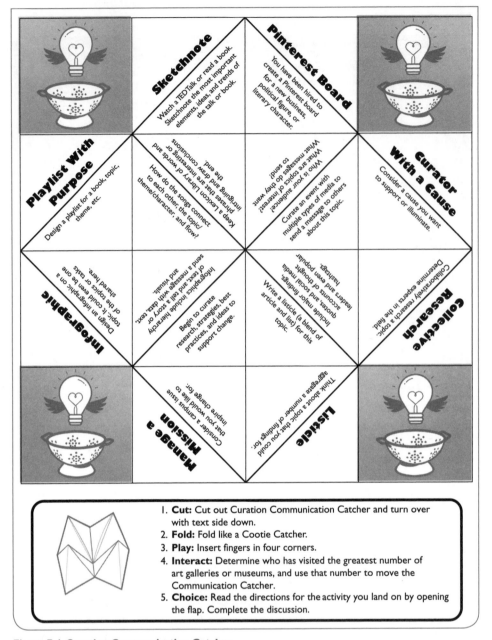

The figure contains the following labels and text:

Sketchnote: Watch a TEDTalk or read a book. Sketchnote the most important elements, ideas, and trends of the talk or book.

Pinterest Board: You have been hired to create a Pinterest board for a new business, political figure, or literary character.

Playlist With Purpose: Design a playlist for a book, topic, theme, etc. Keep a Lexicon Library of words and phrases that are interesting or intriguing and draw conclusions at the end. How do the songs connect to each other; the topic/theme/character and flow?

Curator With a Cause: Consider a cause you want to support or illuminate. Curate an event with multiple types of media to send a message to others about this topic. Who is your audience? What are topics of interest? What messages do they want to send?

Infographic: Design an infographic on a topic. It could even be one of the topics or tasks shared here. Infographics include hierarchy of text, and tell a story or send a message with data, text, and visuals.

Collective Research: Determine experts in the field. Collaboratively research a topic. Begin to curate research, strategies, best practices, and ideas to support change. Write a listicle (a blend of article and list) for this topic. Include major findings, quotes and social media accounts or thought leaders and even popular hashtags.

Manage a Mission: Consider a campus issue that you would like to inspire change for.

Listicle: Think about a topic that you could aggregate a number of findings for.

1. **Cut:** Cut out Curation Communication Catcher and turn over with text side down.
2. **Fold:** Fold like a Cootie Catcher.
3. **Play:** Insert fingers in four corners.
4. **Interact:** Determine who has visited the greatest number of art galleries or museums, and use that number to move the Communication Catcher.
5. **Choice:** Read the directions for the activity you land on by opening the flap. Complete the discussion.

Figure 7.4 Curation Communication Catcher

Available for download at https://resources.corwin.com/cultivatingcomm

- **Sketchnote a TEDTalk or Book:** Watch a TEDTalk and sketchnote the most important elements or trends of the talk. Examples of sketchnotes are included within the book: digital (Figures 4.11 and 7.3) and analog . . . hand-written with paper (Figures 7.2 and 7.8).

- **Curate a Pinterest Board for a Business, Political Figure, or Literary Character:** Design a Pinterest board for a business, literary character, or

Figure 7.5 Student Groups Using Scoop.it to Collectively Curate Materials for an Urban Geography Project

historical figure. What would they wear? What would the titles of their boards be? What would they pin? Who would be their intended audience?

- **Be a Curator With a Cause:** This is probably the purist form of curation. Have students consider a cause they want to support, explore, or illuminate (e.g., perceptions of women in media, gender equality, immigration). Have them curate an event with multiple types of media to send a message to others about this topic. This would be very similar to what galleries do.

- **Collectively Curate Research or Experts on a Topic:** Most curating tools are designed to be collaborative in some form or format. What if instead of having students include a bibliography or reference guide at the end of their paper or essay, they used a curation tool to collect research on the topic? What if part of the research was to determine and follow the experts in the field on the topic and include their major quotes, research, popular hashtags, and even social media accounts?

- **Write a Listicle:** Listicles are by far my favorite curation tool as they blend articles with lists. Think about the last time you clicked on an article like "Six Formative Assessment Tools You Should Use Today in Your Classroom" or "Twenty-One Things Every Teacher Should Do Right Now." Figure 7.6 has been included as an industry example that includes a multitude of sample list post titles to use as a springboard. Remind students that this is not just a list, but a list with rationale and explanation. And the "list with benefits" encompasses information from multiple authors and sources (consider designing a ratio as seen in

130 *Blog Post Headlines*
TITLE TEMPLATES

HOW TO POSTS

1. How To _____ With _____
2. How To Be More _____ When You Feel Like _____
3. How To _____ In _____
4. How To Keep Your Sanity While _____
5. How To Turn _____ Into _____ Every Single Time
6. How To Get Rid of _____ Forever
7. How To _____ Like A Boss
8. How I Almost Got _____ For _____
9. How To Frugally _____
10. How I Made _____ With _____
11. How I Went From _____ To _____ In _____ Days
12. How To Make Your _____ Look More _____
13. How To Start A _____
14. How To Get Your _____ To _____
15. How To Start _____ With No Time

LIST POSTS

16. _#_ Ways To Do _____ While _____
17. _#_ Ways To Increase Your _____ With _____
18. _#_ Habits That Will Make You _____
19. _#_ Changes To Make To Set You Up For _____
20. _#_ Tips For Creating The _____
21. _#_ Ways To Conquer _____
22. _#_ Ways To Sharpen Your _____ Skills
23. _#_ Mistakes I Made When _____
24. _#_ Things The Experts Do Every Day
25. _#_ Weird Habits That _____ People Have
26. _#_ Ways To Make Your Life More Peaceful
27. _#_ Ways To _____
28. _#_ Reasons Why I Chose _____
29. _#_ More Effective Strategies
30. _#_ Tricks You Must Try Today
31. _#_ You Should Be Aware Of
32. _#_ Ways To Get Out Of A _____
33. _#_ Must Haves For _____
34. _#_ Ways To Help A _____
35. _#_ Styles Of _____
36. _#_ Must Ask Questions For _____
37. _#_ Skills That Could Make Or Break _____
38. _#_ Tips For Surviving A _____
39. _#_ Simple Steps When _____
40. _#_ Awesome Activities For _____
41. _#_ Useful And Quick _____ Tips
42. _#_ Tips To Make Your Child More _____
43. _#_ Values I'm Living By
44. _#_ Reasons Why Everyone Does _____
45. _#_ Ways To Find Purpose In _____
46. _#_ Tricks To Jump Start Your _____
47. _#_ Things You Should Do _____
48. _#_ Habits Of Highly Successful _____
49. _#_ Things I Wish I Knew Before I _____
50. _#_ Things You Need To Know Today
51. _#_ Ways To Successful _____
52. _#_ Things A-List _____ Refuse To Do
53. _#_ Steps To Create The Perfect _____
54. _#_ Common _____ Mistakes Everybody Does
55. _#_ Pieces Of Advice For New _____
56. _#_ Hacks That Are Pure Genius
57. _#_ Things I've Learned From _____
58. _#_ Tips To Become A More Productive _____
59. _#_ Resources For The Best _____
60. _#_ Things To Include In Every _____
61. _#_ Little Known Ways To _____
62. _#_ Myths You Should Know About
63. _#_ Ways To Teach _____
64. _#_ Unsuspecting _____
65. _#_ Tips And Tricks To _____
66. _#_ Common Thoughts Everyone Has When _____
67. _#_ Things To Do While _____
68. _#_ Ways To Ease Anxiety During _____
69. _#_ Methods That Work To _____
70. _#_ Things Every _____ Should Know
71. _#_ Steps To Starting a Successful _____
72. _#_ Basics Tips For _____
73. _#_ Fool Proof Ways To Conquer _____
74. _#_ Truths About _____
75. _#_ Ways _____ Can Make Or Break You
76. _#_ Habits of Highly Successful _____
77. _#_ Reasons Why _____ Are Awesome
78. _#_ Shocking Finds That Will Change Your _____

RESOURCES / FREEBIES

79. The Ultimate Guide To _____
80. Ultimate Guide To _____
81. Beginners Guide To _____
82. The Best DIY: _____
83. Quick Guide On _____
84. A Complete Tutorial On _____
85. Step By Step Guide To _____
86. Cheat Sheet For _____
87. An In Depth Guide To _____
88. The Essential Guide To _____
89. The Ultimate _____ Bundle For _____
90. A Cheat Sheet For _____
91. The Best Guide To _____

SCARCITY POSTS

92. The One Mistake You Are Making Every Time You _____
93. Secrets To _____
94. The Top Secrets From _____
95. Mistakes That _____ Never Make
96. My Biggest Mistake With _____
97. Why _____ Is Actually Good For Your _____
98. The Only _____ Things You Need to Succeed In _____
99. Don't Ever _____, Here Is Why
100. Are You Missing These _____ Uncommon Signs To _____?

CONSENSUS POSTS

101. Everyone Does _____, You Should Too
102. The Majority Of _____ Do This Every _____
103. Why No One Is _____ Your _____

UPLIFTING POSTS

104. Want To Be Truly _____? Start Each Day With _____
105. The _____ Best _____ Of All Time
106. Become A Successful _____ By Doing _____
107. 1 Simple Rule To _____
108. Why _____ Love _____
109. Create A Kickass _____
110. Top _____ Tools I Use Every _____

CONTROVERSIAL POSTS

111. Before _____, You Must Do _____
112. If You _____, You Will _____
113. Do _____ If You Want People To _____
114. Why I Still Need _____
115. Why _____ Make The Best Friends
116. Dear _____, This Is Why I Recognize You From A Mile Away
117. Now I Understand Why _____
118. The Do's And Don'ts Of _____
119. Do You Really Know How To _____?
120. Does Having A Bad _____ Make Being A Bad _____?
121. A Quick Way To Deal With _____
122. Why You Need To Get Rid Of _____

HELPFUL POSTS

123. Start A _____ In _____ Easy Steps
124. Super Simple _____ To Get Stuff Done
125. Completely Change Your _____ With _____
126. Critical Steps To _____
127. The Top 100 _____ You Need To _____
128. Start _____ In 15 Minutes
129. The Best Places To Buy _____
130. What To Wear To _____

GET MORE DONE, FASTER!

startamomblog.com

Figure 7.6 130 Blog Post Headlines Title Templates, Including Multiple Listicle Starters

Source: Start a Mom Blog, http://www.startamomblog.com/blog-post-headlines

Figure 7.1 to guide students). A creative spin on this idea can be torn from the pages of *Unstuck* by Noah Scalin as he suggests focusing on seven things. Perhaps this is "Seven Things Our President Could Have Done Differently," "Seven Tips for Studying," "Seven Songs Hamlet Might Have Listened to on His iPod," or even "Seven Preposterous Scientific Experiments." Oftentimes forced constraint to a number helps with creativity too.

- **Manage a Mission:** This example is similar to the "Be a Curator With a Cause," but it focuses on not changing people's ideas or perceptions but their actions. Have students think about a problem that plagues the school (e.g., unhealthy eating, eco-waste, stress) and begin to curate research, best practices, to support change.

- **Playlists With Purpose:** Create a playlist of videos or music that illustrates a greater theme or tone or flows through a character's transitions through the book. This is very similar to creating a score for a movie.

- **Create an Infographic:** Infographics are also a form of curation as they organize content and often elevate and distill a large range of ideas and information on a topic. Any one of the ideas listed above could be distilled into an infographic.

Curation activities can be as simple or complex as you like. The most important things to remember about curation is that it is not just putting a bunch of ideas and topics in an online manila folder; it is the act of carefully selecting relevant information on a topic, pulling from a variety of sources, and making personal connections to and evaluations of the content that adds value. Sometimes it is helpful to talk about what a topic is and what it isn't. To that end, I have adapted a graphic from Austin Kleon to highlight the differences between good curation and bad curation (Figure 7.7).

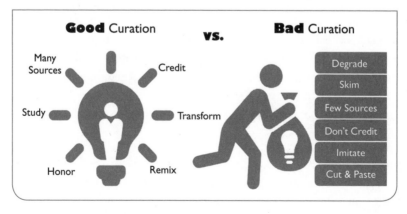

Figure 7.7 Good Curation Versus Bad Curation

Source: Adapted from Austin Kleon (2015)

With this book, I have sought to provide both analog and digital means to improve college and career-ready communication in our students. In each chapter, I have provided both paper-and-pencil, face-to-face, and digital options and activities for fostering these skills. Though curation may appear slanted toward a stylus and a sketchnoting app or tools like Pinterest and Scoop.it, I challenge you to consider curation as a brain dump and distillation practice of knowledge that is not tethered to any tool in particular. For years, I kept handwritten journals and notes. In 2011, I jumped ship and gravitated to Evernote and Pinterest. I used Evernote for all of my notes because I love having access to them on any device, the ease of search tools, and knowing that they were cloud based so I would never lose them. For ideas and inspirations, I chose Pinterest because it was more visual in nature. So, 5 years later, I rarely reference the notes from meetings and professional development in Evernote and only use Pinterest as inspiration file management (similar to a card catalogue, which I actually own). This is not to say that these tools are not beneficial, just that they didn't actually fulfill the entire purpose and need that I had in mind. Many us of may have jumped the shark when new technologies emerged and now may be letting the pendulum swing a little further back to some of our tried and true methods.

I still use these tools, but I found that for certain tasks, analog proved to be better for my own learning style. Rather than typing quotes and notes from a book into Evernote, I will read and highlight the entire book. Once I have finished reading it, I curate my learning and reflections through hand-drawn summaries, graphs, and lexicon libraries (Figure 7.8). Through this thoughtful distillation of content, I remember more of what I have read and access it far more often because all of it is contained in one easy to access book. Apparently, I am not alone in this finding. A recent article "How to Improve Your Reading Retention on Any Device" championed five tips. Three of which were (1) "make reading an active experience" by highlighting or making notes, (2) "repetition" of revisiting the content, and (3) "put it to use," which is a process even Ronald Reagan used to rephrase rather than regurgitate content (DuVall, 2014). And those who summarize what they read versus those who repeatedly reread remember 50 percent more material over the long term ("What's the best way to learn from a book?," 2012). I think the most important thing to remember is that what begins as pencil and paper (or pen and paper in my case) doesn't need to stay that way . . . as you can see these curations can be easily shared and augmented digitally as showcased in Figure 7.3.

Navigating curation, just like the rest of the formats of communication, comes down to purpose. If the purpose is to publish a collaborative collection of multimedia resources on a topic that you plan to add on to, then an online tool would most likely be preferable. But if the purpose is to distill meaning of a work or topic for personal use and have easy offline access to it, then a bound sketchnote or bullet journal might make more sense. If it is indeed a notetaking exercise and not a project, studies have found that laptop notetakers tend to "transcribe lectures verbatim

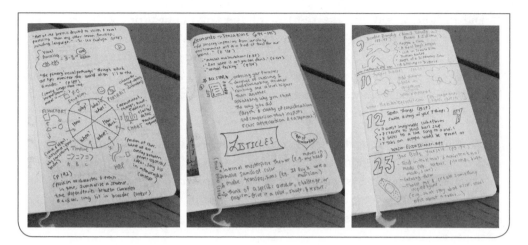

Figure 7.8 Curation Summaries of Books Using a Moleskine

rather than processing information and reframing it in their own words (which proves to be) detrimental to learning" (Mueller & Oppenheimer, 2014). In reality it is not so much digital versus analog but transcription versus transformation.

Yes, this idea tends to bleed into sketchnoting and mind-mapping, which may be somewhat familiar territories. What is important to remember is that curation isn't just the content, but it is how it is organized and structured that matters as well.

Making interesting connections, providing a different angle of the world or a topic, and crafting a new point of view is one way students can practice creativity and innovation. Two of my favorite curations are that of Karen Zack and Diane Muldrow. Karen Zack (Twitter handle: @teenybiscuit) creates mashups of seemingly unrelated items. Seeing a visual connection between a puppy and a bagel, a parrot and guacamole, or a chihuahua and a muffin will most likely not end world hunger, but fine-tuning our ability for inquiry and innovation might. A more refined idea of creative curation is what Diane Muldrow has done with Golden Books where she thoughtfully aggregates pages from 60 different Golden Books that span more than 70 years to tell one unique story about life's lessons, "Everything I Need to Know I Learned from a Little Golden Book."

Before we break out into a Beauty and the Beast showtune and sing from the rooftops about seeing something that wasn't there before, at its core curation is creativity and critical thinking. Back in 2012, I had co-hosted a podcast called "Appy Hours 4 U." At the heart of the show was curation. Each episode brought together a list of apps that all had a common theme (e.g., comics, literacy, screencasting, cautionary). The most popular of these was one we titled "Surprisingly Educational" where we knitted together a flight of seemingly non-educational entertainment apps (like My PlayHome, Snapguide, and Talking Tom) and discussed how they could be used instructionally. While people tuned in for the list of apps, they stayed tuned in for the commentary and insight. Curation, like the rest of the communication skills, isn't about seeking Oz or reaching a pot of instructional gold. It is about creating a magnet for the things we know will make our students workforce- and life-ready. When we start paying attention to these skills all around us, it is very easy to bring these nuggets into our classroom because we are actively paying attention to them in our own surroundings.

Curation can be fun and it can come in a variety of formats (e.g., collages, books, podcasts). But if we don't sharpen our skills and utilize our judgment to process content on a regular basis, it will be much harder when we want to leverage and utilize these skills in academic settings or in careers. Some skills are learned and easy to pick up again, like riding a bike, and others take years of practice and opportunity to hone.

What Is the Value of Critically Evaluating Curation for My Students?

When I started writing this chapter, I found a 2011 post titled "An Open Letter to Everyone Using the Word 'Curate' Incorrectly on the Internet." The biggest issue was that people who were actually curators felt that the term had been hijacked.

> *"I believe curating is the passing of a torch. It is the care and protection of cultural property. It is something not to be undertaken lightly, and it does not happen with the click of a mouse."*
>
> **—Peter Morin** *(Curator)*

While this post was written at the time Pinterest was taking off and I do acknowledge the ever-evolving nature of the English language, I think it important to recognize the legacy of the word in the context of museums, galleries, and data. Curation implies care; care for the work, care for the process, and care for the legacy that is left by collecting and extending the existing body of original work. As I have mentioned in earlier chapters, the Mentorship program is by far one of my favorites, as it provides students with hands-on authentic learning experiences in an area of passion and interest. One of the most memorable was that of Isabella Savage. In her work mentoring with a Curator at the Harry Ransom Center, she was tasked to analyze the curated work of Frank Reaugh for range of media displayed. While these media had been documented in a checklist, Isabella discovered trends on the percentages of pastel works that appeared in each section that could further support and inform the thematic context of various sectors of the exhibition (Savage, 2015).

Beyond the mentorship experience, I remember Isabella stating how excited she was that the Harry Ransom Center published her work on their site alongside popular industry experts. Curation is more than a collection of ideas or artistic works; it is the act of adding value or determining insightful trends within a body of work or topic. There is much information on the Web. We are pummeled by it, but information alone does not impact change; connecting the dots of information to form knowledge and new ideas and perspectives does. Figure 7.9 highlights how creating new recipes led to two innovations created specifically for this book. Information as a stand-alone is rapidly becoming obsolete. Take libraries . . . I have witnessed several libraries weeding books. I don't think it is much of a surprise that the books that are removed are informational in nature, compilations of literature, history, and scientific advances. We can't predict the technological advances and scientific breakthroughs that our students will witness or perhaps engage in within their lifetime, but we can prepare them to connect the dots.

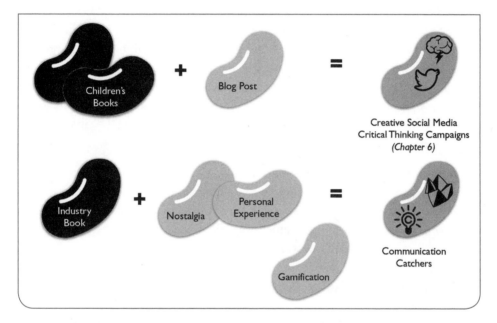

Figure 7.9 Graphical Representation of Idea Recipes

In the last chapter, we established that a good majority of secondary students are online and most likely have a variety of social media accounts. What better way to share content and increase visibility with prospective students than to use curation

> *"Trusted curation is the future."*
>
> —**Mark Cuban** *(Businessman and Investor, via* Shark Tank*)*

and social media tools to share stories and educational media and market your school? A quick Internet search revealed Pinterest boards for Stanford Graduate School of Business, The University of Texas at Austin, University of California, University of Oregon, University of Oklahoma, Ole Miss, Syracuse, Texas A&M, and Duke, just to name a few. They share a variety of content and images ranging from campus photos, traditions, and sporting events to school fashion, dorm hacks, and study tips. Some even have examples of famous alumni and published books by current professors. I share these examples for two reasons: one to state that curation has infiltrated far deeper than just the business realm, but also to make you aware that curation is now a form of marketing and knowledge persuasion.

Just like in the previous chapter on social media where we discussed being critical consumers of content, it is important to think about the underlying strategies of curation as a new way to communicate vision and voice. Now that you have an idea of what curation is, what value it holds for our students, and that it is a very real tool that colleges and careers use to establish thought leadership and visibility in an industry, let's build a deeper understanding of the underlying strategies used and decisions made while curating. While there are multiple ideas and definitions for what curation actually is, I think we can at least agree that curation is more than just the preservation and updating of content on a topic and that it at the very least is a collection of work that tells a story or imparts a message. At its best, curation actually requires a fair number of higher-order thinking skills to artfully analyze, evaluate, and distill content to create something that is original, has value, and offers intrigue and insight into a topic. When students write, oftentimes teachers will share mentor models . . . expert examples to evaluate or to provide insight into their own writing. Before having students curate, have them think critically, observe, and interpret curations of others. These could be infographics, listicles, Pinterest boards, an art gallery or museum exhibit, etc.

The activity in Figure 7.10 offers questions and strategies that can be used with college curations or a peer's curation designed from the Curation Communication Catcher in Figure 7.4. Having students individually review the same curations and/or different curations on the same topic allows for richer discussion on trends and analysis of how the content was organized and distilled.

What Are the Risks Associated With Curation?

Teaching students to think critically about what they curate online is also important. Beyond properly citing and attributing work (as mentioned in Chapter 4), curation also communicates a message about us as people. While curation is an orchestrated organization of a variety of sources and ideas, it too is a form of communication. While most of this chapter focused on the positive aspects of curation, I would be remiss to not include the risks as well. Most curation sites are also social media sites and are easily discovered via a Google search. Imagine a parent Googling your campus or prospective school district and happening on a Pinterest board of one of your teachers. This is exactly what happened to an elementary teacher in a Texas school. The parent found a popular Internet meme that said, "Do you want to hear a secret? You're the reason your teachers are alcoholics" (Ko, 2016) pinned to one of the teacher's personal boards. While I am sure that this Internet meme did not originate with this teacher and fairly certain that it was nothing more than a joke, public perceptions are very difficult to change. I am not saying we are what we pin, but I am saying that the best practices found in the prior chapter on social media also apply to curation. What we curate is a reflection of us and because it is online

Curation Analysis

Select a Curated Work

1. **Individually:** Select a curated work to evaluate. This could be a listicle, sketchnote, infographic, board, etc.

Individually

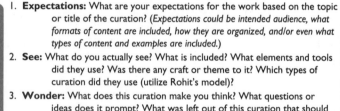

Analyze and Evaluate the Work

1. **Expectations:** What are your expectations for the work based on the topic or title of the curation? (*Expectations could be intended audience, what formats of content are included, how they are organized, and/or even what types of content and examples are included.*)
2. **See:** What do you actually see? What is included? What elements and tools did they use? Was there any craft or theme to it? Which types of curation did they use (utilize Rohit's model)?
3. **Wonder:** What does this curation make you think? What questions or ideas does it prompt? What was left out of this curation that should have been added?
4. **Connect:** What was the most interesting piece of information or artifact included? What new knowledge on the topic did you gain from the curation?
5. **Extend and Explore:** What could I do to extend or expand or modify this collection? Where would I find these items and content to extend this resource? How would I search for them?

Individually

Compare and Contrast Evaluations

1. **Same Curation:** Compare and contrast your findings to another student who analyzed the same curation.
2. **Same Topic but Different Curation:** Compare and contrast your findings to another student who analyzed the same topic but chose a different curation or source.

With a Series of Partners

Figure 7.10 Curation Analysis Handout

Available for download at **https://resources.corwin.com/cultivatingcomm**

and not in a binder that we only share with colleagues, and/or have an opportunity to explain our rationale for selections: We have to be cognizant of what and how we curate. This is also a powerful lesson to share and conversation to have with our students. How would your parents, college admissions board, or future boss feel about the content you curate online?

It is important to remember that with curation comes great responsibility ... responsibility to add value and care to others' content and ideas and responsibility to curate a positive picture of your online digital doppelgänger. We are judged by how we communicate online. We have to remember that this isn't just what we create or say but also our interests and opinions that are conveyed by what we curate, like, pin, and snap.

Chapter Resources

Curation Preparation Inventory Assessment

☐ What is the value of integrating curation activities into my curriculum?

☐ How can curation support lifelong learning?

☐ What activities will I use to explore curation within my curriculum?

☐ What is the value of critically evaluating current curations?

☐ How can I provide opportunities for both analog and digital curation experiences for my students?

☐ What types of curations and topics would I want my students to evaluate?

☐ How can I communicate both the benefits and side effects of curation with my students?

Share your answers using the hashtag #cultivatecomm.

My Students' Self-Assessment Checklist

☐ My students can articulate what curation is and provide examples.

☐ My students can use curation as a way to digest and distill information.

☐ My students can select appropriate tools (both analog and digital) and utilize effective processes for curation and distillation of content.

☐ My students are able to use and create a variety of types of curations.

☐ My students are able to analyze and evaluate a variety of types of curations.

☐ My students understand the perceptions around personal curations.

Additional Resources and Reading

- Curation Communication Catcher (found in Appendix B and on https://resources.corwin.com/cultivatingcomm)

- Curation Analysis Handout (found on https://resources.corwin.com/cultivat ingcomm)

- Suggested List of Curation Tools (found on https://resources.corwin.com/ cultivatingcomm)

- Suggested Reading and Resources (found on www.pinterest.com/techchef4u/ communicating-through-curation)

References

CoSchedule. (2015). How to schedule your social media content curation for massive growth. *Slideshare.net*. Retrieved October 14, 2016, from http://www.slideshare.net/ coschedule/how-to-schedule-your-social-media-content-curation-for-massive-growth -infographic

DuVall, J. (2014). How to improve your reading retention on any device [Crew Blog]. Retrieved July 21, 2016, from https://blog.crew.co/reading-retention/?utm_ content=bufferf4189&utm_medium=social&utm_source=twitter.com&utm_ campaign=buffer

Kleon, A. (2015). *The steal like an artist journal: A notebook for creative kleptomaniacs*. New York, NY: Workman Publishing Company.

Ko, S. (2015). Harlandale ISD teacher investigated for social media posts. *KENS 5*. Retrieved April 7, 2016, from http://legacy.kens5.com/story/news/2015/05/22/ harlandale-posts-teacher-pinterest-columbia-heights-elementary/27825705/

Mueller, P., & Oppenheimer, D. (2014). The pen is mightier than the keyboard: Advantages of longhand over laptop note taking. *Psychological Science, 25*(6), 1159–1168. http://dx.doi.org/10.1177/0956797614524581

Redefining learning in a technology-driven world: A report to support the adoption of the ISTE Standards for Students. (2016). *Iste.org*. Retrieved July 14, 2016, from http:// www.iste.org/docs/Standards-Resources/iste-standards_students-2016_research-validity -report_final.pdf?sfvrsn=0.0680021527232122

Savage, I. (2015). Frank Reaugh's preferred medium. *Cultural Compass*. Retrieved April 9, 2016, from http://blog.hrc.utexas.edu/2015/12/01/frank-reaughs-preferred-medium/

Smith, C. (2014). 270 amazing Pinterest statistics. *DMR*. Retrieved April 7, 2016, from http://expandedramblings.com/index.php/pinterest-stats

What's the best way to learn from a book? (2012). Barking Up the Wrong Tree. Retrieved October 13, 2016, from http://www.bakadesuyo.com/2012/09/whats-the-best-way-to -learn-from-a-book

Book Study and Communication Cohort Challenges

My goal for this book was to create a resource that met the needs of teachers seeking to support their students in the classroom and beyond. My intent was to provide real-world examples, tangible exercises, and easily accessible pedagogical practices tied to research and modeled after industry experts. While the book includes relevant research, I also wanted to make it an enjoyable read for teachers and leave them with something more than just direct applications for the students in the classroom.

To meet and nurture these communication skills, each chapter includes a book study template that can be completed individually as you read and then shared with a fellow colleague as you embark on this learning journey or perhaps even to facilitate an online book club. Figure A.1 depicts one for Chapter 1. All of the book study templates can be found on the companion website at https://resources .corwin.com/cultivatingcomm.

For those of you who would like to be challenged, optional communication exercises that use the tools and best practices highlighted in each chapter but are tailored to classroom teachers' professional learning are provided and found on the companion site as a quick checklist (Figure A.2). Sharing is caring, and learning in tandem with another professional in your hallway, zip code, time zone, or social network is always helpful to gain new insights and perspectives or just have the support of a colleague. Whether you embark on these challenges solo or with a professional posse, it is my hope that through these exercises, you stretch, deepen, hone, and flex your understanding for the content provided within this book.

And one more thing. Subscribe to the "Cultivating Communication in the Classroom" TechChef newsletter to receive valuable updates, the latest research, and additional resources to support fostering college and career readiness skills all year long. A link to subscribe can be found on the companion site.

Email Etiquette

Communicating with PEERS and PROFESSIONALS to elicit an action or response through clear communication, self-advocacy, and due diligence.

Favorite quote or piece of research:

What other C's are addressed (e.g., Critical Thinking, Creativity, Collaboration) in this chapter?

What social and emotional learning core competencies are addressed?

3 strategies I plan to use with my students:

Teacher challenges I plan to tackle OR tools and "suggested reading" I plan to explore:

Additional support and suggested reading can be found at https://resources.corwin.com/cultivatingcomm

Figure A.1 Book Study Guides for Each Chapter

Available for download at **https://resources.corwin.com/cultivatingcomm**

Communication Cohort Challenges

Email

☐ What is the most important takeaway your students should have in regard to the use of email? Craft this in 6 words or 140 characters or less.

☐ **CHALLENGE 1A:** Try to achieve 0 Inbox (an approach at keeping your email inbox empty or almost empty).

☐ **CHALLENGE 1B:** Compose an email of gratitude to a staff member, parent, or student.

Collaboration

☐ What is the most important thing that needs to be in place for collaborative groups to be positively interdependent? Craft this in 6 words or 140 characters or less.

☐ **CHALLENGE 2A:** Recreate the Uffe Elbaek with a curricular spin using different labels for each axis. How might this model be appropriate for a historical character, literary or political figure, or even strategies students use to tackle a math or science problem?

☐ **CHALLENGE 2B:** Create a Cootie (or Communication) Catcher for another group activity. Multiple curricular examples have been curated here: https://www.pinterest.com/techchef4u/surprisingly-educational-paper-fortune-tellers

Visual Literacy & Presentations

☐ As you read this chapter, choose a color, symbol, or image that best represents or captures something you found to be interesting, important, or insightful within this chapter and tweet it.

☐ Consider your current classroom reality and challenge yourself to make it your preferred reality with this sentence completion activity.
  • Student presentations are like _____ because _____.
  • Student presentations can be like _____ if _____.

☐ Which aspects and features of visual literacy, slide design, and presentations were the most interesting or exciting to you?

☐ **CHALLENGE 3A:** Take a look at a previous student presentation and see if you can modify a slide or two with the best practices delineated within this chapter.

☐ **CHALLENGE 3B:** Transform an old syllabus or handout using the tips and best practices shared in this chapter.

☐ **CHALLENGE 3C:** Create the same presentation in three different pieces of software and create a pros and cons list for each tool.

Additional support and suggested reading can be found at https://resources.corwin.com/cultivatingcomm

Figure A.2a Communication Cohort Challenges

Available for download at **https://resources.corwin.com/cultivatingcomm**

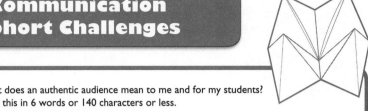

Communication Cohort Challenges

Projects & Publishing

- ☐ What does an authentic audience mean to me and for my students? Craft this in 6 words or 140 characters or less.
- ☐ **CHALLENGE 4A:** Develop a Keep/Change/Improve model to explore and revamp existing projects. What aspects of an existing project do you currently employ that you would like to KEEP? What aspects and parameters do you currently use that you would like to CHANGE (remove and/or replace with a different strategy)? What aspects and parameters do you currently use that you would like to IMPROVE?
- ☐ **CHALLENGE 4B:** Create a school or classroom hashtag and process for sharing student original images.
- ☐ **CHALLENGE 4C:** Explore your own visual style and consider adopting a consistent way of creating documents or media for your students or your teacher blog or class website.

Portfolios & Resumes

- ☐ Complete this following Visible Thinking stem… "I used to think Portfolios… but now I think Portfolios…"
- ☐ What is your WHY for Digital Portfolios for your students? Craft this in 6 words or 140 characters or less.
- ☐ Which aspects and features of a Digital Portfolio platform are most important to you?
- ☐ **CHALLENGE 5A:** Create your own Digital Portfolio Index for your class.
- ☐ **CHALLENGE 5B:** Begin creating your own Teaching Portfolio or Blogfolio.
- ☐ **CHALLENGE 5C:** Update your resume or research visual curriculum vitaes and create one.

Social Media

- ☐ How can I guide my students to create a positive digital doppelgänger? Craft this in 6 words or 140 characters or less.
- ☐ **CHALLENGE 6A:** Create a school or classroom social media account (e.g., Facebook, Twitter, Instagram, Snapchat) and share with parents so they can follow the learning and the stories in the classroom.
- ☐ **CHALLENGE 6B:** Engage in some of the activities and challenges provided for students within the chapter using your own social media accounts.

Curation

- ☐ What will curation mean for me and my curriculum? Craft this in 6 words or 140 characters or less.
- ☐ **CHALLENGE 7A:** Create a curation for your school or PLN. Perhaps it is curating educational articles on a topic, a board of professional books that people post and share reviews of as they read them, or exemplar lessons you would like to explore.
- ☐ **CHALLENGE 7B:** Start a Curation Club where people find great ideas online and actually do them in the classroom (e.g., select a lesson or educational craft your find online, bring supplies to make or execute it, and actually make it).

Additional support and suggested reading can be found at https://resources.corwin.com/cultivatingcomm

Figure A.2b Communication Cohort Challenges

Available for download at **https://resources.corwin.com/cultivatingcomm**

Communication Catchers

Communication Catchers have been included in each chapter to support you and your students. Additionally, blank copies have been included in this book and on the companion site. The Communication Catchers, while not intended to be a comprehensive curricular resource, are designed to support choice, conversations, and creativity. Learning doesn't have to be serious to be impactful. I remember creating these in high school for fun and recently my elementary-age son started making these in school. The beauty of these Communication Catchers, aka fortune tellers, is they blend the old school tangible paper and memories of our olden days with an updated appeal. With these Communication Catchers, I have also baked in tangible and tactile ways to include gamification and customization through inquiry.

If this "craftivity" idea is intriguing to you, visit the companion site where I have curated additional curricular examples of fortune tellers. If you would like to create your own fortune teller and have it featured on the site, please email it to me at techchef4u@gmail.com.

How to Make the Communication Catcher

1. **Cut and Fold:** Cut out the Communication Catcher. Place the square face up and fold and unfold the square in diagonals from corner to corner. The folds should create an X.

2. **Flip and Fold:** Place the square facedown and fold each of the corners to meet the center.

3. **Flip and Fold:** Turn the paper over. The flaps should be face down. Fold each of the four corners so the points meet in the center.

4. **Fold:** Fold the square in half from side to side. Unfold and fold the square from bottom to top.

5. **Wear, Pinch, and Play:** Slide both thumbs and index fingers under the four flaps. Pinch the top corners together with the thumbs and index fingers under the four flaps.

Available for download at **https://resources.corwin.com/cultivatingcomm**

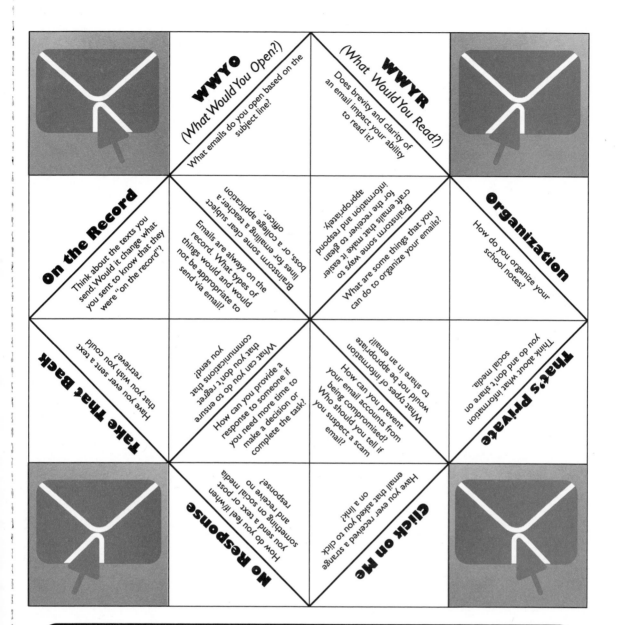

WWYO
(What Would You Open?)
What emails do you open based on the subject line?

WWYR
(What Would You Read?)
Does brevity and clarity of an email impact your ability to read it?

On the Record
Think about the texts you send. Would it change what you sent to know that they were "on the record"?

Emails are always on the record. What types of things would and would not be appropriate to send via email?

Brainstorm some clear subject lines for emailing a teacher, a boss, or a college application officer.

Brainstorm emails that make it easier for the receiver to glean information and respond appropriately.

What are some things that you can do to organize your emails?

Organization
How do you organize your school notes?

Take That Back
Have you ever sent a text that you wish you could retrieve?

What can you do to ensure communications that you don't regret you send?

How can you provide a response to someone if you need more time to make a decision or complete the task?

How can you prevent your email accounts from being compromised? Who should you tell if you suspect a scam email?

What types of information would not be appropriate to share in an email?

Think about what information you do and don't share on social media.

That's Private

No Response
How do you feel if/when you send a text or post something on social media and receive no response?

Have you ever received a strange email that asked you to click on a link?

Click on Me

---

1. **Cut:** Cut out Email Etiquette Communication Catcher and turn over with text side down.
2. **Fold:** Fold like a Cootie Catcher.
3. **Play:** Insert fingers in four corners.
4. **Interact:** Determine who has the greatest number of email accounts, and use that number to move the Communication Catcher.
5. **Choice:** Read the directions for the activity you land on by opening the flap. Complete the discussion.

Email Etiquette Communication Catcher

Available for download at https://resources.corwin.com/cultivatingcomm

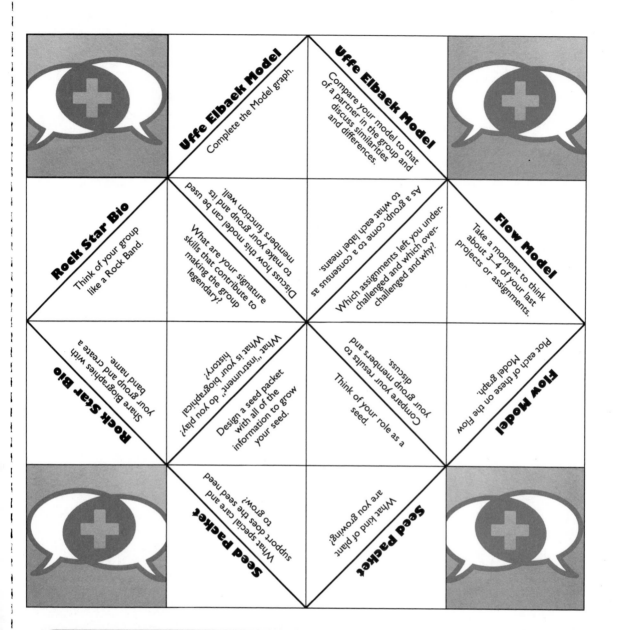

Uffe Elbaek Model
Complete the Model graph.

Uffe Elbaek Model
Compare your model to that of a partner in the group and discuss similarities and differences.

As a group come to a consensus as to what each label means.

Which assignments left you under-challenged and which over-challenged and why?

Flow Model
Take a moment to think about 3–4 of your last projects or assignments.

Rock Star Bio
Think of your group like a Rock Band.

What are your signature skills that contribute to making the group legendary?

Discuss how this model can be used to make your group and its members function well.

What "instrument" do you play? What is your blog/biographical history?

Compare your results to your group members and discuss.

Think of your role as a seed.

Plot each of these on the Flow Model graph.

Flow Model

Rock Star Bio
Share Biographies with your group and create a band name.

Design a seed packet with all of the information to grow your seed.

Seed Packet
What special care and support does the seed need to grow?

What kind of plant are you growing?

Seed Packet

1. **Cut:** Cut out Role and Interactivity Communication Catcher and turn over with text side down.
2. **Fold:** Fold like a Cootie Catcher.
3. **Play:** Insert fingers in four corners.
4. **Interact:** Determine who has the greatest number of pets, siblings, etc., and use that number to move the Communication Catcher.
5. **Choice:** Read the directions for the activity you land on by opening the flap. Complete the discussion.

Role and Interactivity Communication Catcher

Available for download at https://resources.corwin.com/cultivatingcomm

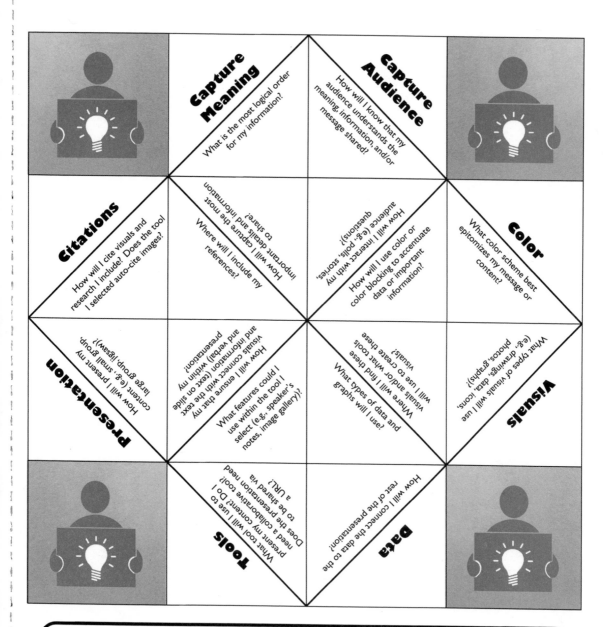

Capture Meaning — What is the most logical order for my information?

Capture Audience — How will I know that my audience understands the meaning, information, and/or message shared?

Citations — How will I cite visuals and research I include? Does the tool I selected auto-cite images?

How will I capture the most important details and information to share? Where will I include my references?

How will I interact with my audience (e.g., polls, stories, questions)?

Color — What color scheme best epitomizes my message or content? How will I use color or color blocking to accentuate data or important information?

Presentation — How will I present my content (e.g., small group, large group, jigsaw)?

How will I ensure that my visuals connect with the text and information (text on slide and verbal) within my presentation? What features could I use within the tool I select (e.g., speaker's notes, image gallery)?

Visuals — What types of visuals will I use (e.g., drawings, data, icons, photos, graphs)? Where will I find these visuals and/or what tools will I use to create these visuals? What types of data and graphs will I use?

Tools — What tool will I use to present my content? Do I need a collaborative tool? Does the presentation need to be shared via a URL?

Data — How will I connect the data to the rest of the presentation?

1. **Cut:** Cut out Presentation Planner Communication Catcher and turn over with text side down.
2. **Fold:** Fold like a Cootie Catcher.
3. **Play:** Insert fingers in four corners.
4. **Interact:** Determine who has the most photo editing apps or tools on their phone, and use that number to move the Communication Catcher.
5. **Choice:** Read the directions for the activity you land on by opening the flap. Complete the discussion.

Presentation Planner Communication Catcher

Available for download at https://resources.corwin.com/cultivatingcomm

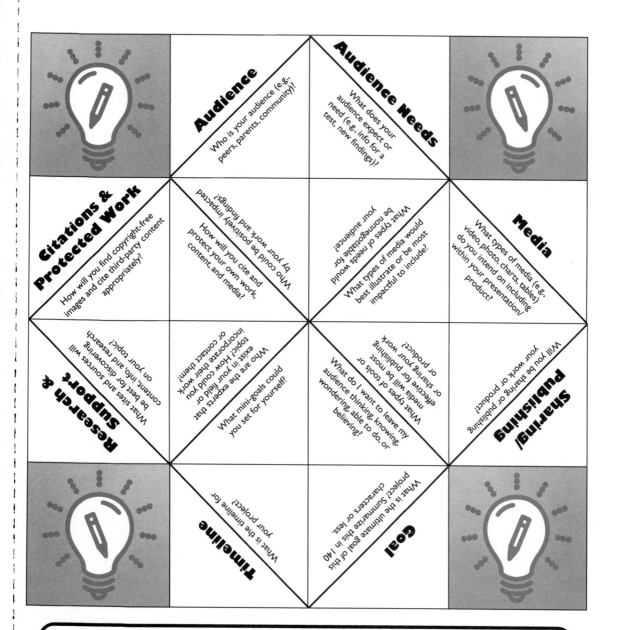

Project Inquiry Communication Catcher

1. **Cut:** Cut out Project Inquiry Communication Catcher and turn over with text side down.
2. **Fold:** Fold like a Cootie Catcher.
3. **Play:** Insert fingers in four corners.
4. **Interact:** Determine who has the most publishing or creating apps or tools on their phone or iPad, and use that number to move the Communication Catcher.
5. **Choice:** Read the directions for the activity you land on by opening the flap. Complete the discussion.

Project Inquiry Communication Catcher

Available for download at **https://resources.corwin.com/cultivatingcomm**

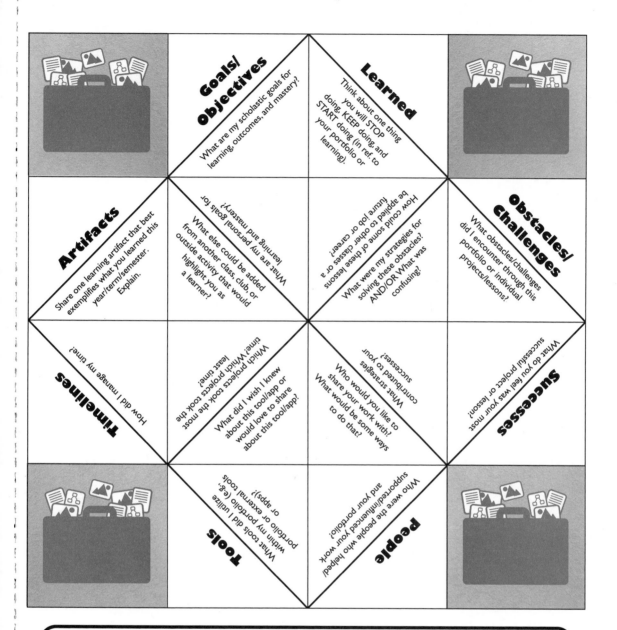

Goals/objectives
What are my scholastic goals for learning, outcomes, and mastery?

Learned
Think about one thing you will STOP doing, KEEP doing, and START doing (in ref to your portfolio or learning).

Artifacts
Share one learning artifact that best exemplifies what you learned this year/term/semester. Explain.

What else could be added from another class, club, or outside activity that would highlight you as a learner?

What are my personal goals for learning and mastery?

How could some of these lessons be applied to other classes or a future job or career?

What were my strategies for solving these obstacles? AND/OR What was confusing?

Obstacles/challenges
What obstacles/challenges did I encounter through this portfolio or individual projects/lessons?

Timelines
How did I manage my time?

Which projects took the most time? Which projects took the least time?

What did I wish I knew about this tool/app or would love to share about this tool/app?

Who would you like to share your work with? What would be some ways to do that?

What strategies contributed to your successes?

What do you feel was your most successful project or lesson?

Successes

What tools did I utilize within my portfolio or supported/influenced your work and your portfolio? external tools or apps?

Who were the people who helped

Tools

People

1. **Cut:** Cut out Peer Portfolio Communication Catcher and turn over with text side down.
2. **Fold:** Fold like a Cootie Catcher.
3. **Play:** Insert fingers in four corners.
4. **Interact:** Determine who has the most summer jobs, and use that number to move the Communication Catcher.
5. **Choice:** Read the directions for the activity you land on by opening the flap. Complete the discussion.

Peer Portfolio Communication Catcher

Available for download at **https://resources.corwin.com/cultivatingcomm**

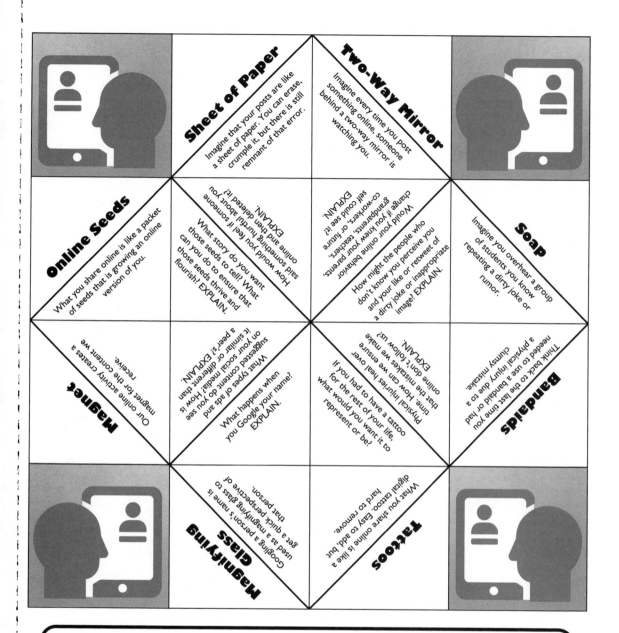

Sheet of Paper
Imagine that your posts are like a sheet of paper. You can erase, crumple it, but there is still remnant of that error.

Two-Way Mirror
Imagine every time you post something online, someone behind a two-way mirror is watching you.

Online Seeds
What you share online is like a packet of seeds that is growing an online version of you.

What story do you want those seeds to tell? What can you do to ensure that those seeds thrive and flourish? EXPLAIN.

How would you feel if someone said something hurtful about you online and then deleted it? EXPLAIN.

Would your online behavior change if you knew your parents, grandparents, co-workers, teachers, self could see it? EXPLAIN.

How might the people who don't know you perceive you and your like or retweet of a dirty joke or inappropriate image? EXPLAIN.

Soap
Imagine you overhear a group of students you know repeating a dirty joke or rumor.

Magnet
Our online activity creates a magnet for the content we receive.

What types of ads and suggested content do you see on your social media? How is it similar or different than a peer's? EXPLAIN.

What happens when you Google your name? EXPLAIN.

If you had to have a tattoo for the rest of your life, what would you want it to represent or be?

Physical injuries heal over time. How can we ensure that the mistakes we make online don't follow us? EXPLAIN.

Bandaids
Think back to the last time you needed to use a bandaid or had a physical injury due to a clumsy mistake.

Magnifying Glass
Googling a person's name is used as a magnifying glass to get a quick perspective of that person.

What you share online is like a digital tattoo: Easy to add, but hard to remove.

Tattoos

---

1. **Cut:** Cut out Digital Doppelgänger Communication Catcher and turn over with text side down.
2. **Fold:** Fold like a Cootie Catcher.
3. **Play:** Insert fingers in four corners.
4. **Interact:** Determine who can name the greatest number of social media accounts, and use that number to move the Communication Catcher.
5. **Choice:** Read the directions for the activity you land on by opening the flap. Complete the discussion.

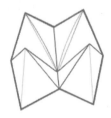

Digital Doppelgänger Communication Catcher

Available for download at **https://resources.corwin.com/cultivatingcomm**

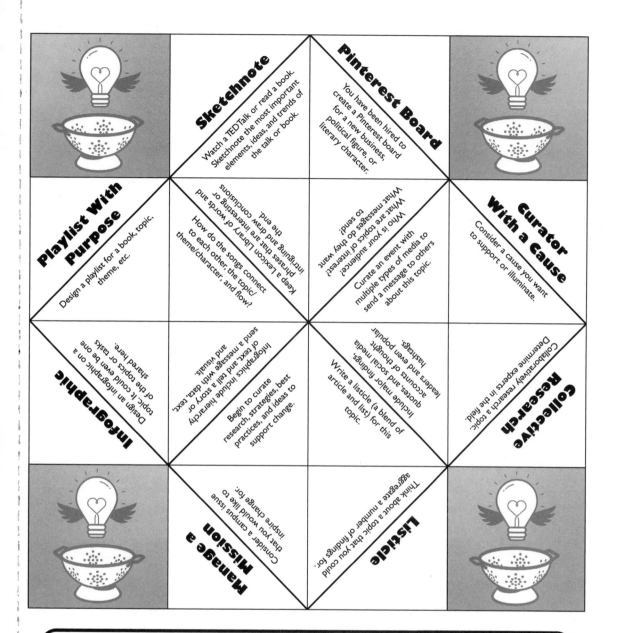

Sketchnote

Watch a TED Talk or read a book. Sketchnote the most important elements, ideas, and trends of the talk or book.

Pinterest Board

You have been hired to create a Pinterest board for a new business, political figure, or literary character:

What messages do they want to send?

Who is your audience? What are topics of interest?

Curate an event with multiple types of media to send a message to others about this topic.

Curator With a Cause

Consider a cause you want to support or illuminate.

Playlist With Purpose

Design a playlist for a book, topic, theme, etc.

Keep a Lexicon Library of words and phrases that are interesting or intriguing and draw conclusions or the end.

How do the songs connect to each other, the topic/theme/character, and flow?

Infographics include hierarchy of text and tell a story or send a message with data, text, and visuals.

Begin to curate research, strategies, best practices, and ideas to support change.

Write a listicle (a blend of article and list) for this topic:

Include major findings, quotes, and social media accounts, or thought leaders and even popular hashtags.

Determine experts in the field.

Collaboratively research a topic:

Collective Research

Infographic

Design an infographic on a topic; it could even be one of the topics or tasks shared here.

Manage a Mission

Consider a campus issue that you would like to inspire change for:

Think about a topic that you could aggregate a number of findings for:

Listicle

1. **Cut:** Cut out Curation Communication Catcher and turn over with text side down.
2. **Fold:** Fold like a Cootie Catcher.
3. **Play:** Insert fingers in four corners.
4. **Interact:** Determine who has visited the greatest number of art galleries or museums, and use that number to move the Communication Catcher.
5. **Choice:** Read the directions for the activity you land on by opening the flap. Complete the discussion.

Curation Communication Catcher

Available for download at **https://resources.corwin.com/cultivatingcomm**

SEL Index

It may not come as a surprise that the industry interviews found all social-emotional learning (SEL) skills to be important and self-management, responsible decision making, and relationship skills to lead the pack. How we communicate with people oftentimes is directly related to our own self-awareness and management. Threading these social-emotional learning competencies throughout the book is vital to students building the foundation for effective communication skills in college, careers, and beyond. While not an exhaustive list, the index below provides a quick reference to locate some of the targeted activities that were thoughtfully designed to tackle and traverse these competencies:

SEL Skill*	Chapter	Activity
Self-Awareness: *Recognizing one's emotions and values as well as one's strengths and limitations*	1, 2, 4, 5, 6	1. Email Etiquette Communication Catcher, Future Me, Anticipate Needs With an Autoresponder 2. Setting Norms, Taking Sides, Role Playing, Flow Model, The Uffe Elbaek Model, Rock Star Bios, Glows and Grows, Independent and Group Rubric, Ideation and Group Think 4. Project Inquiry Communication Catcher 5. Portfolio Index, Peer Portfolio Communication Catcher, Resume and Interview Activities 6. Mirroring Masks, Digital Doppelgänger Communication Catcher
Self-Management: *Managing emotions and behaviors to achieve one's goals*	1, 2, 4, 5, 6	1. Email Etiquette Communication Catcher, Future Me, Ask Me 2. Role Playing, Seed Packet, Flow Model, The Uffe Elbaek Model, Glows and Grows, Independent and Group Rubric 4. Project Inquiry Communication Catcher 5. Peer Portfolio Communication Catcher, Resume and Interview Activities 6. Mirroring Masks

SEL Skill*	Chapter	Activity
Social Awareness: *Showing understanding and empathy for others*	1, 2, 3, 5, 6, 7	1. Emails From the Past, Ask Me, Persuade Me, Miss Me, Embrace Emoticons, Email an Expert, Anticipate Needs With an Autoresponder 2. Setting Norms, Taking Sides, The Uffe Elbaek Model, Glows and Grows, Group Quizzes, Flipped Lit Circles, Problem and Idea Swapping, Ideation and Group Think 3. Presentation Planner 5. Peer Portfolio Communication Catcher, Resume and Interview Activities 6. Mirroring Masks, Digital Doppelgänger Communication Catcher, News and Social Media Analysis 7. Curation Communication Catcher, Curation Analysis
Relationship Skills: *Forming positive relationships, working in teams, dealing effectively with conflict*	1, 2, 3, 4, 5, 6	1. Email Etiquette Communication Catcher, Ask Me, Persuade Me, Embrace Emoticons, Class Newsletter 2. Setting Norms, Role Playing, Seed Packet, Group Shuffle, Rock Star Bios, Glows and Grows, Group Quizzes, Flipped Lit Circles, Problem and Idea Swapping, Ideation and Group Think, Saboteur 3. Presentation Planner 4. Project Inquiry Communication Catcher 5. Peer Portfolio Communication Catcher, Resume and Interview Activities 6. Mirroring Masks 7. Curation Analysis
Responsible Decision Making: *Making ethical, constructive choices about personal and social behavior*	1, 2, 5, 6	1. Ask Me, Persuade Me 2. Setting Norms, Role Playing, Seed Packet, Glows and Grows, Group Quizzes, Flipped Lit Circles, Problem and Idea Swapping, Ideation and Group Think, Saboteur 5. Peer Portfolio Communication Catcher 6. Mirroring Masks, Digital Doppelgänger Communication Catcher, News and Social Media Analysis

Source: *SEL competencies reproduced from Austin Independent School District, https://www.austinisd.org/academics/sel

Ultimately, social-emotional learning skills have to be intertwined with task and career specific competencies to cultivate 21st century communicators that will be effective in college and future careers.

For more information on SEL skills and competencies, visit www.casel.org/social-and-emotional-learning.

> "I think all the SEL competencies are hugely important, but they aren't enough. For example, I recently worked with someone very self-aware, who totally owned their shortcomings and apologized when they made mistakes. But after 10 months of apologies and shortcoming ownership, I was less patient, and it became clear that those limitations were prohibiting that person from executing the tasks they were assigned, [or developed for themselves]. So SEL skills without competency isn't enough."
>
> **—Andrew Gardner** *(VP Professional Learning at BrainPOP)*

APPENDIX D

Industry Insights

The industry insights mentioned in the preface and woven throughout the book are intended to anchor the skills, suggestions, and strategies shared in each chapter. There is no need to speculate how to collaborate within a team or what are the most important things someone looks for in a resume. Technology has broadened our network and in doing so our knowledge base. The industry insights were gleaned from family, friends, and colleagues and a variety of career fields ranging from real estate, litigation, and software design to veterinarians and a makeup and hair artist. While these communication skills and strategies delineated within the book are designed for the classroom, I think you will find that there is no industry or career that isn't impacted.

I want to first thank all of those friends, family, and colleagues that honestly shared their insights with candor and class. Beyond reading these, I hope you consider utilizing this information beyond a cursory glance, so I have provided some jumping-off points.

- **Poll Current Students:** Feel free to use the same questions from the survey with your own students and see how they respond. This serves as a KWL as you will get a good pulse for what they know and don't.

- **Poll Parents:** Parents are such an untapped and underutilized resource. Elementary classrooms have career days but very rarely do we call upon parents in secondary classrooms to offer insight on their own career. Parents would also make a great panel discussion for this topic as well.

- **Poll Former Students:** If you have a way to keep in contact with your middle school students when they go to high school or high school students after they leave your institution, consider polling them and getting their lessons learned and "wish I had known this" truisms.

- **Poll Your Network:** Geography is no longer a barrier to knowledge. Don't hesitate to poll your friends on Facebook or even bring one in using a video conferencing application.

All eight questions for the initial survey have been included below for your reference:

1. How important are these skills (e.g., email etiquette, collaboration and team functionality, visual literacy, social media)?

2. How prepared are applicants for these skills in these areas?

3. How important are SEL skills to your role or and/or profession?

4. What are the most persuasive things you look for in a resume and interview to hire an applicant? Explain.

5. How important is email in your business? What are some best practices you use for email with customers, clients, colleagues, etc.? Explain.

6. What communication skills do you wish you had learned in high school or college that would have better prepared you for your profession/career?

7. How do you ensure that teams are productive, work well together, and meet deadlines? How do you intervene in a group if they are not positively interdependent? Explain.

8. If you could give our current middle school or high school students one piece of advice for the future, what would it be?

INDEX

Abbreviations, 13–14
Accuracy, email best practices, xxx
Action items, in email, 5, 6
Activity buckets, 32
Advertorials, as project idea, 77–79
Advice for future, industry insights, 140
Agendas, collaborative, 35, 42
Ahn, June, 102
ALS Ice Bucket Challenge, 134
Amazon, curation by, 142
American Sign Language (ASL)
    project, 85, 86
Anaphora, visual, 54
App dice, 76, 78
Apple Distinguished Educators, 115
Apples to Apples, 59
Appropriate use in students' projects
    and publishing, 73, 86–92
  credit for and license for work, 91–92
  permissions and copyrights, 87
  plagiarism, 87, 90
  visual style, 88–91
  watermarks, 88
"Appy Hours 4 U" podcast, 151
Archival, online, and social media
    changes, 125
Are They Really Ready to Work?, xix, 1
Art portfolio photographs, 58
Ask 3 model, 6
Ask Me, 11
ASL (American Sign Language)
    project, 85, 86
Assembly app, 59
Attention to detail, in resume
    and interview, 96
Audience
  attention in presentations, 50
  in email, 5
  participation in presentations, 64–65
Authentic audience for students' projects and
    publishing, 73, 84–86
  cross-design within campus, 86

international entities as, 85
local entities as, 85
national entities as, 85
other campuses, 86
school newspapers, 86
Autonomy and choice in student projects,
    73, 74–84
  project ideas, 76–83
  why, how, and what in Golden Circle,
    of project assignments, 74, 83
Autoresponder, in email, 12–13

Badura, Craig, 131–132
Be. (Descoteaux), 136
Beat sheets, as project idea, 76
Bell, Kasey, 89–90
Bellow, Adam, 65
Best practices
  for curation, 154
  for digital portfolios, 99–100
  for drafting presentations, 47, 49–65
  for social media, 154
  for using email, xxx, 2–5
Billboards, 51, 54
Bio, for resume, 114
*Blended Leadership: Six Simple Beliefs
    for Leading Online and Off*, 89
Blog post headlines, title templates, 148
Bloom's Taxonomy, 107–108, 111
Blue Poles (Pollock), 64
Boaler, Jo, 25
Body movement and positions,
    and delivery in presentations, 62
Body shaming, 125
Book Creator app, 85
Book map, xxii
Books, curation summaries of, 150–152
Book study guides, 158–161
Brady, Colin, 141
Brainstorming, collaborative sessions, 37
Branding student images, 20, 88–90,
    115, 117

Bravim, Luiz, 65
Bread crumbs, visual, and delivery
    in presentations, 63–64
Brown, Maureen, xviii
Bulb portfolio, 108–109
Bullying, 125, 127
Burvall, Amy, 89–90
Buzzfeed, 76

*Caffeine for the Creative Team: 150 Exercises to
    Inspire Group Innovation* (Murnaw and
    Oldfield), 30–31, 33
Cannon, Natalie, 75
Canva, 59, 116, 118, 144–145
Career portfolio, 115
Career readiness, xxiii, 113–119
*Careers: The Graphic Guide to Finding the
    Perfect Job for You*, 119
CARP (control, acknowledge,
    refocus, problem-solve), 11
Causes
    curation for, 147
    and social media, 135
Center for High Quality Student
    Work, 111
ChapR.com, 136
Chimenti, Eric, 31
Choice in student projects. *See* Autonomy
    and choice in student projects
"Choose Your Own Adventure," 80, 82
Chua, Sacha, 144
Clarke, Todd, 82, 83
Class newsletter, 14
CNN, as news source, 129
The Coaching Habit, 110
Code switching, as communication skill, 18
Collaboration
    curation of research, 147
    importance to managers, xviii, 20
    remotely, as communication skill, 18
    in resume and interview, 96
Collaboration and positive
        interdependence, 19–40
    building community, 27–30
    collaborative learning, 21–22
    curricular tasks and activities, 35–38
    measuring collaboration, 34–35
    as necessary skill, 20–21
    norms, 23–26
    Role and Interactivity Communication
        Catcher, 33–34, 167
    setting the stage, 22–26
    student strengths and core
        competencies, 30–34

Collaboration Rubric for PBL, 35
Collaboration Self-Assessment tool, 35
Collaborative agendas, 35, 42
Collaborative learning, 21–22
College admissions process, 113–114, 136
College readiness, xxiii, 113
Color
    communicating with, 59–61
    psychology of, 60–61
    slide background, 60
    theory, art history project, 74–75
    See also Visuals, in presentations
Color blocking, 55
Color clashing, 60
Color context, 60
colorhunt.co, 60
Color pairings, 60
Color Picker, 60
Comer, James, 27
Common Core State Standards, 47
Common Sense Media, 135
Communication
    in 1980s compared to current reality, xv
    five styles of, 28
    in resume and interview, 96, 115
    See also Communication skills
Communication Catchers, xxi, 162–177
    Curation, 145–146, 154, 177
    Digital Doppelgänger, 132–133, 175
    Email Etiquette, 4, 165
    Peer Portfolio, 111–112, 173
    Presentation Planner, 68, 169
    Project Inquiry, 93–94, 171
    Role and Interactivity, 33–34, 167
Communication Cohort Challenges, xxi,
    160–161
Communication cultivation. *See*
    Collaboration and positive
    interdependence; Curation; Email
    etiquette; Portfolios, digital;
    Presentation skills; Projects and
    publishing, students'; Social media
"Cultivating Communication in the
    Classroom" TechChef, 158
Communication skills
    within and beyond classroom, xx–xxiv
    importance to managers, xviii
    industry insights, 18
    See also Communication
Community, building with
    collaboration, 27–30
Comparisons, and social media
    changes, 125
Computer science with ASL project, 86

Confidence monitor, 52, 63
Content areas for digital portfolios, 105
Content consumption, in social media
    critical consumption, 128–131
    emotional hygiene, practicing,
        126–128
Content formats, for project ideas, 77
Content, in presentations, 47–48, 50–56
    communication of content
        on a slide, 51–56
    communication of organization
        in slide deck, 50–51
Cooper, Ross, 89–90, 134
Copyright issues, 87, 90
Core competencies of students,
    30–34, 115
CoSchedule, 143
Courtesy, and email best practices, xxx
Cover letters, 113
Creative Commons, 14, 87, 90, 92
Creativity
    importance to managers, xviii
    qualifiers present in, 73
Credit of work done, 87–90
Critical conversation, as communication
    skill, 18
Critical thinking, importance to managers,
    xviii
Csikszentmihalyi, Mihaly, 31
Cuban, Mark, 153
Cue cards, 52
"Cult of Pedagogy," 89, 111
Cultural fit, in resume and interview, 96
Cultures
    collaboration across, 37
    global awareness, advice for future, 140
Curation, 141–157
    analysis of, 154
    defined, 142, 152–153, 154
    good versus bad, 149
    lesson design for classroom, 145–152
    of portfolios, 106
    risks associated with, 154–156
    value of, 142–145
    value of critical evaluation, 152–154
Curation Communication Catcher, 145–146,
    154, 177

Darrow, Melinda, 74
Da Vinci, Leonardo, 106
Dear Abby letters, 11
The Decision Book (Krogerus
    and Tschäppeler), 30–32

Decision making
    email importance for, xxx
    models in collaboration, 31
    as SEL skill, and index to, 180
    as team skill, 42
Decision trees, as project idea, 79–82
Delivery, in presentations, 47–48, 61–65
    audience participation, 64–65
    body movement and positions, 62
    confidence monitor, 52, 63
    connection between talk
        and slides, 63–64
    eye contact, 62
    speed of speech, 62–63
    volume, 62
Depression, and time online, 126
Depth of conversations, social media
    changes, 124
Descoteaux, Koffi, 136
Design projects for using maker parts, 86
Design thinking, in collaborative
    groups, 37
Desmos graphs, 105
Devil's advocates, 36–37
Dewey, John, 29
Digital Citizenship Survival Kit, 131–132
Digital Doppelgänger Communication
    Catcher, 132–133, 175
Digital doppelgängers, crafting
    of, 131–132
Digital portfolios. See Portfolios, digital
Ditch that Textbook, 67
Doctopus, 104
Documentation OF, FOR,
    and AS Learning, 100, 104
Documentation of timelines and
    processes, email importance for, xxx
Duarte, Nancy, 43, 46, 47–48, 51
Duckworth, Sylvia, 89, 91
Due diligence, in email, 6
Duggan, Tara, 28
Duh, Chris, 34
Dunham, Lena, 77
Dupre, Melissa, 36
"Dutch Girl Fakes a 5-Week
    Vacation," 125

Edmodo, 36
Ego Is the Enemy (Holiday), 110
Elmore, Tim, 113
Email accounts, 10–11
Email etiquette, 1–16
    acceptable use policy, 3–5

best practices for, 2–5
clear communication through, 5–10
curricular opportunities with, 11–15
district contract, 3–5
industry insights, xxx
for students, 1–2
troubleshooting with students, 10–11
Email Etiquette Communication
    Catcher, 4, 165
Email file sharing, 10
Emoticons, 13–14
Emotional intelligence, xxiii
The Emotion Thesaurus, 62
Empathy, 18, 96
English, and communicating
    with images, 57
Environmental project, 76–77
ESPN, "Split Image" coverage, 126
Etsy, 77, 79
Evernote, 150
Expectations, setting up 5-star
    norms, 26
Experience, in resume and interview, 96
Experts
    and curation of research, 147
    emailing, 14
Explain Everything, 105
Expository writing handout, 44–45
Eye contact, and delivery
    in presentations, 62

Facebook
    launching of, 126
    as news source, 128
    professional conversations on, 136
    researching by survey, 135
FakeAPhoto, 125
Fear of missing out (FOMO),
    social media changes, 125
Feedback
    advice for future, 140
    real-time audience participation,
        64–65
    in student-led peer conferences, 110
Feedback Model, Bloom's Taxonomy, 111
Feedly, as news source, 128
File management in email, 10
FLAWD (Rigal), 127
Flickr, 59
Flipped literature circles, 36
Flowcharts, decision trees as
    project idea, 79–82
Flow Model, 31–32

FOMO (fear of missing out),
    social media changes, 125
Font size on slide, 51
Formatting, in email, 6
Fortunately, Unfortunately, 134
Fortune tellers, 162
Fotoforensics, 125
4 C's (communication, collaboration,
    critical thinking, creativity), xvi, xvii
Freebies, as project idea, 76, 78
French, Katy, 56
Future Me, 11

Gabaldon, Diana, 93
GAFE (Google Apps for Education), 2, 10
Gallo, Carmine, 47, 58, 62
Gardner, Andrew, 42, 96, 140, 181
Gates, Bill, 119
Gelb, Michael J., 106–107
Geography, and communicating
    with images, 57
Gibson, William, 92
Gilot, Marie, 19
Girls, 77
Global awareness, advice for future, 140
Global Digital Citizen Foundation, xx
Glows and Grows, 34
Goals, as team skill, 42
Godin, Seth, 47
Goldenberger, Maggie, 134
Golden Books, 151
Golden Circle, adapted for projects, 74,
    100–101
Gonzalez, Jennifer, 89–90
Google
    curation and search engines, 142
    on G.P.A.'s, 114
    permissions and licenses, 87
Google Apps for Education (GAFE),
    2, 10
Google Doc Portfolio Index
    template, 104
Google Docs, 36
Google Sites, 115, 117
Google Slides, 55, 60, 67
G.P.A.'s, Google view of, 114
Grading presentations, 66–67
Graphic organizer templates, as project idea,
    76, 78
Green Eggs and Ham, 134
Gregory, Danny, 123
Group projects, 19
Group quizzes, 36

Group rubrics, 35
Guerrieri, Matthew, xxx
Guides, free, as project idea, 76, 78

Hammond, Justin, xxiii, xxx, 18, 96
Hands, and delivery in presentations, 62
Hanson, Jacob, xxx, 18, 42, 96, 140
Hard skills, 20–21. *See also* Soft skills
Harry Ransom Center, 85, 152
Hartmann, Elyse, 101
Harvard Business Review
    collaboration tips, 22–23
    STOP/KEEP/START, 111
Harvard University
    Graduate School of Education Project
        Zero Visible Thinking Routines, 37
    Making Caring Common program,
        xxiii, 136
Hashtag, for school, 88
Hat metaphor, and social media, 127
Hattie, John, 110
Hendricks, Gay, 32
Historical fiction, 92–94
Holiday, Ryan, 110
Holleran, Madison, 126
Home button stud earrings, 77, 79
Honeycutt, Kevin, 88, 89, 98
Hooker, Carl, 11, 65, 134
How to Design Ted Worthy Presentation Skills
    (Karia), 49
How to Think Like Leonardo da Vinci
    (Gelb), 106
Hubspot, 76, 77
Hunt, Cathy, 64

"iAm A Brand Called Me," 88, 115, 117
IBM, xviii
Icons, communicating with, 59.
    See also Visuals, in presentations
Idea assignments, 75
Ideas, number on a slide, 52
Idea swapping, 36
Ideation, collaborative sessions, 37
Ideo, design thinking, 37
If You Give a Mouse a Cookie, 2
"I Have a Dream" speech (King), 54
Imagery, social media changes, 124
Images, communication with, 56–58.
    See also Visuals, in presentations
Independent rubrics, 35
Industry insights, xxiii, 182–183
    on advice for future, 140
    on communication skills, 18

on email etiquette, xxx
    questions in survey, 183
    on resumes and interviews, 96
    on teams, 42
Influence, as communication skill, 18
Infographic, as curation lesson, 149
Information famine, 44
Instagram
    launching of, 126
    as news source, 129
    social media and business, 135–136
International Baccalaureate program, xix
Interpersonal skills, in resume
        and interview, 96
Interviews, industry insights on, 96
Intimacy, social media changes, 124
Intuitions, advice for future, 140
iPad backup decision, 80–81
iPad Base Camp, 104–105
iPadpalooza, 64, 144–145
iPads, 1, 141
ISTE
    1 in 3, 63
    curation standards, 142
    Nets, xix, 47
    Standards for Students, 128
iTunes, 115, 142

Jacomino, Judy, xxx, 18, 96, 140
jamigold.com, 76
Jarche, Harold, 143–144
Johnson, Danny, 18, 96
Johnson, Lisa, 58, 89–90
Johnson, Melissa, xxx, 96

Kahoot, 64
KANBANS, 35
Kanter, Beth, 143
Karia, Akash, 47, 49
Kawasaki, Guy, 47, 54, 57–58
Keep/Change/Delete, 34–35
Keep/Change/Improve, 35
Keynote, 60, 89
King, Martin Luther, 54
Kleon, Austin, 97, 106–107, 110–111, 149
Krogerus, Mikael, 30, 44
KWL chart, 35, 182

LA Fitness, 131
Learners
    proactive, in resume and interview, 96
    support of all, xxii
    See also Students

Learning
    collaborative, 21–22
    curation for, 143–145, 150
    future of, xvi–xix
Learning Curve Report, xviii
Lego Minifigures, 58
Lehmann, Chris, 75
Leitman, Margot, 66
Leveraging situations, advice for future, 140
Libraries, weeding books, 153
License for own work, 87, 92
LinkedIn
    launching of, 126
    professional conversations on, 136
Listening, as communication skill, 18
Listicles
    as curation tool, 147–149
    as project idea, 79
Literature circles, flipped, 36
Little Golden Books, 151
Logos, for school or classroom, 88
*Long Story Short: The Only Storytelling Guide
    You'll Ever Know* (Leitman), 66
Lucas, George, xxiii

Macbeth #killingit, 14
MailChimp, 14
Maker design projects, 86
Making Caring Common, xxiii, 136
MAPS (methodologies for academic
    and personal success), xvi, 86
Margolis, Michael, 114
Martin, Doug, 113
Masada project, 75
Mashable, 76
Mask metaphor, and social media,
    127–129, 131
Matchbox cars, 58
Math, and communicating with images, 57
Mathers, Dani, 131
Matousek, Mark, 127
Mcfarlane, Matthew, 67
Meaningfulness, in creativity, 73
Memes for good, 134
Memory Project, 85
Mentorships
    Bulb portfolio, 108–109
    presentations, xvi
    publishing project, 85, 152
Miles, Sarah, xviii
Minecraft: Story Mode, 80, 82
Mirroring Masks Mixer, 127–129, 131
Mirroring Stories, 127

Missions, managing by curation, 149
Miss Me, 12
Mitchell, Brandon, xxx, 140
Model for Meaningful Feedback, 111
Morin, Peter, 152
Most Likely to Succeed (Wagner), 128
Movies, and social media effects on, 134
MS Paint, 89
Muldrow, Diane, 151
Multimedia theft, 87, 89
Murnaw, Stefan, 30
Myers-Brigg personality tests, 30
Myspace, launching of, 126

National Education Association (NEA),
    on communication skills, xix
National Survey of Student Engagement, 106
Nearpod, 64
Netflix, 76, 142
News, and social media, 128–131
Newsletters/newspapers
    "Cultivating Communication in the
        Classroom" TechChef, 158
    in school, 14, 86
Newton, Claire, 28
Norms, 23–26
North, Ryan, 80
Notetaking, 150–151
Noun Project, 59

Obama, Barack, 129
Office of Educational Technology, xviii, xx
Ohlmeyer, Kati, xxx, 18, 42
Oldfield, Wendy Lee, 30
The Onion, 131
Online archival, and social media
    changes, 125
Oracy, 62
Other side of the coin, 29–30
Outlander series, 93
Ovenell-Carter, Brad, 89, 91
*Overloaded and Underprepared:
    Strategies for Stronger Schools
    and Healthy Successful Kids* (Pope), 106

Padlet, 76, 78
Paper by FiftyThree, 89
Parents and student conferences, 112–113
Partnership for 21st Century Skills, xix
Passion
    intuitions and advice for future, 140
    in resume and interview, 96
    in social media and business, 135

.pdf document format, 10
PechaFlickr, 59
Peer conferences, student-led, 110–113
Peer Portfolio Communication Catcher, 111–112, 173
PenPal Schools, 37
Perceptions of resume, 117–118
Periscope, launching of, 126
Perkins, Cyndee, 42, 140
Permissions for use, 87
Personality, mask metaphor in social media, 127
Personality tests, 30
Personal Knowledge Mastery (PKM), 143
Person, variable, reflection on, 106–107
Perspective, 18, 28
Persuade Me, 11–12
Peters, James, 18, 42, 96
Peters, Kristy, xxx, 18, 42, 96, 140
"Pete the Cat," 132
Phone, as confidence monitor, 52, 63
Photo Booth, 89
Photographs, 57–58, 113, 124–125
Piaget, Jean, 72
Pinterest
    as curation tool, 141–142, 146–147, 150
    as news source, 129
    and risk in social media, 154–156
    university use of, 154
Piracy of media, 87, 90
PKM (Personal Knowledge Mastery), 143
Plagiarism, 87, 90
Playlists with purpose, 149
Pollock, Jackson, 64
Pope, Denise, xviii, 106
Portfolios, digital, 97–122
    archive artifacts, technology to, 97–98
    benefits for students, 102
    challenges to solve, 101–102
    described, 98–101
    developmental (or learning or workspace) portfolio, 103
    entry point into, 104–106
    involving peers in learning process, 110–113
    items to include, 103–104
    main goal of, 102–103
    Peer Portfolio Communication Catcher, 111–112, 173
    platforms for, 102–103
    showcase portfolios. See Showcase portfolios

student reflection on learning journey, 106–109
why and how and what in Golden Circle, 100–101
Positive interdependence, 22–26. See also Collaboration and positive interdependence
Posters, 135
PowerPoint presentations, 46–47
PPT, 60
Practice in art of building a resume, 117
Preparation inventory challenges. See Table of Contents, at end of each chapter
Presentation elements
    content, 47–48, 50–56. See also Content, in presentations
    delivery, 47–48, 61–65. See also Delivery, in presentations
    visuals, 47–48, 56–61. See also Visuals, in presentations
Presentation Planner Communication Catcher, 68, 169
Presentations
    in future of learning, xix
    of mentorship programs, xvi
Presentation satellite cafe, 66
Presentation skills, 43–71
    best practices, 47, 49–50, 65. See also Presentation elements
    discomfort with public speaking, 65–66
    grading presentations, 66–67
    importance for students, 46–47
    three elements of, 47–49
    tools and applications for use with, 65
    visual literacy importance, 44–46
Presentation Zen, 60
The Princess Bride, 73
Privacy, social media changes, 124
Problem swapping, 36
Procrastination, advice for future, 140
Professional learning, support of, xxiii
Professional praise, for resume, 114
Project ideas, 76–84
    advertorials, 77–79
    beat sheets, 76
    content formats, 77
    decision trees, 79–82
    freebies, 76
    free guides, 76
    listicles, 79
    story bibles, 76

templates, 76
visualizations, custom and original, 82–83
Project Inquiry Communication Catcher,
    93–94, 171
Projects and publishing, students,' 72–95
    appropriate use in, 73, 86–92. *See also*
        Appropriate use in students' projects
        and publishing
    authentic audience for, 73, 84–86.
        See also Authentic audience for students'
        projects and publishing
    autonomy and choice in, 73, 74–84
    compared to publishing, 73
    project ideas, 76–84. *See also* Project ideas
    revision of existing project, 92–94
    why, how, and what in Golden Circle, for
        autonomy and choice, 74, 83
Provacateurs, 36–37
Psychology of color, 60–61
Publications, in-campus, as authentic
    audience, 86
Public speaking discomfort, 65–66
Publishing, student
    compared to student projects, 73
    resume templates, 118–119
    See also Projects and publishing,
        students'
Puentedura, Ruben R., 14

Queries, in student-led peer
    conferences, 110
Questions, in email, 6
Quip, 36
Quizzes, group, 36
Quotes, to protect work, 88

RAFTS (role, audience, format, topic, strong
    verb), 11
Ransom, Harry, 85, 152
Reading retention, 150
Reading strategies, 143
Read, Ryan, 76
Reagan, Ronald, 150
Real estate publishing, 79, 83
Reaugh, Frank, 152
Rebbeck, Geoff, 99
Reflection, of students on learning journey,
    99, 106–109
Reflective prompts, 106–107
Relationship skills, as SEL skill, and
    index to, 180
Repetition of content, 54–55

Resonate: Present Visual Stories that
    Transform Audiences (Duarte), 47
Resources, reading, and references.
    See Table of Contents, at end of
    each chapter
Response emails, 5, 8–10
"The Resume Is Dead, the Bio Is
    King," 114
Resumes for career and college readiness,
    96, 113–119
Reynolds, Garr, 44, 47, 56
Richards, Reshan, xxx, 96, 140
Rigal, Emily-Anne, 127
Robinson, Toni, 64
Rock Star Bios, 33–34
Role and Interactivity Communication
    Catcher, 33–34, 167
Role playing, 28–29
Romeo and/or Juliet: A Chooseable-Path
    Adventure, 80
Roosevelt, Franklin D., xvi

Saboteurs, 36–37
Sacco, Justine, 131
Sales copy, 77, 79
SAMR model (substitution,
    augmentation, modification,
    redefinition), 14
Saunders, Elizabeth Grace, 9
Savage, Isabella, 152
SavetheCat.com, 76
Scalin, Noah, 149
Schleicher, Andreas, xv
Scholastic scrapbook, 100, 112
School newspapers, as authentic
    audience, 86
Science labs, and visual lab reports, 57
Scientific American, 72
Scoop.it, 147, 150
Screencastify, 105
Scrolling back, reviewing the past, 135
Search engines, and curation, 142
Seed Packet, 31
Seek, Sense, and Share, 144
Seesaw, 76, 78
Self-advocacy, in email, 6
Self-assessment checklist for students.
    See Table of Contents, at end of
    each chapter
Self-assessment strategies, 106–107
Self-awareness, as SEL skill,
    and index to, 179

Selfies, 135
Self-management, as SEL skill,
     and index to, 179
Self-selected evaluations, 110
SEL (social-emotional learning) skills
   index of activities in each chapter,
        179–181
   support of, xxiii
Seven things, in listicles, 149
Shark Tank, 73
SHARP model (stories, humor,
     analogies, references and quotes,
     pictures and visuals), 50
Showcase portfolios
   and best practices, 99
   building for employment, 115
   for career and college readiness, 113
   defined, 103
   mentorship portfolio using Bulb, 108–109
Signature strengths of students,
     30–34, 115
Sinek, Simon, 74, 100–101
Single Point Rubric, 111
The Sixth Sense (film), 134
Sketchnotes, 144–146, 150–151
*Sketchnotes for Educators: 100 Inspiring
     Illustrations for Lifelong Learners,* 89
Slide deck book, 67
Slide design. *See* Presentations
Slide Design for Students, license, 92
Slide Docs, 66
*slide:ology: The Art and Science of Creating
     Great Presentations* (Duarte), 47
Snapchat
   launching of, 126
   negative example of social media, 131
   as news source, 129
Social awareness, as SEL skill,
     and index to, 180
Social-emotional learning (SEL) skills
   index of activities in each chapter,
        179–181
   support of, xxiii
Social media, 123–139
   changes in communication, 124–125
   critical consumption of content, 128–131
   curation and, 154–156
   digital doppelgängers, crafting of,
        131–132, 133
   emotional hygiene in content
        consumption, 126–128
   negative examples of, 131
   positive integration of, 132–136

Soft skills, 20–21, 113–114
Speaker notes, 52, 63
Speed of speech, and delivery
     in presentations, 62–63
"Split Image," 126
Sprints, as team skill, 42
srsly Hamlet, 14
Stanford University
   Challenge Success program, xxiii
   Institute of Design, 37
"Steal My Slide Design," 65–66
Stevens, Rick, 20
Sticky notes, 25–27, 49, 76, 78
Stock photo images, 57
STOP/KEEP/START, 111
Story bibles, as project idea, 76
Strategy, variable, reflection on, 106–107
Student-led peer conferences, 110–113
Students
   protection of their work, 88–92
   reflection in digital portfolios, 106–109
   signature strengths and core
        competencies, 30–34
   See also Learners
Students' self-assessment checklist.
     *See Table of Contents, at end of
     each chapter*
Subject line, in email, 5
"Surprisingly Educational" app, 151
Survey for industry insights, 182–183
Survey swap, 28–29
SXSWEDU, 57–58, 127

Taking sides activity, 27–28
Talking, in student-led peer
     conferences, 110
Task, variable, reflection on, 106–107
Taylor, Valerie, 50
Teachers Pay Teachers, 135
Teachers, support of, xxiii
Teams, 19, 42
Tear sheets, 6
TechChef4u.com, 115, 158
TEDTalks, 62, 146
Templates, as project idea, 76
Texas School for the Deaf, 85
Texting, as compared to email, 3
Text, lines of, on a slide, 52
Text plagiarism, 90
Text-to-text, text-to-self, and
     text-to-world, 143
That's Good! That's Bad!, 134
Thinglink, 144–145